Policing Matters

Policing
Terrorism

Policing Matters

Policing Terrorism

Christopher Blake, Barrie Sheldon,
Rachael Strzelecki and Peter Williams

Series editors

P A J Waddington

Martin Wright

Los Angeles | London | New Delhi
Singapore | Washington DC

www.learningmatters.co.uk

Los Angeles | London | New Delhi
Singapore | Washington DC

www.learningmatters.co.uk

Learning Matters
An imprint of SAGE Publications Ltd
1 Oliver's Yard
55 City Road
London EC1Y 1SP

SAGE Publications Inc.
2455 Teller Road
Thousand Oaks, California 91320

SAGE Publications India Pvt Ltd
B 1/I 1 Mohan Cooperative Industrial Area
Mathura Road
New Delhi 110 044

SAGE Publications Asia-Pacific Pte Ltd
33 Pekin Street #02-01
Far East Square
Singapore 048763

Library of Congress Control Number available

British Library Cataloguing in Publication Data
A catalogue record for this book is available from
the British Library

ISBN: 978 0 85725 518 1

Editor: Julia Morris
Development editor: Jennifer Clark
Production controller: Chris Marke
Project management: Diana Chambers
Marketing manager: Zoe Seaton
Cover design: Toucan Designs
Typeset by: Kelly Winter
Printed by: MPG Books Group

FSC

Contents

1 Introduction to concepts of terrorism

Barrie Sheldon

About this book

Each chapter provides a number of tasks that help to develop your knowledge and understanding of the subject matter and also give you ideas to develop themes for academic assignments. Access to the internet will be required for completion of tasks and a number of case studies are provided to link theory with practice.

This book provides you with a basic overview of terrorism and counter-terrorism measures with a focus on the United Kingdom (UK) and is an excellent resource for any student undertaking introductory terrorism modules at academic levels 4, 5 and 6. The internet provides a wide range of quality terrorism resources for students and it is recommended that some time is spent getting to know what is available.

PRACTICAL TASK

Go to the 'Useful websites' section at the end of this chapter, where you will find a list of some of the terrorism websites that are available. Access the websites and find out what is available to you, looking particularly for links that provide access to reports and academic publications.

Many of the websites are based within the United States of America (USA) but will be very relevant to terrorism studies. The audacious attack by al-Qaeda on the twin towers of New York on 11 September 2001, which resulted in over 3,000 people losing their lives, saw the USA take the lead role in the current global war against terrorism.

> *We will direct every resource at our command – every means of diplomacy, every tool of intelligence, every instrument of law enforcement, every financial influence, and every necessary weapon of war to the destruction and to the defeat of the global terror network.*
>
> (George W Bush, 2001)

Historical perspective

The problem of terrorism is not a new phenomenon and has been witnessed on a global basis throughout history, from antiquity, through the middle ages and onwards to the twenty-first century. Historical accounts of terrorism can be found in most countries and, when these are examined, there is evidence of many different causes of terrorism; issues that motivate terrorists have existed over the entire span of human history. Many of today's terrorists are still inspired by historical events and it is the connection between past and present that makes the study of the history of terrorism important in understanding modern-day terrorism (Mahan and Griset, 2008).

Early origins of terrorism

Examples of terrorist activity can be traced back well before the first century; however, we will start by examining three early renowned terrorist organisations: the Zealots, the Assassins and the Thuggees.

Zealots

The Zealots of Judea, also known as the 'Sicarii' or 'dagger men', were opposed to the Roman occupation and took part in a revolt that lasted nearly 100 years from the time Herod became king in 37 BC. They were members of an organisation operating underground who had strong religious convictions and believed that they could not remain faithful to the true nature of Judaism while living as Roman subjects. The group carried out assassination attacks targeting Roman occupation forces and Jews who supported and collaborated with the Romans. As the Zealot revolt became more open they were finally trapped and members of the group committed mass suicide in Masada, Judea, in 74 AD.

Assassins

The Assassins of Persia (Iran) and Syria (1090–1275) were a breakaway group of Shi'ites called the 'Nizari Isma'ili' who used the tactic of assassination to target enemy leaders. They were one of the first groups to make systematic use of murder as a political weapon. Their ambition was to overthrow the existing Sunni order in Islam and to replace it with their own, to purify Islam. Because they had limited numbers, restricting the viability of open combat, they resorted to sending lone assassins to kill opposition leaders and then waited with their victim to be killed or captured (an act of martyrdom). This action caused considerable fear within the enemy population.

Thuggees

The Thuggees were an Indian secret society believed to have been responsible for killing tens of thousands of people over a number of centuries. It is not known exactly when they first appeared, but there is evidence they existed in the seventh century and were known to be very active in the thirteenth century. The Thuggees had deeply entrenched religious convictions and carried out their killings as a sacrifice to the goddess 'Kali', the Hindu goddess of creation, preservation and destruction. In this particular case the main audience for the terrorists was the goddess rather than the general public. Their activities and methods of killing were deemed to be acts of terrorism by going beyond the accepted norms that regulate violence.

> *Their deceit, unusual weapon (a noose), and practice of dismembering corpses (thereby preventing cremation or proper burial) made Thug violence outrageous by Hindu standards or by those of any other culture.*
>
> (Mahan and Griset, 2008, p49)

REFLECTIVE TASK

Find out more about the Zealots and consider why this group were considered to be a terrorist organisation. The link www.asiantribune.com/?q=node/12854 will take you to an article written by Professor Fernando of the University of Columbo titled 'The Menace of Terrorism and Its Early Origins'. Read the article and then consider how the reasoning for defining the Zealots as terrorists could be applied to both the Assassins and Thuggees (further research may be required to find out more about the two groups).

Seventeenth to nineteenth centuries

Throughout this period there were many examples of global terrorist activity and the following case studies highlight some key historical events that assist with the understanding of terrorism:

- Guy Fawkes, 1605;

- the French Revolution, 1793;

- the People's Will (Narodnaya Volya), 1879.

Guy Fawkes

During the reign of Henry VIII (King of England 1509–47), the King asked the Pope to annul his marriage to Catherine of Aragon after she had failed to provide him with a male child. His intention was to marry Anne Boleyn, but the Pope refused his request, so Henry declared himself head of the Church of England and separated from the Catholic Church. This was followed by a period of action directed against the Catholic Church, including the dissolution of monasteries, destruction of churches and seizure of lands. Catholics who failed to recognise the king as supreme head of the Church were repressed and persecuted. The persecution continued when Elizabeth I took the throne in 1558, and when she was succeeded by James 1 in 1603 it was hoped that he would be more tolerant as his mother was a Catholic; however, he continued to persecute the Catholics.

A small group of Catholic men led by Robert Catesby decided that the use of violence was the only answer and they planned to blow up the Houses of Parliament when the King and other officials would be present during its opening on 5 November 1605. They managed to smuggle explosives into the building but, following a tip-off, Guy Fawkes was captured while guarding the explosives. The rest of the group were soon captured and put to death for treason. Today these conspirators would be considered as extremists or terrorists.

The French Revolution

This period of revolution within France was considered as a prelude to modern terrorism and was referred to by the British statesman and philosopher Edmund Burke (1729–97) as the *régime de la terreur*, translated as the 'Reign of Terror' (Martin, 2009).

The revolution came about following a period of recession, a deteriorating economy and imposition of taxation. France was a feudal state with an absolutist monarch (King Louis XVI) and there was much disquiet about the inequalities of social life. Most people lived in poor conditions, had to work hard and suffered deprivation, while a minority enjoyed excessive riches and a life of luxury. On 14 July 1789 the Bastille prison in Paris was stormed by rioters supported by a group of radical revolutionaries who murdered the guards and later took control of government. The King was later tried and executed in January 1793, following which a revolutionary tribunal led by Maximilien de Robespierre began the reign of terror. Thousands of people opposed to the new dictatorship were arrested, sometimes on the flimsiest of evidence, tried by the tribunal and beheaded by guillotine.

This is a good example of state terrorism, which is explored further in the next chapter. The revolutionaries who had taken control of a mainly Jacobin-dominated government adopted tactics of terror to achieve the goals of their revolutionary ideology. The ideology was related to justice, freedom and equality; however, there was a smaller group of Jacobin socialites who supported complete state control and believed that equality should be enforced by the state (O'Carroll, 1994).

The People's Will: Narodnaya Volya

This group was founded in 1879 as a protest against the tsarist regime in Russia. In 1861 Tsar Alexander II abolished serfdom. The serfs expected to acquire new land and also be given land that they had previously tended, but instead wealthy landowners would only provide the land at excessive prices. This resulted in the Tsar being publically criticised for his enslavement of the lower classes.

In 1876 a revolutionary society, 'Land and Liberty' (Zemlya Volya), was founded. Its membership consisted of many university students who had developed Marxist views and who championed the rights of the people, particularly the peasant classes. In 1879 the group was split into two following a series of arrests and trials. One of these groups was Narodnaya Volya, whose members saw terrorism as an important tactic to achieve their political objectives. The group carefully selected their targets and used tactics of shooting, knifing and bombing directed against government officials. In 1881 Tsar Alexander II was assassinated by a Narodnaya Volya bomb, following which members of the group were quickly arrested and hanged, resulting in the group's demise. The impact of the group was not forgotten and it provided some stimulus for the later Bolshevik Revolution of 1907, which brought about the communist era in Russia (Mahan and Griset, 2008).

Colonialism

REFLECTIVE TASK

The following provides a definition of colonialism:

The colonial system of political government or extension of territory, by which one nation exerts political control over another nation, territory, or people, maintaining the colony in a state of dependence, its inhabitants not having the same full rights as those of the colonial power. The controlling power is typically extended thus by military force or the threat of force.

(Webster's Dictionary, 1913)

Consider the ramifications of colonialism and how it may contribute to terrorist activity.

Colonialism has influenced the development of terrorism in many corners of the globe and is a political process that, according to Smith (2005), can:

- usurp political control;
- ignore ethnic boundaries;
- strip away economic resources;
- alienate the population;
- undermine cultural hegemony.

These factors invariably produce an emotionally charged environment that can lead to the development of terrorism in the name of nationalism or ethnic causes (Smith, 2005).

There are many historical examples of terrorist uprisings linked directly to colonialism, and the two terrorist groups considered below demonstrate such links.

Hindustan Socialist Republican Association
During the nineteenth century Britain took political control of India and it wasn't until 1947 that India achieved independence from British rule. During this time many Indians were opposed to British rule and a group led by Mahatma Gandhi campaigned to end it. Gandhi did not believe in violence and rejected terrorism; however, another group known as the Hindustan Republican Army (HRA), inspired by the Bolsheviks' role in the Russian Revolution during 1917, supported the idea of terrorism. Initially their aim was to organise an armed revolution to end colonial rule and replace it with a Federal Republic of the

United States of India. In 1928, following a speech given by Bhagat Singh, leader of one the groups, the aims of the group were stated as creating an India based on the socialist ideals of Lenin and Marx, and the group's name changed to the Hindustan Socialist Republican Association (HSRA).

The group was responsible for a number of terrorist attacks, including the looting of a train in Kakori carrying Government money (1925), the shooting of two police officers in Lahore (1928) and the bombing of the Government's Central Assembly in Delhi (1929). It is believed that the HSRA ceased as an organisation following the death of certain leaders and activists, but it provided the inspiration for future revolutionary groups:

> Bhagat Singh thus symbolised all that was best in our struggle for national liberation and that is why he is still a mighty source of inspiration for the present generations – as he was for the earlier ones.
>
> (Surjeet, 2006)

REFLECTIVE TASK

Go to the following website link and read through the 1929 manifesto of the HSRA: *www.shahidbhagatsingh.org/index.asp?link=hindustan_socialist.*

- *What does the manifesto say about the use of violence and its legitimacy in the struggle against the British rulers?*

- *Why do you think that the HSRA advocates the use of terrorism as being the most effective means of retaliation against British rule?*

Make a list of the arguments put forward to support the use of terrorism and then consider them further when the causes of terrorism are explored.

Basque Fatherland and Liberty

Basque Fatherland and Liberty (ETA) is a left-wing terrorist group whose primary objective is to create an independent Basque state in northern Spain and south-west France based on Marxist principles. The group emerged in 1959 to oppose the dictator General Franco (Spain's head of state 1936–69), who was suppressing the Basque language and culture. Other political groups such as the Basque Nationalist Party were renounced by ETA as being collaborators with the Spanish Government and, by the 1960s, ETA had developed into a revolutionary group adopting terrorist tactics to achieve their goals. They targeted and killed Government officials using both firearms and bombs, and more recently have targeted and bombed tourist areas within Spain.

ETA has attempted to enter the political process through the 'Batasuna' political party, but in 2003 the Spanish Supreme Court banned the party, which was considered as the political arm of ETA. More recent attempts by the Government to negotiate with ETA have failed.

These examples demonstrate the power of a large state exerting political control over a territory and its people, where certain members of the population have become disaffected and see the only means of changing the political process as being through violence. In contrast with ETA, the Irish Republican Army (IRA) and its political wing 'Sinn Fein' have now become an integral part of government in Ireland.

REFLECTIVE TASK

Does terrorism work? The IRA has been able to enter the political process and successfully change the face of politics in Northern Ireland, yet ETA has failed legitimately to become part of government and influence policy. Why do you think this is?

Academics generally purport that terrorism does not work. Carr (2002) suggests that the strategy of terror is a spectacularly failed one; however, Gould and Klor (2010) argue that terror attacks carried out by Palestinian terrorist factions between 1988 and 2006 have moved the Israeli electorate towards a more accommodating stance regarding their political objectives. The effectiveness of terrorism as a strategy is discussed further in Chapter 3.

The modern era

Within the modern era a new type of terrorism has emerged. The events of 9/11 refocused thinking on counter-terrorism strategy and the world was waking up to a new-found realisation that certain terrorists are intent on causing mass destruction.

The traditional type of terrorism throughout much of history has seen clearly identifiable groups with explicit grievances who carefully select their targets and use conventional weapons such as firearms and explosives. Some of the examples provided above demonstrate this, for example the HSRA and ETA. In contrast, the new terrorism is a worrying development with very loosely based networks, vague, religious or mystical motives and the use of asymmetrical methods to maximise casualties. The new terrorists seek weapons of mass destruction and are adept at using modern technology such as the internet to serve their purpose and to manipulate the media to obtain maximum publicity (Martin, 2009).

Al-Qaeda provides a good example of the new type of terrorism. It has no hierarchical structure but a very loose global network that supports the group's religious ideology based on eradicating Western influences from the Muslim world and imposing a strict and exclusive form of government based on Sunni Islam. Al-Qaeda has been linked to other terrorist organisations, groups and individuals worldwide:

> the main threat no longer comes from the organisation called Al Qaeda, but from the bottom up – from radicalized individuals and groups who meet and plot in their neighbourhoods and on the Internet.

> (Sciolini and Schmitt, 2008, p1)

The attack on the World Trade Center in New York resulted in mass casualties, using commercial jet airlines as unconventional and unique weapons. There have been similar attempts since and those groups aligned to the new terrorism will not shy away from utilising weapons of mass destruction. These terrorists are ruthless in seeking maximum publicity and impact, and will target populations indiscriminately, hoping to cause mass casualties. The new terrorism brings with it new challenges for world security and counter-terrorism has become a major international issue.

PRACTICAL TASK

Draw a simple table to show the differences between the new and traditional types of terrorism. To assist with this task consider two groups, such as al-Qaeda and the Provisional IRA, and explore their structures, targets and tactics, which will highlight a number of differences.

REFLECTIVE TASK

The attack on the World Trade Center on 11 September 2001 was considered as 'The Dawn of a New Era' (Martin, 2009). Why and how has this event changed the terrorism landscape?

Defining terrorism

The word 'terrorism' became more widely used following its association with the *régime de la terreur* in 1793 (see page 4). A good starting point for defining terrorism is to examine some dictionary definitions.

PRACTICAL TASK

Using both academic texts and the internet, explore the range of definitions that are provided for terrorism.

During your research you will discover that there are many different definitions of terrorism and this makes understanding the term difficult. So why is there a need to define terrorism? A definition of terrorism is necessary to assist with the development of effective counter-terrorism strategies, and to provide a basis in law, to enable the prevention and disruption of terrorist activity and the prosecution of terrorists.

In November 2005 Lord Carlile of Berriew, QC was tasked by the UK Government to review the definition of terrorism. He started by stating that there was no universally accepted definition of terrorism and that it continues to be the subject of much debate within the international community (Carlile, 2007).

Within the UK a definition for terrorism is provided by section 1 of the Terrorism Act 2000. The definition has not been simply constructed but carefully drafted to ensure that UK law is fit for purpose to tackle the terrorist threat effectively. Table 1.1 outlines elements of the UK definition.

Table 1.1 Definitions of terrorism

Terrorism means the use of, or threats of, action . . .

What? (action)	• serious violence against a person • serious damage to property • endangering another person's life • creating a serious health and safety risk to public • seriously interfering with or disrupting an electronic system.
Why? (purpose)	• to influence government or international government organisation, or to intimidate the public • to advance a political, religious or ideological cause.
Where?	• the UK and anywhere else in the world.

Source: Adapted from section 1, Terrorism Act 2000, as amended by section 34(a) Terrorism Act 2006

By comparison, a leading expert in the field of terrorism defines it as *The deliberate creation and exploitation of fear through violence or the threat of violence in the pursuit of political change* (Hoffman, 2006, p40). Another expert highlights the fact that the USA has a range of different definitions across government agencies, but that there is evidence of commonality, including *premeditation, unlawfulness, groups or agents, force or violence, human or property targets, intimidation, and a political objective* (Martin, 2009, p57).

PRACTICAL TASK

Complete some further research and study a range of definitions of terrorism used by other governments and terrorism experts. Identify commonalities of definition and attempt to produce a definition of your own.

Considering terrorism from different perspectives can also present difficulties in defining it. For example, who decides that a person or a group are terrorists? Consider the phrase 'One man's terrorist is another man's freedom fighter.' People and groups often see their actions of violence as justified and part of a legitimate campaign to achieve freedom, fairness and justice.

CASE STUDY

Nelson Mandela

The National Party in South Africa promoted a scheme of 'apartheid' – a policy of racial segregation within society. The African National Congress (ANC) actively opposed the policy and embarked on a campaign of violence, sabotaging both Government and military targets. The ANC was led by Nelson Mandela, who was convicted of sabotage in

1961 and jailed for 27 years. The ANC was considered to be a terrorist group, but following democratic elections in 1994 the ANC took control of government. Mandela was released from prison and in May 1990 he became the President of the Republic of South Africa.

CASE STUDY

Hamas

Hamas (Harakat al-Muqawamah al-Islamiyya) is a Middle Eastern Islamic terrorist organisation operating primarily in the Gaza Strip and the West Bank in Israel. Their aim is to replace the Jewish state of Israel with an Islamic Palestinian State, bridging two terrorist trends of the Palestinian fight against Israel and the wider struggle of establishing Islamic governments (James et al., 2003).

Hamas believes that it must resist Israel through armed insurrection known as 'jihad' (holy war). However, it also recognises the need to build a working relationship and avoid conflict with the Palestinian authorities. On 26 January 2006 Hamas won a landslide victory in the Palestinian elections – 76 of 132 seats on the Palestinian Legislative Council – and Ismail Haniyeh was appointed Prime Minister. He is considered to be a moderate and was willing to engage in peace talks; however, following the election victory, both the USA and the European Union (EU) threatened to cut funding to the Palestinian Authority unless it renounced violence and recognised the state of Israel. This was clearly unacceptable to Hamas and they argued that Palestinians were entitled to continue to seek independence but would willingly talk with international mediators to resolve the conflict.

> Our government will spare no effort to reach a just peace in the region, putting an end to the occupation and restoring our rights.
>
> *(Haniyeh, 2006)*

In this particular case study we have a group who have achieved political legitimacy but are still considered to be terrorists because of the violent tactics they adopt to achieve their aims.

REFLECTIVE TASK

Find out more about Hamas and consider whether you believe its members to be freedom fighters or terrorists. 'Al-Qassam', the military arm of Hamas, has a website: www. qassam.ps/index.html – consider whether the information provided here supports the

REFLECTIVE TASK *continued*

premise that Hamas members are freedom fighters rather than terrorists. In contrast, consider the position of Israel and ask whether it is a victim or an aggressor. To help with this, complete a Google search using the parameter 'Israel a victim or an aggressor'.

Extremism and terrorism

In understanding the term 'terrorism' it is also important to consider the role of extremism. Extremism can be associated with a group or a person who has radical beliefs, political views and opinions, which are not the norms of society. It is quite often a precursor to terrorism but only manifests itself as terrorism when violence is used. An extremist may be active in promoting his or her beliefs through peaceful protest, propaganda or causing disruption or damage, but these acts in themselves do not necessarily constitute acts of terrorism.

Consider the case of Islamic fundamentalist clerics who preach against the evil infidels of the West and promote a jihad (holy war) to expel crusaders (Jews, Christians and Westerners) and to purify their homelands with the aim of establishing an Islamic government. The clerics' interpretation of the Qur'an (Islamic holy book) is used to justify their political views and to encourage their more militant followers to engage in violence with promises of martyrdom and salvation. The Qur'an outlines two types of jihad – a greater jihad, which is a personal struggle to find faith and God within each person, and a lesser jihad, which relates to an external struggle against forces of evil and non-believers. It does not permit war, the killing of people or suicide, but some extremist clerics have distorted the information provided by the Qur'an to support their own motives (Mattil, no date). Islamic extremism has been recognised as a major global problem and there is evidence of widespread radicalisation of individuals encouraged to commit acts of terrorism, such as the 7 July 2005 bombings in London. The problem of radicalisation by extremists needs to be tackled and is currently a major tenet of the UK counter-terrorism strategy (see Chapter 9).

Causes of terrorism

PRACTICAL TASK

Before reading this section of the chapter, write down a list of things that you believe may contribute to individuals, groups and states committing acts of terrorism.

You may have produced a long list of potential causes of terrorism, but what does research tell us? There is no simple explanation, but it is important that we understand the driving forces (ideology and motivation) behind terrorism so that appropriate action can

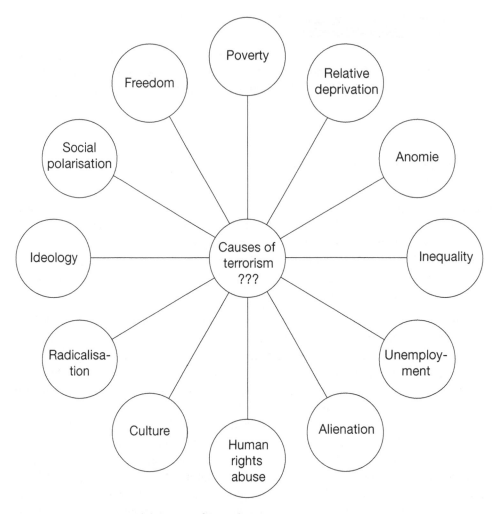

Figure 1.1 Some potential causes of terrorism

be taken to reduce and prevent it. Figure 1.1 shows some potential causes of terrorism, but it is important to highlight that defining and identifying the causes and motivations for terrorism are not simple or straightforward.

Causes can be examined from an individual, group and state perspective. Various forms of terrorism have different ideologies and motivations, and the causes will be diverse and many. It is not possible to find a single explanation for terrorism and models that are produced consider many factors, such as political history, government policy, cultural tensions, ideological and economic trends, individual idiosyncrasies and many other variables (Martin, 2009).

Extremist ideology

Ideology can be defined as a body of ideas reflecting social needs and aspirations of an individual, group, class or culture. It is a set of doctrines or beliefs that form the basis of political, economic or other systems (Free Dictionary, 2010); for example, anarchism, Marxism and fascism are political ideologies.

Extremist ideology can motivate individuals to become terrorists and influence communities to sympathise with terrorists. Terrorism occurs when opportunity, motivation and capability are present, and ideology is one of a number of factors that can motivate a person to commit terrorism (Hassan, 2006). The nature and impact of the extremist ideology is an important consideration to make when attempting to understand the causes of terrorism.

Table 1.2 shows some examples of terrorist goals and objectives that give us clues to the groups' ideologies and motivation.

Having established the ideology and motivation of a terrorist group, what is it that drives an individual or group member to carry out acts of terrorism?

Table 1.2 Examples of terrorist goals and objectives

Hezbollah (Lebanon)	Radical Islamic group – liberation of Jerusalem, destruction of Israel and establishment of Islamic state in Lebanon.
Armed Islamic Group (Algeria)	Radical Islamic group – overthrow of secular government, replacing it with a fundamentalist state based on Islamic law.
Kahane Chai (Kach) (Israel)	Radical Jewish group – restoring biblical state of Israel, by annexing the West Bank and Gaza and parts of Jordan. Expelling all Arabs and introducing strict implementation of Jewish law.
Real Irish Republican Army (Northern Ireland)	Expelling British troops from Northern Ireland and unifying Ireland.
Aum Shinrikyo (Japan)	Control of Japan and the world to create a global utopian society.
Revolutionary Armed Forces of Colombia (FARC)	Establishing a Marxist state in Colombia.

Source: Adapted from Cronin (2004)

Individual motivations

Academics provide various models and explanations for individual terrorist motivation. For example, Miller (2006, cited in Mahan and Griset, 2008, p10) provides a three-stage process.

1. *Unacceptable conditions:*   *(It's not right).*
2. *Resentment and feeling of injustice:*   *(It's not fair).*
3. *Cause of the injustice is personified:*   *(It's your fault).*

In contrast, Martin (2009, p65) provides a further three explanations of what motivates an individual to commit terrorism.

1. *Considers goals and options and makes a cost benefit analysis (rational).*
2. *Personal dissatisfaction with life and accomplishments (psychological).*
3. *Perception of 'outsiders' and their threat to ethnic group survival (cultural origins).*

Further, can an individual terrorist be identified through personal traits and where is a terrorist most likely to come from? Study the opposites in Table 1.3, which summarises research findings (not exhaustive) of terrorist profiles and where terrorism occurs.

Table 1.3 Terrorist profiles

Deprived and uneducated people	Affluent and well-educated people
High proportion of young males	Both sexes and all ages
Rich countries	Poor countries
Modern industrialised world	Low-development areas
During a process of transition and development	Prior to, or after, such a process
Former colonial state	Independent state
Established democracy	Less democratic regime

Source: Adapted from Lia and Skjolberg (2004, p8)

Terrorist profiles

In view of the atrocities that terrorists commit, is it reasonable to suggest that a terrorist has some sort of mental deficiency or has a deviant character? The psychopathy of a terrorist has been studied by many academics and there is little evidence to support the supposition made. Crenshaw (1981, p390) remarked:

Terrorists do not show any striking psychopathy; on the contrary the most outstanding characteristics of terrorists seem to be their normality.

PRACTICAL TASK

The four 7/7 bombers – Khan, Tanweer, Lindsay and Hussain – were young men who led what appeared to be unremarkable lives. Find out more about them – how did they become terrorists, and what were their personality and character traits? Consider whether you (on the evidence available) would describe them as ordinary people, or were certain traits evident that gave clues to their destiny?

Profiles of the four bombers can be found online at:

- *http://news.bbc.co.uk/1/shared/spl/hi/uk/05/london_blasts/investigation/html/bombers. stm*

- *www.militantislammonitor.org/article/id/794.*

Post-investigation evidence linked the 7/7 bombers to the international terrorist group al-Qaeda. Both Khan and Tanweer had visited Pakistan prior to the 7/7 bombings, where it is suspected they visited terrorist training camps and made contact with the al-Qaeda network. Khan described himself in a video released after the attack as *'a soldier' fighting a war against Western governments and their supporters in the general population* (*BBC News*, 2007).

All four of the bombers were connected with the Islamic faith and, prior to committing terrorist acts, had been indoctrinated with extremist beliefs (radicalised), which manifested themselves in the planning and execution of one of the UK's most terrifying and deadly attacks.

Understanding the psychology of the terrorist, the ideology and the motivations that drive the terrorist agenda is important, so that effective counter-terrorism policies can be developed. Subsequent chapters outline the UK counter-terrorism strategy (CONTEST), certain sections of which, such as the 'Prevent' workstream, directly tackle the problem of 'radicalisation', which is attributed with developing potential terrorists.

C H A P T E R   S U M M A R Y

A brief historical perspective has provided evidence that the phenomenon of terrorism is nothing new. It has been with us since time immemorial in various forms, with individuals, groups and states participating in terrorist activity. What is new is globalisation, where technology and sophisticated media services have opened up a more diverse range of opportunities for the terrorist. The new terrorism knows no boundaries, has loose networks, seeks mass casualties and will use new methods of attack to seek the spectacular, such as the use of jet airlines as lethal weapons. The use of weapons of mass destruction by terrorist groups or states is a potential reality for the future.

Extremism has been identified as a precursor to terrorism, but extremist behaviour in itself is not a crime. Terrorism only occurs when violence is used by the extremist in support of his or her beliefs. The term 'terrorism' is hard to define and there are well over 100 definitions available (Hewitt, 2008), which can be confusing. The UK definition of terrorism (s1, Terrorism Act 2000) is designed to allow the creation of a range of offences and powers to deal effectively with the terrorist threat.

Similarly, the causes of terrorism are many and diverse, but it is important to establish the causes so that effective counter-terrorism strategies can be developed. Terrorist ideology and motivations must be understood and provide a good starting point for the study of any terrorist group.

REFERENCES

BBC News (2007) Profile: Mohammad Sidique Khan. Available online at http://news.bbc.co.uk/1/hi/uk/4762209.stm (accessed 30 November 2010).

Bush, George W (2001) Transcript of President Bush's Address. Available online at http://archives.cnn.com/2001/US/09/20/gen.bush.transcript (accessed 3 September 2010).

Carlile of Berriew, Lord (2007) *The Definition of Terrorism*. Norwich: The Stationery Office.

Carr, Caleb (2002) *The Lessons of Terror: A History of Warfare Against Civilians: Why It Has Always Failed and Why It Will Fail Again*. New York: Random House.

Crenshaw, Martha (1981) Causes of Terrorism. *Comparative Politics*, 13(4) (July): 379–99. Available online at www.ukrainianstudies.uottawa.ca/pdf/Crenshaw%201981.pdf (accessed 1 November 2010).

Cronin, Audrey Kurth (2004) *Foreign Terrorist Organizations*. Washington, DC: Congressional Research Service.

Free Dictionary (2010) Ideology. Available online at www.thefreedictionary.com/ideology (accessed 30 November 2010).

Gould, Eric D and Klor, Esteban F (2010) Does Terrorism Work? Social Science Research Network. Available online at http://papers.ssrn.com/sol3/papers.cfm?abstract_id=1413329 (accessed 29 November 2010).

Haniyeh, Ismail (2006) Profile: Hamas PM Ismail Haniyeh. *BBC News*, 14 December 2006. Available online at http://news.bbc.co.uk/1/hi/world/middle_east/4655146.stm (accessed 20 September 10).

Hassan, Muhammad Haniff Bin (2006) Key Considerations in Counterideological Work against Terrorist Ideology. *Studies in Conflict and Terrorism*, 29: 531–58.

Hewitt, Steve (2008) *The British War on Terror.* London: Continuum.

Hoffman, Bruce (2006) *Inside Terrorism.* New York: Columbia University Press.

James, Matthew May, Outman, James L and Outman, Elisabeth M (2003) *Terrorism Reference Library – Vol. 1: Almanac.* Detroit, MI: UXL.

Lia, Brynjar and Skjolberg, Katja (2004) Causes of Terrorism: An Expanded and Updated Review of the Literature. Kjeller, Norway: Forsuarets Forsknings Institutt (FFI) Norwegian Defence Research Establishment. Available online at http://rapporter.ffi.no/rapporter/2004/04307.pdf (accessed 1 November 2010).

Mahan, Sue and Griset, Pamala L (2008) *Terrorism in Perspective*, 2nd edition. London: Sage.

Martin, Gus (2009) *Understanding Terrorism: Challenges, Perspectives and Issues*, 3rd edition. London: Sage.

Mattil, James F (no date) What in the Name of God? – Religious Extremism, Fear & Terrorism. Global Focus: Open Source Intelligence. Available online at www.globalfocus.org/GF-Religion.htm (accessed 22 September 2010).

O'Carroll, Aileen (1994) What's the Importance of the French Revolution? Available online at http://struggle.ws/wsm/talks/france1793.html (accessed 6 September 2010).

Sciolino, Elaine and Schmitt, Eric (2008) Al-Qaeda Threat has Analysts Split into 2 Opposing Camps. *International Herald Tribune*, 8 June 2008. Available online at www.iht.com/articles/2008/06/08/america/terror.php (accessed 13 September 2010).

Smith, Jonathan B (2005) Colonialism – A Catalyst for Ethnic Terrorism. Michigan State University. Available online at www.whisprwave.com/msu-hs-class/issues-in-terrorism/colonialism-ethnic-terrorism.htm (accessed 11 September 2010).

Surjeet, Harkishan Singh (2006) Baghat Singh Remains Our Symbol of Revolution. *People's Democracy (Weekly Organ of the Communist Party of India)*, 30(12), 19 March. Available online at http://pd.cpim.org/2006/0319/03192006_surjeet.htm (accessed 12 September 2011).

Webster's Dictionary (1913) Available online at www.webster-dictionary.org/definition/Colonialism (accessed 6 September 2010).

USEFUL WEBSITES

http://terrorism.about.com/od/groupsleader1/a/TerroristGroups.htm (About.com – Terrorism Issues)

http://wn.com/terrorismworld (Terrorism World)

http://worlddefensereview.com/index.shtml (*World Defense Review: News, Commentary & Analysis*)

www.cdi.org/terrorism/terrorist-groups.cfm (Center for Defense Information (CDI) – List of known terrorist organisations)

www.ctc.usma.edu (Combating Terrorism Center at Westpoint)

www.homeoffice.gov.uk/counter-terrorism (Home Office – Counter-terrorism)

www.icst.psu.edu/index.shtml (International Center for the Study of Terrorism (Pennsylvania State University))

www.manhattan-institute.org/html/cpt.htm (Center for Policing Terrorism)

www.manhattan-institute.org/tools/bytopic.php (Manhattan Institute for Policy Research)

www.mi5.gov.uk/output/international-terrorism-and-the-uk.html (MI5 Security Service – International Terrorism and the UK)

www.mideastweb.org/Middle-East-Encyclopedia (*Encyclopedia of the Middle East*)

www.mipt.org (Memorial Institute for the Prevention of Terrorism)

www.nctc.gov/site/index.html (National Counterterrorism Center (NCTC) – Counterterrorism Calendar 2010)

www.nps.edu/library/research/subjectguides/specialtopics/terroristprofile/terroristgroupprofiles.html (Naval Postgraduate School – terrorist group profiles)

www.pbs.org/newshour/topic/terrorism (PBS Newshour (Terrorism))

www.rand.org/research_areas/terrorism (RAND Corporation)

www.satp.org/satporgtp/site.htm (South Asia Terrorism Portal)

www.start.umd.edu/start (START: National Consortium for the Study of Terrorism And Responses to Terrorism)

www.terrorism101.org/index.html (Terrorism 101)

www.terrorismanalysts.com (*Perspectives on Terrorism: a journal of the Terrorism Research Initiative*)

www.terrorism-info.org.il/site/home/default.asp (Intelligence and Terrorism Information Center) www.terrorism-research.com/groups/categories.php (Terrorism Research)

www.worldstatesmen.org/Terrorist.html (World Statesmen – Global Terrorist Organizations)

Should you find any of the web links do not work, use a search engine (e.g. Google or Bing) to find a new link.

Terrorism Act 2000

Terrorism Act 2006

2 Who are the terrorists?

Chris Blake

CHAPTER OBJECTIVES

By the end of this chapter you should be able to:

- describe the characteristics of state sponsored terrorism;
- debate the issues around revolutionary dissident terrorism;
- understand the debate around religious terrorism;
- discuss violent left- and right-wing ideologies, including terrorism.

Introduction

You have already examined the concept of terrorism in Chapter 1 and it follows that the label 'terrorism' will be used in this chapter to describe the application of unlawful violence to advance a political, religious or ideological cause. This might involve overthrowing or changing a government, replacing officials, revising an economic or social policy, disseminating a socio-economic ideology, or pursuing religious or nationalistic goals.

Hoffman (2006) reminds us that terrorism has endured for over 2000 years and as a term in political science since the French Revolution. It has survived by being able to adapt and adjust to new challenges and countermeasures, and by exploiting opponents' vulnerabilities. To remain one step ahead of the counter-terrorism 'initiative', terrorists have to be determined and extremely sophisticated. Of course, the mantra as to whether such action is politically or morally justified remains a vital question; *Osama Bin Laden was a freedom fighter for Ronald Reagan but a terrorist for George W Bush. One can change sides without changing tactics* (Neilsen, 2003, p430).

Is terrorism liberating?

There have been many attempts to rationalise terrorist activity using political, nationalistic or social justifications and alternative terms have been used to describe terrorist activity: guerrilla movements, commando units and national liberation movements, for example.

These terms are often used to endow the terrorist and terrorism with legitimacy and a more positive foundation. Syria has repeatedly emphasised that it does not assist terrorist organisations, but rather 'national liberation' movements. In a speech to the 21st convention of union workers in 1986, former president Hafez al Assad remarked:

> *We have always opposed terrorism. But terrorism is one thing and national struggle against occupation is another. We support the struggle against the occupation being waged by national liberation movements.*

(Hatzav, 1986, p5)

This attempt to justify terrorism using 'national liberation' arguments is reflected in various Arab forums and debates that differentiate between criminal acts of terrorism. Hatzav (1987, p18) refers to terrorism as *liberation from the yoke of foreign conquest*. Ganor (2005) suggests that national liberation is at one end of a continuum of violence and 'terrorism' at the other end.

REFLECTIVE TASK

The following statement by Leohnid Brezhnev, former president of the USSR, was made in 1981 during a visit by Libyan leader, Muamar Qaddafi. It seems to polarise freedom fighting and terrorism.

> The imperialists have no regard for the will of the people or the laws of history. Struggle for national liberation makes them bitter. They call it terrorism.
>
> *(Cline and Yonah, 1986, p24)*

Before reading further, decide whether 'one man's terrorist is another man's freedom fighter' or do you believe that killing cannot be justified in the name of 'liberation'?

It should be emphasised that the political goal in and of itself, whatever it might be, does not legitimise terrorist activity. Of course it's possible that a terrorist organisation can also be a national liberation movement, but any attempt to rationalise terrorist activity using political, nationalistic or social justifications deviates from the range of otherwise legitimate acts of protest.

The war on terror

The phrase 'war on terror' was first used by President George W Bush to indicate a global military, political, legal and ideological struggle against designated terrorist organisations and regimes, with a particular focus on militant Islamists and al-Qaeda.

The main challenge that we now face is to identify and understand the rationale and inner logic that both motivates and animates terrorism. This can be characterised by the cardinal rule of warfare, 'know your enemy', and looking beyond the simple caricature of a hate-filled, mindless fanatic.

It is easy to dismiss terrorism as an irrational, homicidal obsession. Instead, we need to understand more about how core aims and motivations affect the choice of tactics and targets. For example, terrorist organisations which, by their very nature, act in order to achieve some political aim can be influenced by the amount of support and assistance received from state sponsors. It will suffice briefly to mention that this is usually expressed politically and/or ideologically or in providing economic and military aid, operational training and weapons, perhaps by providing assistance in committing terrorist acts. The notion or paradigm of the state as a 'sponsor' of terror is discussed later in the chapter.

Although briefly discussed in the previous chapter, the point is made here again. Terrorism needs to be considered both as an extreme form of political protest and as aggressive warfare. This is key to developing an appropriate response, whether in the form of safety and security measures and/or offensive measures that target the infrastructure, facilities or activists and leaders. This is discussed in more detail in Chapter 5.

PRACTICAL TASK

The notion of a 'war on terror' has been criticised for lacking definition and an identifiable enemy, which some critics argue provides an agenda or framework for 'perpetual' military action and the pursuit of other goals.

Go to the following link and debate the merits of this assertion: http://dsc.discovery. com/convergence/koppel/highlights/highlights-05.html

---

Categories of terrorism

Terrorism can be divided into two broad categories: domestic and international. Domestic terrorist organisations have long been able to cause harm within a host country where both the perpetrators and targets tend to be 'home-grown'. In 2004 Chechen terrorists took over a Beslan school in Russia's North Ossetian region. In the resulting siege close to 350 civilians, mainly women and small children died and more than 700 people were injured (CNN International.com). International terrorism, on the other hand, involves victims, targets, institutions or citizens of another country, as in the case of the 9/11 attacks where the hijackers had previously lived and trained in Germany, Pakistan, Afghanistan, Chechnya and the USA. International terrorism, though, does not require perpetrators to leave their home countries. It can strike at targets in the home country with symbolic international links and/or interests such as diplomats and military personnel.

Martin (2009) draws attention to the trend in which terrorists recognise no qualitative difference between their victim group and the enemy interest that it represents. We are reminded of the Lebanese Civil War in which domestic attacks against victims with an international profile were commonplace. A prominent characteristic of the Lebanese war was the kidnapping by Islamic extremists of foreign nationals who were considered to be legitimate targets and 'fair game' for terrorist violence (Martin, 2009).

International terrorism is aimed at impeding and undermining political progress, economic prosperity, the security and stability of the international state system and the future of civil society. Moreover, globalisation and the nature of free and open societies enable international terrorist networks to take advantage of freedom of movement, communications, financial systems and logistical support. Extremist networks are able to operate in, and exploit seams between states, between the military and police forces, and between international and local laws. Consequently, Western democracies are highly vulnerable to terrorist violence.

Al-Qaeda (AQ) is probably the most widely known international terrorist organisation. Following the elimination of the AQ network base of operations in Afghanistan, the remaining leadership and key operational elements dispersed globally, effectively decentralising control and franchising its extremist efforts to affiliated groups within a developing network. The resulting Al-Qaeda Associated Movement has extended extremism and terrorist tactics well beyond the original organisation. It exploits Islam and purposefully targets 'ordinary' people to create fear and intimidation in nation states in the pursuit of its political, religious and ideological goals.

AQ is not only responsible for the 9/11 attacks, but is credited with the 1995 bombing of the World Trade Center, the 1998 attacks on the US embassies in Kenya and Tanzania, the 2000 attack on the USS *Cole* in Yemen and with the attacks on Indonesian and Turkish targets. These incidents have had economic and security implications worldwide and subsequent changes in visa procedures, airport security, target fortification and other counter-terrorism measures are indications that international terrorism now represents the greater concern to authorities.

The modern era of international terrorism began in 1968 following the Arab–Israeli conflict and Israel's subsequent occupation of captured territory. The Palestinians resorted to international terrorism to publicise their cause to the international community and to gain recognition by the Israelis. Levels of international terrorism hit a new plateau in the early to mid-1970s as terrorist methods were copied by non-Palestinian groups; for example, by left-wing nihilist groups, which sprang up throughout Western Europe believing that religion and nationalism were at the root of ignorance (Martin, 2009).

PRACTICAL TASK

Use academic texts and the internet to identify some of these 'copy cat' groups. Were they domestic or international in nature? Draw up a table that lists their key functions, processes and resources – compare and contrast. Why is it important to identify key functions, processes and resources in determining a counter-network strategy?

Terrorism – a shifting paradigm

From the late 1960s until the late 1980s international terrorism was primarily motivated by secular nationalism, separatism, Marxist ideology and nihilism, although the collapse of many communist regimes in the post-cold war era saw a reduced interest in Marxism and a subsequent decline in terrorism (Wilkinson, 2001). The shift in Soviet attitudes towards the United Nations was signalled as early as 1985, when the Soviet Union endorsed a Security Council resolution (579) condemning hostage-taking and reminding all states of their obligation to *secure the safe release of the hostages* and to prevent future incidents (Luck, 2004, p90). Since the 1990s the ideologies of class conflict and secular nationalism have been challenged by a new infusion of religious-based fundamentalist groups; religious 'extremism' is now seen as the predominant model for political violence in the modern world and a central issue for the global community.

Religious and secular terrorism

Hoffman (2006) has described religious terrorism as a sacramental act or divine duty of unquestionable faith. It is contingent on trends within specific religions, the historical experiences of ethno-national groups and the unique political environment of nations. Moreover, it tends to be unconstrained by political, moral or other practical considerations and large-scale violence is considered as morally justified, necessary and expedient for the attainment of terrorists' goals. It should be noted that, while religious justification of such attacks is important for many Muslims, secular groups related to Fatah, such as Tanzim and Al-Aqsa Martyrs' Brigade, have resorted to similar tactics. However, secular terrorism generally regards indiscriminate killing as counterproductive, if not immoral.

Secular and religious terrorism also differ in their constituencies. Secular terrorism seeks to appeal to the communities it purports to 'defend', or people for whom it claims to speak. It regards violence as a legitimate means of correcting or creating new systems and/or processes. Religious terrorism appeals to its own constituency. It is not the component of any 'system' but, rather, the 'outsider' that seeks fundamental change to the existing order. This sense of alienation allows the religious terrorist to engage in a 'total' war that can, and often does, result in limitless violence against a virtually open-ended category of targets; that is, anyone outside the terrorists' religion or religious sect. This goes some way towards explaining the rhetoric of 'holy terror' and the use of denigrating language, such as 'infidels', 'dogs', 'children of Satan' and 'mud people'. The deliberate use of such language portrays victims as either subhuman or unworthy of living, and further erodes constraints on violence and bloodshed.

These distinguishing factors can also serve to make religious terrorism much more dangerous. In some environments, religion is more the overarching cultural identity for politically violent movements. But where religion becomes the primary motive for terrorism – the sacramental act rather than a device for achieving political goals – there are no moral limits to what might be done and seemingly little chance for a negotiated settlement.

PRACTICAL TASK

Neat categories exist in academia, but how easy is it to differentiate between religious and secular terrorism? Research and prepare a model that compares the fundamental characteristics of religious and secular terrorism. Pay particular attention to the type and extent of violence used as well as the constituency profile.

State-sponsored terrorism

State-sponsored terrorism is firmly rooted in the story of human civilisation. Religious impulses have not been the only driving forces behind terrorism; the Enlightenment and other intellectual movements of the eighteenth century challenged the divine rights of the monarchy, arguing instead for a political system that recognised the equality of men. Hereditary rulers and their representatives were the target of assassins, and revolutionary governments have themselves turned on their citizens, launching terrorist attacks of an extreme nature. In 1789 radicals forced King Louis XVI to move to Paris, where he was later tried by the revolutionary court and then executed. This saw the establishment of a revolutionary Tribunal and Committee for Public Safety and the start of the *régime de la terreur*, mentioned in Chapter 1. Hoffman (1998) estimates that 40,000 people were victims of French, state-sponsored terrorism with the 'new' government targeting, arresting and executing opponents in the name of the revolutionary cause. Like modern terrorists, the revolutionaries used advances in modern technology. Dr Joseph Guillotine saw himself as a humanitarian, inventing a machine intended to make capital punishment less painful to the victim. Fearing that they might also be on a list of state enemies, the regime was finally ended when a group staged a *coup d'état.*

Characteristics of state terrorism

Participation in terrorist and extremist behaviour incorporates direct and indirect sponsorship in both the domestic and international policy domains. At one extreme, a government can operate its own death squads for the express purpose of advancing the state's interests. At the other extreme it can simply provide a safe haven for terrorists, allowing them to operate with impunity. Lying somewhere in the middle is the provision of financial assistance, or perhaps the refusal to assist another state in extradition proceedings.

Direct sponsorship in an international context

According to Martin (2009) direct sponsorship, or the 'patronage' of terrorism, involves overt participation in, and the encouragement of, repression, violence and terrorism both domestically and internationally. Active methods are used to initiate terrorism and other subversive activities, which include direct arms supply, training and providing sanctuary for terrorists. A prime example is Syria's support of various radical Islamist organisations, such as Hezbollah, Hamas, Palestinian Islamic Jihad and the Popular Front for the Liberation of Palestine, and other terrorist organisations aspiring to eradicate the nation of Israel. Not only does Syria provide money, arms and training for terrorists, but it also allows other countries, including Iran, to use its territory to ship aid to terrorists (Mahan and Griset, 2008).

International support can be framed in a 'foreign policy' that directly supports a group, or proxy, in its cause and continues to do so even when the proxy is known for committing acts of terrorism. Labeviere (2000) refers to US policy in Afghanistan, suggesting that guiding the evolution of Islam and helping Islamists worked well for the USA. He also suggests that the same doctrines can be used to destabilise what remains of Russian power, and especially to counter the Chinese influence in Central Asia. In other words, the Central Intelligence Agency (CIA) had always seen vast potential in using the terrorist network established by bin Laden during the cold war in an international framework in Eastern Europe, the Balkans and Central Asia. In fact, the Balkans provides confirmation of this assertion and is an example of how Western foreign policies can directly undermine Western national security by forming alliances with terrorist forces. Bodansky (1996), a former director of the Congressional anti-terrorism task force, draws attention to the intelligence and military training provided by the USA and Great Britain to the Kosovo Liberation Army (KLA), despite its links to Albanian mafia allies and AQ. There were also concerns that a major portion of the KLA finances were derived from drug trafficking and terrorist organisations motivated by radical Islam, including the assets of Iran and of bin Laden (Craig, 1999). Indeed, the KLA was associated with AQ as early as 1998, but despite these reports US and British military intelligence continued to work with them, providing further training and assistance.

Direct sponsorship in a domestic context

Direct sponsorship or 'patronage' is characterised by the use of state security personnel in an overt policy of sponsored, political violence. According to Martin (2009), state patrons typically rationalise policies of repression by arguing that they are necessary to:

- *suppress a clear and present domestic threat to national security;*

- *maintain law and order at a time of national crisis;*

- *protect fundamental cultural values that are threatened by subversives; or*

- *restore stability to governmental institutions that have been shaken, usurped or damaged by a domestic enemy.*

(Martin, 2009, p104)

Since 1980 politically motivated violence against non-combatants has evolved from a tool used against the state into an instrument of the state. Organised acts of political terrorism in Iran were evident between the 1905 revolution and the rise of Reza Shah to power in 1925. Several political groups were formed in this period to eliminate politicians, journalists and even religious leaders accused of working for foreign powers, notably Great Britain and tsarist Russia. A more recent example of the clandestine use of state resources is South Africa's assignment of the military and security personnel covertly to suppress opponents of racial separation. The South African Government began a direct campaign to flush out anti-apartheid leaders and supporters, which included those offering support to the Inkatha Freedom Party in its violence against the ANC.

In its worst form, domestic 'patronage' can amount to genocide, where resources of the state are employed to eliminate or culturally suppress a people, religion or other demographic group. One such example is the Anfal, anti-Kurdish campaign led by the former Iraqi regime between 1986 and 1989, which involved a series of military campaigns against the Kurdish Peshmerga fighters as well as the mostly Kurdish civilian population of northern Iraq and southern Kurdistan.

Research the 1994 Rwandan Genocide, which was the culmination of ethnic competition and tensions between the minority Tutsi and the majority Hutu. Decide if this is characteristic of domestic state 'patronage'.

Indirect sponsorship in an international context

Indirect sponsorship, or state 'assistance' is characterised by a tacit, indirect link with terrorist behaviour, albeit directed by government. Unlike 'patronage', those who 'assist' are less explicit in what they do and links to 'outsiders' and international foreign policy tend to be more ambiguous. According to Martin (2009), state 'assistance' is usually channelled through sympathetic extremist proxies and agents who will engage in terrorist violence, whereby the state will indirectly arm, train and provide sanctuary for terrorists. This serves to shift the actions of government beyond 'normal politics', which has implications should the proxy's terrorism become known. For example, the notion of pursuing terrorists within a human rights framework lays emphasis on evidence, trial and punishment. And yet this is often in tension with the direct, repressive and often violent methods used by extremist proxies. The ambiguity built into the relationship, though, allows for denial and if the 'assister' is accused of complicity they can:

- *deny the relationship;*

- *admit the relationship but mitigate the outcomes;*

- *admit or deny the relationship but justify the role of the perpetrators and the cause.*
  (Martin 2009, p105)

You have already considered the clandestine use of South African security forces to violently assert authority in the elimination of ANC members and supporters. Now, consider the difference between this and clandestine support provided for anti-ANC death squads or Askaris, which were later responsible for targeting ANC members suspected of being dissidents or sympathisers both inside South Africa and in neighbouring countries.

It has been alleged that the CIA actively supported the military Junta after the overthrow of Dr Salvador Allende in the early 1970s. Access the National Security Archive, excerpts from 'CIA Activities in Chile,' via the link below and decide whether US involvement is an example of international 'state-assisted' terrorism: www.gwu.edu/~nsarchiv/news/200009 19/index.html

Indirect sponsorship in a domestic context

State 'assistance' is characterised by the use of sympathetic proxies in policies of 'assisted' political violence. This can occur in an environment that includes 'patronage' as well as indirect, repressive state 'assistance'. As a mode of surrogate warfare, 'assisted' violence is a useful 'weapons system' and a means of engaging in war against domestic opponents. 'Assisted' proxies can offer a cheap, deniable alternative to open, state violence. Nations that are unable to mount a conventional military challenge may see terrorism as an attractive alternative. The consequences are that it places additional resources in the hands of the terrorists: money, munitions, intelligence and technical expertise. It also reduces the constraints on terrorists by permitting them to engage in operations without fear of alienating perceived constituents or provoking public criticism, since they do not depend on local constituents for support.

State 'assisters' typically rationalise policies of indirect repression by adopting official positions that:

- *focus blame on adversaries for any breakdown in social order;*

- *seek to provide reassurance that efforts are being conducted to restore order;*

- *point to proxy violence as evidence of patriotic sentiment and necessary to suppress threats to law and order.*

(Martin 2009, p107)

Dissident terrorism

Sometimes referred to as 'terrorism from below', Martin (2009) suggests that dissident terrorism is motivated primarily by the desire for some degree of national autonomy or 'self-determination' and is usually directed against existing governments and political institutions. It also champions the aspirations of those distinguished by their culture, religious, ethnic or racial heritage. The championed group may be a minority living among a majority group or it may be a majority national group in a region that is dominated by the government or another ethnic group, such as the domination of Tibet by China. In Latin America, as well as in India and Algeria, terrorism was tied to colonial rule and the desire for self-determination; resistance to the Spanish conquistadors dates from the sixteenth century. Other examples include the Spanish anti-Francoist movement during the Franco dictatorship, the KLA in the Kosovo War and the IRA during the Irish War of Independence. Most factions of the Taliban, the Iraqi Insurgency and Colombia's revolutionary armed forces (FARC) are believed to have engaged in some form of guerrilla warfare.

PRACTICAL TASK

Before continuing, research and write down a list of things that might explain the Russian Federation's refusal to recognise Chechnya as an independent republic.

Chechnya

In 1991 Chechnya declared its independence during the pending collapse of the Soviet Union. Its rationale was that some other Central Asian, Eastern European and Baltic states had also declared independence. The Russian Federation refused to recognise this independence and by 1994 the conflict with Chechen separatists had grown into a war. This concluded in 1996 and was followed with a peace agreement that granted Chechnya substantial autonomy. Russian troops returned in 1999, following the attempt by Chechen separatists to enter bordering Dagestan and a series of bombings in Russia attributed to Chechen militants. The weight of the Russian military response led to an expanded role for women in terrorism; the presence of female suicide bombers within the Chechen resistance movement belies the common presumption that terrorism is purely a male preserve (Torbakov, 2004).

Research the 'Black Widows' and document their involvement in notable acts of separatist violence. What were the reasons for an influx of female terrorists into the Chechen rebel movement?

By the beginning of 2008, Russia claimed to have stabilised the region and the Russian war in Chechnya seemed to be over. But its legacy will continue as Chechen separatism, sporadic terrorist attacks and the spill-over into nearby republics continues. Torbakov (2004) points out that the Chechen war will serve as a reminder and as an object lesson to other groups seeking independence or wishing to leave the Russian Federation.

The notorious 2006 assassinations of highly respected Russian authors Anna Politkovskaya and Alexander Litvinenko have been traced directly to the Chechen conflict and are widely attributed to the Russian regime. Were these assassinations excusable in any way or have they served to taint all of Russian society?

Terrorism and politics

Achieving a psychological impact is ultimately the goal of those engaged in terrorism. It is equally the case that the principal focus of dissident terrorism is to achieve some political objective(s). As Hoffman states, *terrorism is ineluctably political* (1998, p43). We are also reminded that dissident violence has long been viewed as a necessary evil by those sympathetic to its cause, with revolutionaries, terrorists and assassins justifying their actions to defend a higher cause (Martin, 2009). While numerous groups have laid the foundation for contemporary terrorism, one of the earliest revolutionary groups was the Narodnaya Volya, meaning the 'People's Will'. In the late nineteenth century they engaged in a wide variety of terrorist acts ranging from assassination to suicide bombing against officials in tsarist Russia. What was particularly striking about this group is that they specifically sought to avoid the killing of innocent bystanders. They also deliberately called themselves terrorists as opposed to freedom fighters, believing that the former were morally justified in their battle against an 'oppressive state'.

The urban guerrilla

PRACTICAL TASK

Before continuing, refer to the Minimanual of the Urban Guerrilla *by accessing the following link: www.marxists.org/archive/marighella-carlos/1969/06/minimanual-urban-guerrilla/index.htm. We are informed by Hanrahan (1985) that this has been used by many terrorist organisations, including the Italian Red Brigade, the German Red Army Faction and the IRA.*

- *To what extent was Marighella able to influence ideological activism?*

- *Identify the ideological differences between Marighella and Che Guevara, the Argentinian revolutionary who was a major figure of the Cuban Revolution.*

Guerrilla warfare

The term 'guerrilla', meaning 'little war' in Spanish, is a form of warfare in which the combatants are irregular military, rather than regular forces. Mao Zedong began his revolution in the Chinese countryside, as did the Algerian National Liberation Front, although Marighella initially pursued an urban-based campaign. This was based on a scorched-earth policy, the sabotage of transport and oil pipelines, and the destruction of food supplies. He believed that urban terrorism would create a crisis atmosphere and that ordinary people would become a source of rebellion. Like Guy Fawkes, he overestimated the will of the people and was killed in a police ambush in 1969.

CASE STUDY

MNLF, MILF and Abu Sayyaf

The conflict in the Philippines is mainly a legacy of Spanish and American colonialism. In the 1960s the Muslim/Moro separatist movement in the Philippines emerged among a small number of students and intellectuals, articulating widespread grievances concerned with discrimination, poverty and inequality. The movement gained popular support, coalescing into an armed group, the Moro National Liberation Front (MNLF). But factional fighting led to the founding of the Moro Islamic Liberation Front (MILF) and in 1991 the Abu Sayyaf group split from the MNLF intent on the establishment of an Islamic state.

Access the links below and examine the collective and independent roles of the MNLF, MILF and the Abu Sayyaf group. Discuss whether the methods used were justified in the attempt to secure equality and a recognised homeland.

- *www.strategicstudiesinstitute.army.mil/pdffiles/PUB625.pdf*

- *http://rspas.anu.edu.au/papers/conflict/may_ADSC.pdf*

Communal terrorism

Dissident, communal terrorism is also referred to as separatist, nationalist, tribal, racial, indigenous or minority terrorism and it usually occurs where sub-populations wage war on each other. It is also based on perceived racial, religious, ethno-national and/or ideological differences and/or to defend a cultural identity. Africa ranks at the top for communal conflicts with long-term disputes in Sierra Leone, Liberia, Chad, Sudan, Congo, Burundi and South Africa. Disputes can involve genocide in the extreme or occur where a politically dominant ethnic or racial group seeks to control a subordinate ethnic or racial group, such as the domination of African-Americans by white supremacists in the American south at the turn of the twentieth century.

Right-wing extremism

Right-wing political extremism can take various forms, with some individuals and groups advocating stringent and immoderate measures, including violence and intimidation to promote their beliefs, and their priority over other cultures and communities. They generally seek strong centralised government and the preservation of a national, domestic culture. Beginning in the nineteenth century, groups of native Americans, primarily Protestants, began to form protective associations to dispel the influence of immigrant groups and foreign religions. As an urban Protestant movement, the Know Nothings formed a secret anti-Catholic society to discourage Irish immigration. Perhaps the most notorious group in the immediate post-Civil War period was the Ku Klux Klan (KKK), a religious organisation that used terror and intimidation to progressively disenfranchise and effectively relegate Republicans and freed slaves to the political margins of society.

Left-wing extremism

Left-wing extremism developed from working-class movements that sought to create a class, or national consciousness, and to eliminate, not preserve, social and economic inequalities. Leftist terrorism in post-war Argentina presented serious challenges for established governments and eventually led to the downfall of the military junta in 1973. The Revolutionary Armed Forces of Colombia (FARC) formed in 1964 as the armed wing of the originally pro-Soviet Colombian Communist Party. It successfully 'liberated zones' in central Colombia by using guerrilla tactics, including kidnapping and assassinations. The Red Brigade, an Italian Marxist-Leninist revolutionary movement, was perhaps the most threatening and ideological terrorist group in Europe during the 1970s and early 1980s, and was responsible for the kidnap and murder of former Italian Prime Minister Aldo Moro in 1978.

CASE STUDY

Hanns-Martin Schleyer

A woman stepped out in front of a car in Cologne, forcing the driver to stop. He was chauffeuring one of West Germany's most powerful industrialists. The woman revealed two machine guns and, along with her accomplices, she bundled Hanns-Martin Schleyer out of the car.

PRACTICAL TASK

Research and discuss the incident. What were the motivating influences behind the Red Army Faction? The group was severely weakened by the fall of the Berlin Wall and shortly afterwards its dissolution was announced along with an accompanying statement: 'The revolution says I was, I am, I will be again.' What do you understand by this statement?

Religious terrorism

Religious terrorism usually occurs between different religious groups, particularly when one or more becomes segregated. Martin (2009) explains that cultural identity is defined partly through religious ideals and that religious terrorism tends to have an element of religious 'quality'. The Sri Lankan Tamil Tigers, for example, were able to force the Government into negotiations through their lengthy guerrilla and terrorist campaigns. The dismantling of former Yugoslavia similarly led to violence between Orthodox Christian Serbs, Muslim Bosnians and Roman Catholic Croats and the forced removal of rival groups from their claimed territory. In Israel both Jewish and Muslim militants have engaged in sectarian violence against each other, with both justifying their actions as reprisals for attacks on their peoples and territory. In Northern Ireland the mainly Protestant unionist and mainly Catholic nationalist communities have been waged in communal unrest since 1969. The principal issue at stake is the constitutional status of Northern Ireland. Terrorist attacks by the Provisional IRA and republican splinter groups have been directed mainly against the British administration both in Northern Ireland and in the UK. During the same period loyalist paramilitaries have targeted pro-IRA Catholics, civilian leaders, opposition sympathisers and random victims rather than symbols of republican authority. The future of Northern Ireland is now the subject of intense negotiations, but without IRA violence it is unlikely that the British would have considered negotiations or that the Protestant majority in Northern Ireland would have consented to any reduction in its control (Alonso, 2007).

A night of street fighting between hundreds of Muslims and Christians left at least 12 people dead and two churches in flames on Sunday in the latest outbreak of sectarian tensions in the three months since the revolution that ousted President Hosni Mubarak.

(New York Times, 2011)

Decide whether tensions in this case stem from religious or political disagreements. Will this hamper Egypt's move to democracy and what can be done to prevent a recurrence?

Terrorism in the name of a religion

Religious violence often stems from events that occurred hundreds, even thousands, of years ago. Indeed, the tactics used by many of the twenty-first-century terrorist organisations have been inspired by much earlier theoretical and theological arguments. The Jewish Zealots referred to in Chapter 1 constitute one of the earliest large-scale terrorist organisations. Guy Fawkes was part of another religiously inspired terrorist group and, like other instances of 'holy terror', the origins of the gunpowder plot are related to events that occurred long before.

Prior to the 9/11 attacks terrorism was primarily a mechanism of revolutionary violence derived mainly from the political grievances of secular extremists. This chapter has previously examined how the emanation of Marxist-inspired ideologies, rightist reaction, ethno-nationalist imperatives or amalgams of these tendencies threatened governments and 'enemy peoples'. But the past two decades have witnessed 'new' forms of terrorism. In the 1980s state-sponsored terrorism became the new face of warfare. In 1983 the suicide bomber rose to prominence as an unstoppable form of terrorism. This older, cold war-influenced era was gradually replaced by a mainly sectarian terrorist environment that became the driving force behind international terrorist violence. Religious terrorism remained in the shadows of secular ideology until the mid-1990s (Martin, 2009). Then, the rise of Christian Identity violence in the USA and the Aum Shinrikyo attack in Japan steered the spotlight on to religious terrorism, which is now the predominant model for political violence in the modern world (Martin, 2009).

Religious terrorism has increased in its frequency, scale of violence and global reach. In disparate places around the globe, from Indonesia to the Caucasus and from Pakistan to Western Europe, jihadist ideology has become the banner under which an array of violent grievances is being expressed. In many of these regions, local and global grievances are merging into a pervasive hatred of the USA, its allies and the international order they uphold.

Radicalisation

Previously discussed in Chapter 1, 'extremist ideology' is naturally aligned with the notion of radicalisation and the way that people move towards extremist beliefs. Quite simply, it is a process by which religious and ideological beliefs are interpreted. This can involve a sense of personal injustice, alienation or community disadvantage that arises from socio-economic factors such as discrimination, social exclusion and lack of opportunity, although setting out these factors does not in any way imply their validity. While an individual may not be relatively disadvantaged, he or she may identify with others who are seen as less privileged; also, different generations within the same family may have significantly different views about these issues. The process of globalisation can also become a catalyst for radicalisation, not simply in economic terms but also through the modernity of social and cultural traditions.

Understanding jihad

In the Islamist context, jihad refers to the duty of Muslims to strive 'in the way of God'. The plasticity of the word, however, has made it the source for much debate and, in the West, it has become a synonym for the terms 'holy war' and 'terrorism' (Martin, 2004). The literal meaning of jihad is a sacred 'struggle' or 'effort', which refers to:

- a believer's internal struggle to live out the Muslim faith as well as possible;

- the struggle to build a good Muslim society;

- holy war: the struggle to defend Islam, with force if necessary.

Developing the notion of a 'holy war', Martin (2009) explains that not all Muslims support jihad or terrorism. He suggests that *Pigeonholing of both the term and its range of meaning does [it] a disservice and often leads to a misunderstanding of Islamic behaviour* (p151). He also reminds us of the many Muslim lives lost in violent conflicts between Iran and Iraq, and in the civil wars of Afghanistan and Algeria.

Historically, Islamic authorities have set clear boundaries on the use of indiscriminate violence; the killing of non-combatants, women, children and fellow Muslims has been almost universally condemned throughout history. But with 'Islamic jurisprudence' at the core of Osama bin Laden's thinking, he has been responsible for promoting the indiscriminate use of terrorism, including the killing of Muslims. This would appear to be based on the work of Sayyid Qutb, the enormously influential Islamic thinker of the past century, and a group of contemporary Saudi apocalypticists (Benjamin and Simon 2002).

State sponsorship of religious and revolutionary movements

Hezbollah

Iran has been very open with its 'patronage' of Hezbollah, the Lebanese movement that has been effective in using terrorism to advance its political agenda. Hezbollah has previously targeted foreign forces in Lebanon, including the US marines and French paratroopers who were serving as peacekeepers, as well as units of the Israeli Defence Force. Continuing pressure against the Israelis eventually led to the evacuation of their foothold in southern Lebanon. These tactical victories helped the group to become one of the major political forces in Lebanon, and the Lebanese Parliament (Kydd and Walter, 2006). Iran has also promoted other religious movements, including Palestine Islamic Jihad and Hamas, the Islamic Resistance Movement.

PRACTICAL TASK

Research the role of Syria in supporting radical Islamist terrorists, which includes Hezbollah, Hamas, Palestinian Islamic Jihad and the Popular Front for the Liberation of Palestine.

Muslim Kashmir

In the Jammu and Kashmir regions of India, a sustained insurgency, supported by the Pakistani authorities, led to a protracted campaign of terror between Pakistani proxies and Muslim Kashmir on one side, and the Indian army on the other side. Islamic fighters, supported by Pakistan, have waged a protracted war against the Indian presence, using terrorism to attack Indian forces and interests in the pursuit of an independent Jammu and Kashmir.

The Mujahidin – Holy Warriors of Faith

Accepting the title of Mujahidin means that one must live, fight and die in accordance with religious teachings (Martin 2009). The modern conceptualisation of the Mujahidin, or 'holy warrior', can be traced back to the Soviet invasion of Afghanistan where, in 1979, the fight against Marxist and Soviet regimes reflected a long-established tradition of uprising against oppression reaching back to the wars against the British in the mid- and late nineteenth century. In Afghanistan, the Mujahidin called upon their allies from all over the Muslim world to assist in the Soviet fight and, after ten years, they scored a stunning victory, forcing the communists to retreat unconditionally from Afghanistan.

C H A P T E R S U M M A R Y

This chapter has discussed the notions of state and dissident terrorism, religious violence and violent ideologies, including terrorism from the left and the right. Religious violence was defined and examples of religious movements, united by their identity and belief systems, were provided. The reader was introduced to state-sponsored terrorism and examples of guerrilla and conventional warfare were presented. The reader was introduced to methods of state sponsorship – patronage and assistance. Patronage is characterised by its active, direct participation in terrorism. The assistance model is characterised by the tacit, indirect sponsorship of terrorism. The scale of support and directness of involvement were discussed in both the foreign and domestic policy domains. The chapter provided readers with an understanding of the nature of dissident terrorism, including revolutionary, nihilist and nationalist dissident terrorism. Communal terrorism – group against group – includes ethno-nationalist, religious and ideological communal terrorism. Anti-state dissident terrorism is defined as terrorism directed against governments and other centres of power. The chapter provided readers with an insight into the characteristics of left-wing, Marxist-inspired terrorism, which is characterised by democratic socialism. Though much less ideologically centred, right-wing terrorism emphasises nationalism, racism, anti-democracy and a strong executive. Finally, religious terrorism was discussed, with a focus on radicalisation, jihad and examples of state-sponsored religious movements.

Alonso, R (2007) *The IRA and Armed Struggle*. Oxford: Routledge.

Benjamin, D and Simon, S (2002) *The Age of Sacred Terror*. New York: Random House.

Bodansky, Y (1996) *Some Call It Peace: Waiting for War in the Balkans*. London: International Media Corporation.

Cline, R and Yonah, A (1986) *Terrorism as State-sponsored Covert Warfare*. Fairfax, VA: Hero Books.

CNN International.com (2004) Russia School Siege Toll Tops 350. CNN International, 5 September. Available online at http://edition.cnn.com/2004/WORLD/europe/09/04/russia.school/index.html (accessed 10 May 2011).

Craig, LC (1999) The Kosovo Liberation Army: Does Clinton Policy Support Group(s) with Terror, Drug Ties?: From Terrorists to Partners. United States Senate Republican Policy Committee, Washington, DC, 31 March. Available online at www.fas.org/irp/world/para/docs/fr033199.htm (accessed 19 May 2011).

Ganor, B (2005) *The Counter-terrorism Puzzle: A Guide for Decision Makers*. New Brunswick, NJ: Transaction Publishers.

Hanrahan, G (trans.) (1985) *The Terrorist Classic: Manual of the Urban Guerrilla* by Carlos Marighella. Chapel Hill, NC: Documentary Publications.

Hatzav (1986) 25 November 1986, originally in *Tishrin*, Syria, 17 November 1986.

Hatzav (1987) 11 February 1987, originally in *Al-Anba'a*, Kuwait, 30 January 1987.

Hoffman, B (1998) *Inside Terrorism*. New York: Columbia University Press.

Hoffman, B (2006) *Inside Terrorism*, 2nd edition. New York: Columbia University Press.

Kydd, AH and Walter, BF (2006) *The Strategies of Terrorism. International Security*, 31(1): 49-80.

Labeviere, R (2000) *Dollars for Terror: The United States and Islam*. New York: Algora Publishing.

Luck, E (2004) Tackling Terrorism, in Malone, D (ed.) *The UN Security Council from the Cold War to the 21st Century*. Boulder, CO: Lynne Reinner.

Mahan, P and Griset, P (2008) *Terrorism in Perspective*, 2nd edition. London: Sage.

Martin, G (2004) *The New Era of Terrorism*. London: Sage.

Martin, G (2009) *Understanding Terrorism: Challenges, Perspectives and Issues*, 3rd edition. London: Sage.

Neilsen, K (2003) On the Moral Justifiability of Terrorism (State and Otherwise). *Osgood Hall Law Journal*, 41(2&3): 427–44.

New York Times (2011) Clashes in Cairo Leave 12 Dead and 2 Churches in Flames, 8 May. Available online at www.nytimes.com/2011/05/09/world/middleeast/09egypt.html?_r=1 (accessed 16 May 2011).

Torbakov, I (2004) Assessing the Moscow Subway Blast: Tragic Incident or Lethal Spillover from the War in Chechnya?, in Sageman, M (ed.) *Unmasking Terror* (pp110–12). Washington, DC: Jamestown Foundation.

Wilkinson, P (2001) *Terrorism Versus Democracy: The Liberal State Response*. London: Frank Cass.

3 Terrorist tactics and targets

Rachael Strzelecki

CHAPTER OBJECTIVES

By the end of this chapter you should be able to:

- understand the theoretical concepts relating to terrorist targets and tactics;
- outline the selection of targets and methods used by terrorist groups;
- explore the effectiveness of terrorism and how success is measured;
- analyse the implications of weapons of mass destruction as a mode of terrorism.

Introduction

Wardlaw (1997) describes terrorism as *violence for effect* and notes that *the actual physical damage it causes is not important; the aim is to have a dramatic impact on the audience* (p43).

This chapter explores a number of theoretical concepts to explain the rationale behind the tactics adopted and targets selected by terrorist groups. It also examines tactics used by terrorist groups to achieve their goals and why terrorists in certain circumstances change tactics. Selecting a target for an attack, whether it be a physical target such as a building or a person, or a psychological target such as a government, is a crucial element of the decision-making process. The rationale for target selection is explored together with the methods employed by terrorist groups to achieve their objectives and how success is measured.

Throughout history terrorist groups have been altering their tactics and methods in order to achieve their end objectives. More recently a more radical form of terrorist has been introduced to the world stage, which has led to new and more sinister approaches to methods used by terrorist groups. Mass killing by terrorists has been witnessed in New York, Bali, Mumbai, London and Madrid, and there is a real desire by terrorist groups to obtain weapons of mass destruction. The chapter will conclude by briefly exploring this emerging threat.

Theoretical concepts: terrorist targets and tactics

Before delving into the theoretical concepts that explain tactics and target selection processes of terrorist groups, consider what is meant by an objective and the difference between an objective and a goal.

An objective is an incremental step in the overall process that leads to an ultimate goal. A goal is the final result of the process, the terminal point of a series of processes.

(Martin, 2009, p339)

Each terrorist group has its own goals and objectives primarily defined by political views and ideologies. For example, the end goal for a right-wing terrorist is to overthrow an existing regime and replace it with a fascist-orientated or nationalist one. To achieve this goal a number of objectives may be necessary, such as recruiting, training, marketing, promotion of racism and the use of violence.

When discussing terrorist objectives you inevitably stumble across moral arguments, such as a terrorist group believing they are freedom fighters fighting for a just cause, whereas the majority of the community would consider their actions of violence to be terrorism (see previous comments on pages 8–11). Large sections of a population may agree or sympathise with a terrorist group but oppose the way that their goals and objectives are met.

To the majority of the global population acts of terrorism may appear random and senseless acts of violence; however, to the terrorist group they are neither of these two things. Violent acts are often methodically planned and rarely senseless, with a mindset that the actions taken are merely a consequence of war in support of their cause. The targets are rarely chosen at random but are selected to meet a political agenda or ideology. Martin suggests that extremists have an almost *universal acceptance that terrorist violence is a kind of 'poor man's warfare' used by the weak against strong opponents* (2009, p338).

Violence is justified as an acceptable weapon for certain members of society to oppose regimes that do not share the same political views or other agendas such as extreme religious views. It also provides a clear message to adversaries who do not understand peaceful ways of negotiating.

Terrorist methods are adopted by extremists for a number of reasons:

- *terror tactics are relatively easy to employ and are useful for organisations that lack sophisticated weapons or popular support;*

- *terrorism attracts a substantial amount of publicity that can achieve global notoriety and attention; and*

- *it questions the ability of a government to rule, and if perceived as weak, may result in an over-reaction by law enforcement and security forces (this may also engender support for terrorist group).*

(Martin, 2009, p338)

Although terrorist groups are very different, there can be certain similarities between objectives based upon scales of minimum and maximum desirability. The minimal objective for most terrorist groups is public recognition of existence, with the most desirable objective being the achievement of their main political goal (Weimann and Winn, 1994). For example, in the instance of the IRA in Northern Ireland their minimal objective was met when they were recognised as a terrorist group with their purpose known and publicly debated. Their most desirable objective was to have a united Ireland with no British influence present in the north.

A number of central objectives can be shared between violent extremist groups, such as seeking to change an existing order, causing psychological and social disruption, winning media awareness and publicity, and creating a revolutionary environment (Martin, 2009).

PRACTICAL TASK

Find out about the terrorist bomb attack in Omagh, Northern Ireland (August 1998) carried out by the Real Irish Republican Army (RIRA) and write down what you think the objectives of the RIRA were. Comprehensive information about the attack can be found at www.wesleyjohnston.com/users/ireland/past/omagh/main.html.

In 1997 the RIRA (Oglaigh na hEireann) split from the Provisional IRA (PIRA) and their political arm Sinn Fein (SF) after denouncing their involvement in the peace process. Their ultimate objective was to disrupt the peace process and create a unified Ireland. Their immediate goal was to embarrass the SF leadership as they engaged in the peace process and their early tactics included attacking Northern Ireland's economic structure by bombing town centres. This event created intense public outrage within the community and the RIRA suspended its military operations (Anatalio, 2002).

Selection of targets

How does a terrorist group select a specific target? There is not a 'one model fits all' approach and a terrorist group's selection of targets can be unique in many ways depending on the type of people that make up the group, their ideologies and beliefs, and the way that each group operates.

When a group is deciding which target to attack it can be faced with several possible legitimate options. The group considers the likely impact and reaction of the attack to achieve and promote its political agenda and in some cases may redefine target selection. The ideology of the group helps to identify targets and group objectives assist in selecting suitable targets to attack (Hoffman, 2006). Symbolic targets and those that provide propaganda value are very often selected by the terrorist.

REFLECTIVE TASK

The Olympic Games attract immense global media coverage and public interest. Consider why the Games are always a potential target for terrorist groups and how an attack can contribute to the goals of a terrorist group. The following websites have information about terrorist attacks at Olympic Games:

- *http://olympics.pthimon.co.uk/terrorism.htm (terrorist attacks – Germany and Atlanta*

- *http://history1900s.about.com/od/famouscrimesscandals/p/munichmassacre.htm (Munich massacre).*

When selecting a target some terrorist groups will want to avoid disaffecting a community that supports their cause and shares their ideologies. Strong support is necessary to secure funds, new recruits, weapons, forged documents and other items required for effective terrorist operations. The right target selection is key to maintaining the trust and interest of those who support or sympathise with a terrorist group. The Omagh bomb attack provides an example where the terrorist group failed dramatically in maintaining popular support.

Terrorists can be constrained by the capabilities and size of the group, whose aspirations may be limited by several factors such as availability of materials and resources and even abilities of members within the group (Drake, 1998). A terrorist group may also need to consider security risks, such as evading police surveillance and arrest, for the attack to be carried out successfully. Sometimes security forces themselves can become a target, such as police stations and police officers as witnessed in Northern Ireland.

Table 3.1 provides examples of terrorist groups, their objectives and potential targets.

Table 3.1 Terrorist groups, objectives and potential targets

Terrorist group	Objectives	Potential targets
Al-Aqsa Martyrs' Brigade (Palestinians)	To achieve a Palestinian state	Israeli civilians Military personnel
Secular Iraqi insurgents (Iraqi people)	To establish a national government and remove occupying military forces	Military personnel Foreign workers Iraqi collaborators
Al-Qaeda (AQ) (devout Muslims)	To achieve a global Islamic uprising	The West Secular Islamic governments
Irish Republican Army (IRA) (Roman Catholics)	A united Ireland without British influence	British people Ulster Protestants
Bosnian Serb Militias (Bosnian Serbs)	To achieve a Serb state	Bosnian Muslims Bosnian Croats

Source: Adapted from Martin (2009, p344)

A terrorist group will want to gain both physical and psychological impact from their chosen targets. A successful attack will ultimately result in the physical destruction of a target, but the primary aim may force a psychological target to react in a particular way; for example, choosing a physical target such as a police station to cause a reaction from a psychological target such as local government. Once a group has selected appropriate targets and assessed their capability and security measures they are ready to make an attack, most likely against the most vulnerable of their chosen targets.

PRACTICAL TASK

Consider further the Olympic Games and draw up an additional list of potential security measures that a terrorist group may have to overcome.

Methods of terrorism

There are many ways in which terrorist groups carry out violent attacks. Some groups use specific forms of violence that become their signature, such as the IRA who kneecapped kidnapped victims. Signature methods are rarely replicated by other terrorist groups but, like terrorist objectives, there are some commonalities between the various groups. The most common methods shared between different groups include:

- firearms;

- kidnapping;

- hijacking;

- explosive devices.

Firearms

Firearms are used to ambush and attack terrorist adversaries. They are the most commonly used weapon among terrorist groups and include pistols, rifles and assault rifles such as the AK47 or the M-16 and machine guns such as the Uzi or the Ingram. In more recent years other firearm weapons have been utilised by terrorist groups, such as mortars, rocket-propelled grenades such as the RPG-7 and precision-guided munitions such as the Stinger or the SA-7. The RPG-7 is a favourite among global dissident terrorist groups as it is a light, self-propelled munition. The SA-7 is less commonly used by dissident groups but is a very effective weapon that can be guided to its specified target by remote technologies.

Kidnapping

There are several potential motives behind the use of kidnapping by terrorist groups, including financial gain and propaganda to spread the terrorist cause. This can help to raise the profile of the group, especially if a hostage is a public figure or of a different nationality, for example the kidnap of Gordon Brown. He was a British tourist who was kidnapped by members of AQ in North Africa. The kidnap was arranged so that AQ could request a member of their group to be released from a prison in Worcestershire, England (Bentham, 2009). Many kidnappings that involve foreign nationals end in execution and sadly Gordon Brown was executed by AQ in 2009 after four months as a hostage.

Hijacking

This is mainly associated with terrorist attacks on board an aircraft, although hijacks take place on other modes of transport such as trains and maritime vessels. The main aim of this type of attack is to maximise the propaganda potential by taking hostage large numbers of victims. The starting date of modern aviation terrorism was 22 July 1968, when the Popular Front for the Liberation of Palestine (PFLP) hijacked an Israeli passenger plane bound for Tel Aviv from Rome and demanded the exchange of hostages for comrades in arms imprisoned in Israel.

> *It was the first time that an aircraft had ever been hijacked not out of criminal motivation or for personal reasons, but with the specific goal of politically pressuring an opponent and using the incident as a propaganda message to bring a political cause to the world's notice.*

(Arsley, 2005, p76)

Explosives

Explosives are an old favourite with terrorist groups as they provide a very effective method of creating both a physical and psychological impact on the selected target. There is a vast array of explosives, such as dynamite, TNT, plastic explosives, Semtex and composite 4 (C-4). Commercial explosives such as dynamite and TNT are readily available and have been used by terrorist groups in the past. Dissident groups now favour more sophisticated explosive compounds such as RDX, found in commercially made plastic explosives.

Semtex is a powerful explosive favoured by the IRA and used in many of their bombings in Northern Ireland together with C-4, an extremely powerful high-grade plastic explosive. Explosives can also be made by soaking ammonium nitrate fertiliser with fuel oil (ANFO). The ammonium nitrate can be used as a base for a bomb and added to other composite compounds to intensify the explosion. This method of attack was used by the IRA in 1996, when they planted a car bomb in the Docklands area of London causing extensive damage to property.

Many terrorist groups use the bomb and some of the most common types are as follows.

Petrol bombs or Molotov cocktails
These are very easy to construct and cost-effective, and are made by filling a glass bottle with petrol and igniting a rag used as a trigger. The glass bottle can then be thrown at the desired target. To create a greater and more damaging effect the glass bottle can be filled with other substances such as 'styrofoam', which sticks to a target and aids combustibility. This simple bomb has been used by terrorist groups worldwide.

Pipe or nail bombs

A length of piping is filled with explosives and other shrapnel such as nails to create maximum impact when the bomb explodes. This type of bomb was used at the 1996 summer Olympics in Atlanta, where two people died and hundreds more were injured.

Vehicular bombs

A vehicle is usually loaded with explosive (e.g. large quantities of ANFO) and then driven to the chosen place of attack to be detonated. Vehicular bombs are used by several dissident terrorist groups and they were a favoured choice of the IRA. The devastating attack on the town of Omagh in Northern Ireland was the result of a detonated car bomb.

Improvised explosive devices

Improvised explosive devices (IEDs) are home-made devices designed to cause death or injury by using explosives alone or mixed with toxic chemicals, biological toxins or radiological material. They are unique because the builder has to improvise with whatever materials are available and they are designed to defeat a specific target or type of target, and are becoming more difficult to detect and protect against as they become more sophisticated (Globalsecurity.org, 2011). IEDs have been used widely by the Taliban in the war against terror in Afghanistan.

Suicide bombs

More recently some terrorist groups have moved away from using traditionally recognised bombs to using human suicide bombers (the ultimate smart bomb). Suicide bombers are often religious terrorists who commit violence as acts of symbolism. A suicide bomber can maximise the damage potential for both physical and psychological targets and, as WuCh'i, a Chinese military philosopher, stated, *one man willing to throw away his life is sufficient to terrorise a thousand* (Sun Tzu, 1963, p9). The use of suicide bombers is increasing as they are a very cheap and flexible weapon that can attack a target directly. Suicide bombers are regularly used by AQ and dissident groups in Israel with 9/11 providing the most spectacular example of a series of targets being hit by four terrorist teams using jet airliners as bombs to commit suicide and inflict mass murder and destruction. In more recent times suicide bombings have become the signature methods of both Chechen rebels and Iraqi insurgents (Martin, 2009).

PRACTICAL TASK

Continuing with the Olympic Games scenario, draw up a list of potential methods of attack a terrorist group could use together with the rationale for choices made.

Suicide terrorism

Suicide terrorism has become an increasing challenge for security services and it could be argued that it is the most aggressive form of terrorism. One of the first known suicide bomb attacks in the modern era was carried out in Lebanon in 1981 during a civil war between Christian and Muslim militants (Lamb, 2011), and the massacre of 29 Palestinians in Hebron by a Jewish settler named Baruch Goldstein in 1994 sparked off the first of many suicide attacks by Hamas (Litvak, 2010). This type of attack is a growing phenomenon among terrorist groups as it attracts wide media coverage due to the nature of the violence and also the large numbers of casualties and amounts of devastation that an attack can create. During the past decade there has been an increase in the use of female suicide bombers, including attacks in Russia and Sri Lanka (Speckhard and Ahkmedova, 2006).

Religious beliefs and ideologies are reinforced during terrorist training but are not the main contributing factors for an individual suicide bomber. Other driving forces can motivate the suicide bomber, such as anger or revenge. Some female suicide bombers join terrorist groups after losing loved ones through war, with a motive of seeking revenge (Silke, 2001). (See the task on page 28 of Chapter 2, concerning the Chechen 'Black Widows'. See also below on 'Suicide terrorism as a tactic'.)

Effectiveness of terrorism

For a terrorist to measure the success of an attack, links are made between the goals and objectives, the method of attack adopted and the impact of the attack, to assess whether a successful outcome has been achieved.

Martin (2009) suggests that *the effectiveness of a terrorist attack is measured by unconventional criteria* (p374). This includes achieving both media and political attention; having an impact on an audience; gaining concessions; disrupting normal routines; and provoking state overreaction.

In Chapter 1 (page 7) it was suggested that terrorism generally does not work; however, there is evidence available to suggest that successful outcomes can be achieved.

Suicide terrorism as a tactic

As mentioned above, since 1981 more than 50 terrorist groups across the world (e.g. Algeria, Argentina, Croatia, China and India) have adapted and used a variety of mechanisms to deploy suicide bombs, including explosive belts, vests, toys, motorcycles, bikes, boats, backpacks and false pregnancy stomachs. Over a 25-year period 1,840 suicide bombings have occurred (86 per cent since 2001), including 920 in Iraq and 260 in Afghanistan, many of which have killed US troops. The exact number of troops killed is classified information and an army major within Iraq claimed that he had not been given the numbers *because it might show the effectiveness of the enemy's weapon* (Wright, 2008).

In a study relating to suicide bombers it was found that suicide terrorism can persuade a state to abandon limited or modest goals such as withdrawal from a territory of low strategic importance. But a state was unlikely to abandon goals central to their wealth or security where the loss of territory could weaken economic prospects and strengthen rivals (Pape, 2003). In a more recent study that considered a hypothesis that deaths from suicide terrorism were continuing to rise, suggesting that suicide terrorism is becoming more efficient, it was found that it had become less efficient in killing and injuring victims (Asthappan, 2010).

REFLECTIVE TASK

How effective do you think modern terrorism tactics are? Do the tactics selected enable successful outcomes in line with planned objectives, or is there evidence to suggest that in the main terrorist tactics are ineffective?

In cases of failure terrorists are very adaptable and are prepared to make changes to achieve their goals and objectives. A good example of this is provided by AQ, who used young females as suicide bombers during early bombing campaigns but later had to change tactics to infiltrate and attack potential targets. They deployed a 64-year-old male suicide bomber who drove a lorry to a target area in Algeria and killed over 50 civilians (Boccolini, 2007).

Weapons of mass destruction

Weapons of mass destruction (WMDs) was a term originally used by the former Soviet military to represent nuclear, chemical and biological weapons and has now been broadened to include radiological weapons. In the past terrorists' use of WMDs has been constrained, with groups seeking to gain politically from attacks by drawing a large audience but also wanting to maintain support and sympathy. One terrorist expert noted that terrorists want a lot of people watching but not a lot of people dead (Bowman, 2002). New trends are emerging and, as highlighted in Chapter 1 (pages 7–8), modern terrorists are prepared to use WMDs to inflict mass casualties. The use of jet airliners by AQ on 9/11 is a prime example of this.

The term WMD is synonymous with causing mass casualties and this can be achieved by various means; however, for the purposes of the remainder of this section the focus will be on chemical, biological, radiological and nuclear (CBRN) weapons.

Sarin nerve gas, ricin, anthrax and cyanide are some examples of substances that have been used by terrorists to target individuals and crowded places. Terrorists will continue to seek and broaden their use of CBRN weapons, and there is a growing concern globally of their capability to develop and deploy them. Materials required for CBRN weapons are becoming increasingly easier to obtain, due to less stringent controls within the former Soviet states specifically, and the increased information and technological advancements that are available to individuals through the internet (Bowman, 2002).

To date CBRN attacks remain rare. There may be a number of reasons for this, such as the risk being too high; lack of materials and capability to build/deploy; or concerns about the ramifications of an attack. However, evidence has long been available to suggest that certain terrorist groups are actively pursuing the acquisition and use of CBRN weapons.

CBRN weapons acquisition

There is much speculation about CBRN weapons and their capability to cause spectacular levels of destruction and mayhem. The speculation alone, spurred on by the media, can create its own destruction in the form of mass panic. To this end, are terrorist groups relying purely on a fear factor to create panic or are CBRN weapons a viable global threat?

Chemical weapons

Certain chemical agents such as chlorine or phosgene are easily available and require little expertise to convert into a weapon. However, the production of nerve agents can be technically unfeasible without access to a sophisticated laboratory infrastructure. High temperatures are required for production that can generate corrosive and dangerous by-products such as hydrogen cyanide gas, which is produced during the process of making the nerve agent 'Tabun' (Hinton, 1999). To disperse a chemical agent the most effective method is using an aerosol or vapour, in the form of a spray or explosive. Chemical agents are vulnerable to temperature, moisture or wind and are more effective when deployed on an indoor population (Bowman, 2002).

Using a chemical weapon as a WMD is unpredictable due to the vulnerability of the agents and they do not necessarily cause mass casualties. The nerve agent Sarin, released in a Tokyo subway in 1995, killed only 12 individuals.

Since 9/11 there has been increasing concern that an attack would be made on facilities housing toxic chemicals, allowing a terrorist to achieve the devastating effects of a chemical attack without manufacturing a weapon. The effects of such an attack were illustrated in Bhopal, India, in 1984 when an employee of a pesticide plant released 40 metric tons of methyl isocyonate into the atmosphere, killing over 3,000 people and injuring hundreds of thousands more, some of whom were left with permanent disabilities (Broughton, 2005).

Biological weapons

Many biological agents (pathogens) can be obtained and grown with relative ease, but there are significant steps that need to be taken in order to convert them into effective weapons. A terrorist group would have to overcome extensive operational and technical challenges to convert biological materials successfully into a weapon capable of causing mass destruction (GAO, 1999). The agents most likely to be used by a terrorist are anthrax, smallpox, botulinum toxin and bubonic plague (Martin, 2009).

The use of biological weapons does not necessarily result in mass casualties, as witnessed in 2001 following a series of anthrax attacks in the USA. Intelligence suggested that the anthrax was obtained from a government laboratory, alluding more to the security of the laboratory, rather than the harm caused by the pathogen.

A further concern relating to biological agents is their use against agricultural targets (agroterrorism), which has the potential to cause mass economic and social destruction in a country (Cameron et al., 2001).

Radiological weapons

A radiological weapon is far less destructive than a nuclear weapon. Radiological material such as plutonium, uranium, cobalt 60 or strontium can be mixed with high-end explosives to disperse the radioactive material. This type of weapon does not have the capability to cause the mass casualties attributed to a nuclear explosion, but if targeted appropriately can still cause severe radiation contamination (Bowman, 2002).

Nuclear weapons

These are the most destructive WMD but also the most difficult for a terrorist group to create. They are dependent on the availability and exact quantities of the key ingredients of either plutonium or highly enriched uranium. If these exact quantities are acquired it is believed that a capable terrorist group would be able to manufacture a nuclear weapon (Falkenwrath, 1998). The release of any nuclear weapon by a terrorist, whether it be a state, group or individual, would have a devastating global effect and it is a scenario that needs to be avoided at all costs.

Iran has the potential to construct a nuclear weapon and this has caused tensions with the West and more specifically Israel. American intelligence agencies believe that it would take at least a year for Iran to convert nuclear material into a working weapon. There is some confidence that international inspectors would identify any attempt to construct a weapon within weeks, giving the USA and Israel ample time to consider military strikes (Mazzetti and Sanger, 2010).

CASE STUDY

Al-Qaeda

In December 1998 Osama bin Laden was interviewed on Al Jazeera television and, when asked about the intentions of AQ to obtain a nuclear weapon, he replied:

> There is a duty on Muslims to acquire them, and America knows today that Muslims are in possession of such a weapon, by the grace of God Almighty.
>
> *(Lawrence, 2005, p72)*

In 2009 the UK government provided further evidence of the threat posed by AQ:

- AQ established facilities in Afghanistan during reign of the Taliban to research CBRN weapons, and provided training for use of contact poisons;
- AQ met with disaffected Pakistani nuclear scientists to assist them in acquiring and developing radiological weapons (2001);
- AQ developed a device to produce hydrogen cyanide gas capable of deployment in crowded places (2003);
- AQ terrorist cells within the UK considered the use of radiological devices (2004);
- AQ leader in Iraq appealed for nuclear scientists to join AQ and attack US bases in Iraq using unconventional weapons (2006);
- AQ deployed explosive devices utilising chlorine gas cylinders in Iraq (2007).

(Home Office, 2009, p127)

CASE STUDY *continued*

The following is an extract from a report considering the threat posed by AQ:

> President Obama recently said that al Qaeda remains the greatest threat to the United States. In his words, 'If an organization like al Qaeda got a weapon of mass destruction on its hands – a nuclear or a chemical or a biological weapon – and they used it in a city, whether it's in Shanghai or New York, just a few individuals could potentially kill tens of thousands of people, maybe hundreds of thousands.' Organizing a coherent strategy to prevent this nightmare from occurring begins with a clear recognition that WMD terrorism is a real and imminent threat.
>
> *(Mowatt-Larssen, 2010, p3)*

REFLECTIVE TASK

In light of the information provided in the case study above, consider the likelihood of the world witnessing a major CBRN attack in the near future that might result in unprecedented mass casualties. (See 'Useful websites' for a number of links that will assist with this task.)

PRACTICAL TASK

To conclude, find out more about the attack records of various terrorist groups (see 'Useful websites') and establish the tactics for attack adopted, the type of weapons deployed and any changes in the tactics adopted.

C H A P T E R   S U M M A R Y

This chapter has identified a number of theoretical concepts, providing some explanations of tactic and target selection by terrorist groups. Although terrorist groups differ in their ideologies and beliefs, many share common traits in their overall goals and objectives, their selection of tactics for an attack and their methodology in choosing a target. Terrorist attacks are not usually random and senseless, but methodically planned and rarely senseless.

Common methods of attack can be found across terrorist groups, such as firearms, explosives, kidnappings and hijacking. Globalisation and the fast growth of new technologies are providing the terrorist with more sophisticated and deadly weapons, providing new challenges for security services. CBRN weapons pose a significant threat but to date their use has been limited; however, it is recognised that some terrorists are intent on both acquiring and deploying them.

The success of terrorist activity is measured by the achievement of goals and objectives. Successful outcomes can include attracting media and political attention, winning the support of the population and provoking state reaction, which may lead to social, economic or political change.

REFERENCES

Anatalio, Monica (2002) In the Spotlight (The Real IRA). Available online at www.cdi.org/terrorism/rira.cfm (accessed 29 April 2011).

Arsley, Jangir (2005) Terrorism and Civil Aviation Security: Problems and Trends. Available online at www.comw.org/tct/fulltext/0503arasly.pdf (accessed 29 April 2011).

Asthappan, Jibey (2010) The Effectiveness of Suicide Terrorism. *Journal of the Washington Institute of China Studies*, 5(1) (Summer): 16–25.

Bentham, M (2009) Kidnapped British Man is Beheaded by AQ. *London Evening Standard*. Available online at www.thisislondon.co.uk/standard/article-23702891-kidnapped-british-man-is-beheaded-by-al-qaeda.do (accessed 2 April 2011).

Boccolini, H (2007) Algeria – AQ Uses Elderly Terrorists in Change of Tactics. Available online at www.adnkronos.com/AKI/English/Security/?id=1.0.1665340094 (accessed 18 April 2011).

Bowman, S (2002) *Weapons of Mass Destruction: The Terrorist Threat*. Washington, DC: Congressional Research Service.

Broughton, E (2005) The Bhopal Disaster and Its Aftermath: A Review. *Environmental Health* (e-journal), 4(6). Available online at www.ncbi.nlm.nih.gov/pmc/articles/PMC1142333/ (accessed 1 May 2011).

Cameron, G, Pate, J and Vogel, K (2001) Planting Fear: How Real is the Threat of Agricultural Terrorism? *Bulletin of Atomic Scientists*, September/October: 38.

Drake, C (1998) *Terrorists' Target Selection*. Basingstoke: Macmillan.

Falkenwrath, R (1998) Confronting Nuclear, Biological and Chemical Terrorism. *Survival*, 40(4): 168–83.

GAO (General Accounting Office) (1999) *Combating Terrorism: Need for Comprehensive Threat and Risk Assessments on Chemical and Biological Attacks*. Washington, DC: National Security & International Affairs Division.

Globalsecurity.org (2011) Improvised Explosive Devices (IEDs)/Booby Traps. Available online at www.globalsecurity.org/military/intro/ied.htm (accessed 29 April 2011).

Hewitt, C (1992) Public's Perspectives, in Paletz, D and Schmid, A (eds) *Terrorism and the Media*. California: Sage.

Heymann, P (1998) *Terrorism and America: A Commonsense Strategy for a Democratic Society*. Cambridge: MIT Press.

Hinton, Henry L (1999) Combating Terrorism: Assessing the Threat of Bio Terrorism. Statement before the House Committee on Government Reform, October 20. Available online at www.chem-bio.com/resource/1999/hinton102099.html (accessed 23 June 2011).

Hoffman, B (2006) *Inside Terrorism*, 2nd edition. New York: Columbia University Press.

Home Office (2009) *Pursue, Prevent, Protect, Prepare: The United Kingdom's Strategy for Countering International Terrorism*. London: Home Office.

Howatt-Larssen, Rolf (2010) *Al Qaeda Weapons of Mass Destruction Threat: Hype or Reality*. Cambridge, MA: Harvard Kennedy School.

Kershaw, S (2002) Even 6 Months Later, 'Get Over It' Just Isn't an Option. *New York Times*, 11 March, p9.

Lamb, R (2011) How Suicide Bombers Work. Available online at http://science.howstuffworks.com/suicide-bomber3.htm (accessed 6 April 2011).

Lawrence, Bruce (2005) *Messages to the World: The Statements of Osama bin Laden*. London: Verso.

Litvak, M (2010) Martyrdom is Life: Jihad and Martyrdom in the Ideology of Hamas. *Studies in Conflict & Terrorism*, 33: 716–34.

Martin, Gus (2009) *Understanding Terrorism: Challenges, Perspectives and Issues*, 3rd edition. London: Sage.

Mazzetti, Mark and Sanger, David E (2010) US Assures Israel That Iran Threat is Not Imminent. *New York Times*, 19 August. Available online at www.nytimes.com/2010/08/20/world/middleeast/20policy.html (accessed 5 June 2011).

Pape, Robert (2003) The Strategic Logic of Suicide Terrorism. *American Political Science Review*, 97(3): 1–19.

Rodgers, W (1996) Hamas Admits to Fatal Israeli Bus Bombings. CNN World News, 25 February 1996. Available online at http://edition.cnn.com/WORLD/9602/israel_explosion/02-25/pm/ (accessed 8 April 2011).

Silke, A (2001) Terrorism. *The Psychologist*, 14: 580–1.

Sigler, R and Curry, B (1992) Handling the Hostage Taker: Public Perceptions of the Use of Force by the Police. *American Journal of Police*, 11(3): 113–27.

Speckhard, A and Ahkmedova, K (2006) Assessment of Attitudes Towards Terrorism, in Alder, L and Denmark, F (eds) *Violence and the Prevention of Violence*. Westport, CT: Praegar.

Sun Tzu (1963) *The Art of War* (reprint). New York: Oxford University Press.

Wardlaw, G (1997) *Political Terrorism: Theory, Tactics and Counter-measures*, 2nd edition. Cambridge: University Press.

Weimann, G and Winn, C (1994) *The Theatre of Terror: Mass Media and International Terrorism*. New York: Longman.

Wright, Robin (2008) Since 2001, a Dramatic Increase in Suicide Bombings. *Washington Post*, 18 April. Available online at www.washingtonpost.com/wp-dyn/content/article/2008/04/17/AR2008041703595.html (accessed 3 June 2011).

www.thesmokinggun.com/documents/crime/terrorism-101-how-guide (Copy of a document seized in Manchester, entitled *Military Studies in the Jihad against the Tyrants*, which includes sections on weapons, tactics and methods)

Information on weapons of mass destruction

http://belfercenter.ksg.harvard.edu/files/al-qaeda-wmd-threat.pdf (*Al Qaeda Weapons of Mass Destruction Threat: Hype or Reality*, by Rolf Mowatt-Larsen)

http://belfercenter.ksg.harvard.edu/files/uploads/Islam_and_the_Bomb-Final.pdf (*Islam and the Bomb*, also by Rolf Mowatt-Larsen)

www.cia.gov/library/reports/general-reports-1/terrorist_cbrn/terrorist_CBRN.htm (*Terrorist CBRN, Materials and Effects*, by the CIA).

www.preventwmd.org/report (Commission on the Prevention of WMD Proliferation and Terrorism (USA))

www.stratfor.com/weekly/20100210_jihadist_cbrn_threat (*The Jihadist CBRN Threat*, by Scott Stewart)

Information on attack records of terrorist groups

www.start.umd.edu/gtd (Global Terrorism Database)

www.state.gov/s/ct/rls/crt/2009/index.htm (US Department of State – Country Reports)

4 Irish terrorism: the UK experience

Peter Williams

> **CHAPTER OBJECTIVES**
>
> By the end of this chapter you should be able to:
>
> - understand the unique development of the province of Ulster in Ireland;
> - describe significant key events that have contributed to dissident Irish nationalism and the adoption of terrorist strategies;
> - appreciate the ideology and motivation of certain Irish dissident groups, and their choice of tactics and targets;
> - understand how policing in Northern Ireland has developed to tackle the problems of terrorism;
> - analyse how the terrorism problem has been tackled and resolved to some extent by political agreement.

Introduction

Who would govern Ireland must have much patience.

(Sir Thomas Larcom, cited in Townsend, 1983)

To set the scene adequately regarding the events in Ireland over the past centuries that have led to acts of terrorism and the formulation of terrorist groups on both sides of the argument would require several volumes.

This chapter looks at the key events that have led to several nationalist-inspired terrorist campaigns, involving the Irish Republican Army (IRA), that could easily fall into the definition of a limited war, given that mainly discriminating force has been used against adversaries – in this case the British state, with the objective of defeating it and bringing about a political goal (Martin, 2010), that is, to get the British out of Ireland and reunite the country into one state.

A key element also focuses on the state in terms of responses via agents of the state, such as the military and the police.

Some of the main political events over this long historical period will also be highlighted. Loyalist violence during the period will not be looked at here. It must be stressed that it was equally as violent as that of the nationalists.

Historical perspective

Exploring and analysing the history of Northern Ireland presents a dilemma for any student or teacher owing to the rich tapestry of information available. For many centuries the British had a presence in Ireland clustered around the Dublin area, referred to as 'The Pale' (see Figure 4.1).

For the purposes of this chapter the most logical place to start a historical analysis is with the 'Plantation of Ulster'.

Plantation of Ulster

Ireland is divided into four historical provinces with the most north-easterly being Ulster, which consists of nine counties. These include the counties that currently form Northern Ireland and are part of the UK, and also the counties Cavan, Monaghan and Donegal, which are situated within the Republic of Ireland. This anomaly is a direct result of the 'Partition of Ireland', which occurred in 1921 (see pages 61–3 for further explanation).

Figure 4.1 The Pale

The Plantations are a crucial element in the modern history of this troubled area of Ireland and it is important to understand their significance and lasting legacy within Irish history.

Figure 4.2 The four historical provinces of Ireland

Practical
Task to do.

Go to *www.bbc.co.uk/northernireland/ashorthistory/archive/topic86.shtml*, read through the information and answer the following questions.

1. What would a Plantation do for Ulster?

2. By what name were the largest group known and what nationality or religion did they have to be?

3. According to the special proclamation by King James to the people of Scotland, who or what was to be 'freed and disburdened'?

4. *According to this proclamation, what were the three key things King James intended to establish by the Plantation?*

5. *What was the purpose of the King's ambitious scheme?*

(See Appendix A on page 189 for answers.)

The planters were initially attracted to Ulster by the prospect of economic development, primarily farming. Many originated from the Scottish lowlands and, as time progressed, were often referred to as the 'Ulster Scots'. The two counties most favoured by the planters were the two situated nearest to Scotland: Antrim and Down. It is often said that a person originating from Ballymena in County Antrim speaks with a dialect more akin to a Scottish accent than Northern Irish.

As well as their enterprise in the economic field, the planters also imposed English property law, which invalidated the Irish equivalent (Foster, 1988). They also imported their cultural diversity and perhaps more importantly their religion, which was almost exclusively Protestant, to a land that was almost exclusively Catholic. Most regrettably, the religious mix became contentious as opposed to consensual and led to eventual and clear discrimination against Catholics.

Perhaps the contention can be understood in some respects when the issue of religion is viewed retrospectively. It must be stressed, however, albeit unfortunately, that the matter of religion in Northern Ireland has pervaded all aspects of political, economic and civil life. Policing, which is examined later, provides a first-class example of this regrettable schism within Northern Irish society.

Taking a retrospective look at Ulster society in the post-Plantation period leads to some key events and milestones, none more so than the penal laws.

PRACTICAL TASK

Go to www.libraryireland.com/articles/Eighteenth-Century-Ireland/Irish-Penal-Laws.php, read the article by Edgar Sanderson (1898) and answer the following questions.

1. *What was subject to robbery in the days of James I?*

2. *What was subject to a capital offence?*

3. *In 1699 what was excluded from English and foreign markets and why?*

4. *In 1779 what was the religious make-up of the raised militia?*

5. *What were violent men working against?*

(See Appendix A on page 189 for answers.)

To summarise what could appear to be a complicated area: the primary purpose of the penal laws was to prevent Catholics gaining economic and political power (Boyle et al., 1975) and to ensure Protestant supremacy. Ulster continued to develop on a different economic track from the remainder of Ireland and one that was almost exclusively agrarian in nature. Economically at least, together with all that it entailed, Ulster began to break away.

English law was stacked against Catholics!

Ulster 'departs' Ireland

From the outset of the Industrial Revolution in the eighteenth century, the economy of Ulster began to diversify towards heavy engineering with shipbuilding, foundries and textiles, creating an allegiance with British cities developing in a similar vein at that time, notably Liverpool (Foster, 1988). In 1849 the steam power for the linen factories of Ulster required 250,000 tons of coal to be imported from Britain annually. By the end of the century imports had multiplied fourfold and there was a constant stream of ships carrying coal bound for Belfast from Liverpool. Later in the nineteenth century an industrial axis formed between the heavy engineering and shipbuilding ports of Belfast, Merseyside and Glasgow.

This was not the only issue in common between these great shipbuilding ports and conurbations. The planters imported the Protestant religion and the 'Orange Order', closely identified with the Protestant religion, was fully ingrained into civil daily life in Ulster.

The Orange Order emerged in Ulster following sectarian disturbances around 1790, which became violent, and as a consequence the Orange Order developed across the country (Boyle et al., 1975). Ironically, other places situated on the British mainland where the Orange Order thrived and still does today include Liverpool and Glasgow.

Orange order. Violent. 1790

Given this major economic expansion in Ulster based on industrialisation, Dublin and the remaining three provinces of Ireland were excluded and remained primarily a rural economy based on agriculture.

In 1861 the population census in Belfast indicated that the city was only one-third Catholic and the workforce was separated along sectarian lines with Protestants holding the skilled jobs. Traditional 12 July marches held by the Orange Order during the 1850–70 period regularly developed into major disturbances (Foster, 1988).

1861 ⅓ of city was Catholic!! Protestants holding key & skilled jobs!

REFLECTIVE TASK

Go to www.grandorangelodge.co.uk and answer the following questions.

1. What happened in 1795?

2. When was the Grand Orange Lodge of Ireland established?

3. According to the website, what does the Loyal Orange Institution continue to do in modern times?

Complete online

REFLECTIVE TASK continued

4. Go to the tab marked 'history' and having drawn up the menu click on 'The Order's Fight for the Union 1886–1921'. What did Bonar Law tell the crowd on Easter Tuesday, 1912?

5. Given what you have read so far, why do you think he said that?

(See Appendix A on page 189 for answers.)

Early beginnings

The disturbances referred to above were largely urban in nature and this is a feature of life in Northern Ireland that has been witnessed periodically for some considerable time.

Not all the disturbances were based in the urban north and protest in the 1830 period, often called the Irish Tithe War (rent-related), led to the passing of repressive or coercive legislation – the Suppression of Disturbances Act 1833 (Townsend, 1983).

This Act should not be seen in isolation. Between 1800 and 1921 the British Government passed 105 'Coercion Acts' in an attempt to establish law and order in response to outbreaks of political violence. Many of these Acts allowed for detention without trial and habeas corpus was suspended for as long as it was in force during the nineteenth century (Farrell, 1986). *normal legal practice was not awaile - detention/no trial!!*

PRACTICAL TASK

Go to www.constitution.org/eng/habcorpa.htm and identify the main purpose of the Habeas Corpus Act 1679.

This approach ideally illustrates the duplicity in respect of responses by law enforcement in Ireland. Around the same time in southern England, the so-called 'Swing' disturbances, involving rural violence and damage targeted at freshly introduced farming machinery, were responded to via the ordinary criminal law (Townsend, 1983).

These disturbances were dealt with by the 'new police', introduced in September 1829 by Robert Peel, who ironically before his appointment as Home Secretary had been the Chief Secretary to Ireland. He was considered the 'father' of the British Police Service; however, it was in Ireland where he spent his formative years in respect of policing and where he introduced a centralised policing service. The disturbances on the mainland were considered a threat to public order, whereas similar disturbances in Ireland were considered a threat to the state, hence the unequal response.

From these early beginnings we can track the Irish dissident movement into what it eventually became – a politicised organisation, via legitimate political parties such as Sinn Fein, and proscribed armed groups such as the IRA.

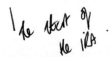

Martin agrees, when he states that:

> *political violence, including terrorism, has systematic origins that can be ameliorated. Social and economic pressures, frustrated political aspirations, and in a more proximate sense, the personal experiences of terrorists and their relations, all contribute to the terrorist reservoir.*
>
> (Martin, 2010, p6)

Initially, however, the disputes concerned rents over land, or the tithe, which at first sight may appear somewhat removed from the events of the late twentieth century; but the underpinning cause certainly is not.

Taking shape

The Special Irish Branch of the Metropolitan Police was introduced during the 1880s as a result of a bombing campaign on the British mainland by Irish nationalists, known as the Fenian Brotherhood (FB). The campaign against British presence in Ireland was clearly gaining ground and, following this campaign and other political arrangements involving the FB which effectively fell through, the republicans re-formed in New York, USA, and established the Irish Republican Brotherhood (IRB) (Maloney, 2002). They also formed a group known as the Clann na Gael, which at one stage had plans to invade Canada and demand a British withdrawal from Ireland. The Fenians completely rejected any negotiation with the British authorities and were totally committed to a violent approach to a British withdrawal from Ireland (Powell, 2008).

In a rather quirky similarity with policing in Ireland relating to direct lineage of historical development impinging on structures, the IRA established not only its roots, but also its optimal objective (Martin, 2010), which was to get the British out of Ireland.

Sinn Fein (translated as *we ourselves*), the Irish republican political party founded in 1905 by Dublin journalist Arthur Griffith, joined the newly named United Irish League. This had previously been known as the Home Rule Party, led by Charles Parnell, who had enjoyed some limited success at Westminster. In a statement released by Sinn Fein almost a hundred years later, the ideology of the republicans is adequately summarised:

> *The root cause of the conflict in Ireland is the denial of democracy, the refusal by the British government to allow the Irish people to exercise their right to national self-determination. The solution to the conflict in Ireland lies in the democratic exercise of that right in the form of national reunification, national independence and sovereignty.*
>
> (Martin, 2010, p53)

In 1885 the Home Rule Party led by Parnell had won 85 seats at Westminster, including 17 of the 33 available in Ulster. This left them in a position of some political clout in London, as they held the balance of power in Parliament and eventually forced the then Prime Minister William Gladstone, in 1886, to introduce the first Home Rule Bill. The proposal involved plans for limited self-government, but this was unacceptable to Ulster business-men who felt their economic prosperity was threatened. As a consequence, an alliance was formed with the Conservative Party on the mainland. The Bill also had the effect of bolstering membership of the Orange Order, which took an overt anti-Catholic stance.

However, as often occurs in politics, other events intervened and the Bill failed due to a revolt within the Liberal Party. A further attempt was made to introduce another Bill in 1893, but this too was defeated in the House of Lords (Farrell, 1976).

A further General Election was held in 1910 and another Home Rule Bill was expected, but Ulster continued to resist fiercely any suggestion of Home Rule. Ulster, with its nine counties, had a population of over 1.5 million people, which represented 36 per cent of the total population of Ireland. In relation to the religious composition of Ireland, Protestants accounted for 26 per cent of the total population, but in Ulster this was 56 per cent. In the six most north-easterly counties – Antrim, Armagh, Derry, Down, Fermanagh and Tyrone – the Protestant majority was greater at 66 per cent (Farrell, 1976). In terms of industrial-isation, Ulster contained almost half of the industrialised workers in Ireland; Belfast, with only 8.8 per cent of the population, contained 21 per cent. The economic powerhouse of Ireland was centred in Belfast.

The unionists felt threatened by the attempts at another Home Rule Bill and the emerging ascendancy of nationalist parties, such as Sinn Fein. Accordingly, the Ulster Unionist Council, led by Dublin lawyer Edward Carson, was founded. He had earlier threatened to establish a provisional government in Ulster, if the Bill had been passed. The unionists began to train a private army, raised via the Orange Order, and later renamed as the Ulster Volunteer Force (UVF). In April 1914 they landed 25,000 rifles at Larne, County Antrim (Farrell, 1976). Both loyalists and nationalists were positioning themselves for an anticipated confrontation that led directly to a significant event in 1916 – the Easter Rising.

Easter Rising, 1916

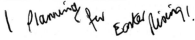

At the time of this major event in Irish history, Britain was heavily embroiled in the First World War against Germany and heavily committed as a consequence in terms of military resources in Belgium and northern France. Unprecedented loss of life occurred during the war and the British military needed regular reinforcements of trained soldiers, and con-scription to the military had been imposed on the British mainland.

Skilled men of military age were exempted from military service on the grounds that their skills were more urgently needed on the home front as opposed to the battle front. The Irish were largely unskilled and perceived as a viable answer to the recruiting problem (Caulfield, 1995). The problem was that the majority of Irish people of military age felt no loyalty towards Britain and felt that the war was between Great Britain and Germany, and not a matter for Ireland. This was a major factor within the Easter Rising.

PRACTICAL TASK

Go to www.easter1916.net, read the main article and answer the following questions.

1. Following the formation of the 'Provisional Government', what organisation was formed under the leadership of James Connolly?

2. According to Benian (1959), what was the major cause of the rebellion?

PRACTICAL TASK *continued*

3. What saved Eamon DeValera's life?

4. What had been decided by the IRB during the early stages of the war?

5. According to the website, what was this event the 'opening act' of?

(See Appendix A on page 190 for answers.)

Life was never going to be the same again and had the effect of bolstering nationalist support against Britain, although the planned uprising in rural Ireland failed to materialise and there is evidence that some Dubliners, who did have sons away fighting in the British forces, were openly hostile to the rebels. While the nationalist position consistently refers to the Easter Rising, which has been repeatedly remembered in the intervening years, perhaps in the wider context of events the Irish newspapers at the time accurately summarised the insurrection as the 'Sinn Fein Revolt' (Taylor, 1997).

As we have seen from the above task, the repercussions from the British administration were unequivocal and justify further investigation, particularly as to the implications of the action. This might possibly explain why the Easter Rising has such status within Irish nationalism and why the immediate subsequent events did more to bolster and stir Irish nationalism, rather than the uprising itself. Sadly, this will not be the first time that we witness action by the British Government playing directly into the hands of the republican extremists.

The leaders and signatories to the 'Proclamation' (see previous task) were tried by a military court martial presided over by General Blackadder. Not surprisingly they were convicted, then sentenced to death and executed by firing squad over a two-week period in the outside yard at Kilmainham Gaol. This action alone gave them martyrdom status and prompted William Butler Yeats' poem 'Easter 1916', in which he referred to 'a terrible beauty' being born (Taylor, 1997).

REFLECTIVE TASK

An internet search will easily find a copy of the poem written by Yeats. Read through the poem and write down your thoughts on what you feel the poet was trying to represent. Consider whether a certain landmark had been reached at this time that made Irish constitutional change inevitable.

When the First World War was over, the British turned their attentions to resolving the Irish problem. The signing of the Armistice agreement in November 1918 signalled the end of hostilities in France and one of the first tasks for the British Government was to hold a General Election, which became known as the 'khaki election', for a peace-time Westminster government that included Ireland.

At the conclusion of the election, Sinn Fein had gained 73 of the 105 Irish seats available. These seats were for the Westminster Parliament, but Sinn Fein MPs established their own parliament in Dublin, declaring it the 'Dial Eireann', and proclaimed an Irish Republic (Powell, 2008). The unionists won 26 seats, all but three of them within Ulster.

The stand-off was set. Sinn Fein claimed victory in that it represented the majority of the people in Ireland and formed an independent parliament based in the Mansion House, Dublin, with one Michael Collins as the Minister of Finance (Taylor, 1997).

The British immediately proscribed the embryonic Irish Parliament. This signalled the start of a war of independence (Powell, 2008), which became known as the Anglo-Irish War, starting on 21 January 1919, the day the Dial Eireann first met (Taylor, 1997).

It was at this time that the IRA was officially formulated from the IRB/Irish Volunteers with the same Michael Collins as the Adjutant General. A war had been declared and, from a British perspective in the first instance, the need for effective policing was required.

Policing in Ireland

As mentioned previously, the early foundations were laid by Robert Peel as Chief Secretary to Ireland who, building on the existing and centralised Peace Preservation Force, formed the Irish Constabulary in 1822. This force was a centralised organisation controlled from Dublin Castle. The structure adopted is closely akin to a military one, with an Inspector-General in overall command. Some years later, when Peel attempted to introduce a similar organisational structure on mainland Britain, it was rejected out of hand as being too close to a continental gendarmerie; hence, the constabulary-style structure of police forces of England, Wales and Scotland in contemporary times. Their legacy is a rejection of Peel's original proposal, but this was not so in Ireland.

In terms of Ireland, with its officers housed in barracks, it was the most suitable arrangement to protect the interests of the state aided by the military, to deal with republican insurrections. The British military in the immediate aftermath of the First World War was in the process of demobilisation, therefore there were fewer troops available for deployment to Ireland and this is perhaps one reason why the approach from government was to treat these insurrections as a threat to law and order as opposed to war. Given this situation, it was clear that the police, by then called the Royal Irish Constabulary (RIC), required assistance.

A solution was reached by deploying police auxiliaries and forming an auxiliary army, who were mainly ex-soldiers returning from the front. They and their policing methods became infamous, as did their sobriquet – the Black and Tans.

PRACTICAL TASK

Go to www.bbc.co.uk/history/british/easterrising/aftermath/af05.shtml, read the contents and answer the following questions.

PRACTICAL TASK *continued*

1. *What was launched in January 1920 and why?*

2. *Why were they known as the Black and Tans?*

3. *How many were enlisted into the Auxiliaries?*

4. *What were the costs of unofficial reprisals?*

5. *What would the British public not accept any further?*

(See Appendix A on page 190 for answers.)

The Partition of Ireland

Eventually, an Anglo-Irish Treaty was agreed between Michael Collins and Prime Minister David Lloyd George in 1921, bestowing upon what was initially known as the 'Irish Free State' dominion status, similar to that of Canada at that time (Powell, 2008).

However, within the republican movement itself, a civil war ensued between those in favour of the Treaty and those against. Basically, the pro-Treaty element prevailed, which led to the Government of Ireland Act 1920. Ireland divided into the Irish Free State in the south, now known as the Republic of Ireland, and Northern Ireland in the north, which remained part of the UK. This process was known as the Partition of Ireland.

While events in the south were very much concerned with removing the British from Ireland, in Ulster the opposite was true. The Protestant majority had been busy arming themselves via organisations such as the UVF. By wishing to retain Ulster as part of the UK, both politically and constitutionally, formulating an armed force in order to protect the union, the Protestant majority in Ulster exercised considerable influence on the British Government. So much so in fact that, when the boundary between northern and southern Ireland was decided and effectively drawn up, the population of Ireland was not consulted (Powell, 2008).

The decision as to where certain individual counties should sit rested solely on the religious profile of each county; hence, three of the Ulster counties – Donegal, Monaghan and Cavan – were placed in southern Ireland. The remaining six counties of Ulster, the most north-easterly and the home of the original planters, which had an in-built Protestant majority within the population, formed the new province of Northern Ireland.

When viewed retrospectively, this decision effectively doomed Northern Ireland from the start in terms of integrating the people of the province and, given its history, the terrorism that subsequently occurred should not have come as a surprise. As there was no consultation, the creation of the state was considered illegitimate (Powell, 2008) and it was not recognised by nationalists. This explains why unionists would refer constantly to 'the province' and republicans to the 'six counties'. Unionists recognised Northern Ireland, whereas nationalists did not and considered Ireland as a 32-county state, the ultimate goal (Martin, 2010) of the republican terrorist groups, not the 26 that formed the Irish Free State (Republic of Ireland).

The map in Figure 4.3 outlines the six counties of the province and the newly drawn boundaries of Northern Ireland.

Unfortunately, Northern Ireland didn't grasp this new beginning as a new opportunity and it quickly became a dominant Protestant state in which Catholic resentment towards this situation was being stoked up.

James Craig, the first Prime Minister, set the tone when he said:

> *I have always said that I am an Orangeman first and a politician and member of this Parliament afterwards. All I boast is that we are a protestant Parliament and a protestant state.*

(Powell, 2008, p42)

Catholics refused to sit in the Northern Ireland Parliament, situated at Stormont, until 1926, and Craig was able to abolish proportional representation and bring about a gerrymandering of political boundaries to ensure one-party (Unionist) rule (Powell, 2008). Public disturbances continued and the response was to introduce the Ulster Special Constabulary (USC) to assist the Royal Ulster Constabulary (RUC) (previously the RIC), who

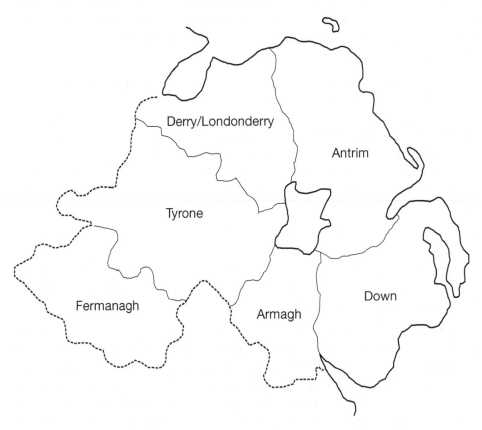

Figure 4.3 Outline map of Northern Ireland showing the six counties

had adopted the new name following Partition. The RUC retained the same centralised military-style structure with an Inspector-General in overall command.

The USC was largely recruited from the existing UVF and contained three classes: A, B and C. Class A became a full-time reserve force and Class B a part-time reserve, both of which were armed while on duty. Class C were available in times of emergency. Like the RUC, the USC was almost entirely Protestant in membership and the Catholic population suffered blatant discrimination from the police.

The 'B' Specials (USC – Class B) were a feature of life in Northern Ireland until the Hunt Report into policing in 1969 recommended abolishing them; it was this report that substituted the title Chief Constable for that of Inspector-General. The then RUC was a legacy of the Irish Constabulary, put in place many years before by Robert Peel as Chief Secretary and for reasons that effectively hamstrung the legitimacy of policing in Northern Ireland. This situation prevailed until the Patten Report into policing in 1999, after the 1998 Good Friday Agreement – the all-Party political agreement into the future of Northern Ireland, which brought about a cessation of violence and has delivered relative peace.

Discrimination against Catholics in all aspects of economic and civil life continued in Northern Ireland until 1967, when the Northern Ireland Civil Rights Alliance (NICRA) (Powell, 2008) started campaigning against discrimination in housing, gerrymandering of political boundaries and policing, specifically the 'B' Specials, which by now were a well-established, overwhelmingly Protestant, armed force. These issues were at the root of the Catholic community grievances and sectarian violence was commonplace.

Street disturbances followed and the RUC was unable to cope; as a result British troops were deployed by the Government on the streets of Northern Ireland in August 1969. This, together with other events, signalled the start of the so-called 'Troubles', which lasted for almost 30 years and heralded the rebirth of nationalist extremism in the form of the IRA and the start of a terrorist war.

The IRA

The IRA had never really disbanded, although it does appear they were somewhat caught off-guard when violence did erupt on the streets of Northern Ireland in the late 1960s. Within its ranks differences of opinion emerged as to policy, so much so that in December 1969 the split was irreconcilable and a 'Provisional' leadership was elected. The organisation basically split into two: the 'Official IRA', known as the National Liberation Front, and the 'Provisional IRA' (PIRA) (Taylor 1997) – the organisation that became most associated with republican extremism and violence during the Troubles and is more chillingly and colloquially referred to as 'the provos'.

They are associated with shootings, mainly of police and military personnel in Northern Ireland, and bombing campaigns on the British mainland, with an objective of removing the British administration from Ireland and an overall goal of a united, 32-county independent state. Scotland was largely excluded from IRA operations due to the large number of emigrant Irish living there (O'Callaghan, 1998) – potential supporters of the republican cause.

The IRA used bombings to great effect during the campaign. This method has the advantage of causing maximum physical and psychological damage with the minimum of casualties (Martin, 2010). Recruits to the IRA received training in explosives, timers, booby traps, clocks, detonators, gelignite and material for making homemade bombs (O'Callaghan, 1998).

The Czech-manufactured Semtex plastic explosive became a favoured tool of the IRA during the bombing campaign (Martin, 2010), along with the ArmaLite rifle, the submachine gun and the RPG7 anti-tank rocket launcher, which became available to the IRA when first landed at Shannon airport in 1972 (O'Callaghan, 1998).

PRACTICAL TASK

Go to http://news.bbc.co.uk/hi/english/static/in_depth/northern_ireland/2001/provisional _ira/default.stm, which provides multi-media services, and click on the highlighted year '1971'. Listen to the statement regarding internment made by the Northern Ireland Prime Minister, Brian Faulkner, and answer the following questions.

- *Who are the main targets in relation to internment?*

- *Who is causing the present threat?*

This is an excellent internet-based resource and careful navigation around it can provide a sequential overview of the operations of the IRA mainly within Northern Ireland during the period of the Troubles.

(See Appendix A on page 190 for answers.)

The issue of internment has been specifically selected for further investigation as it quite simply backfired on the British authorities, just as many of the initiatives introduced in Ireland historically and designed to protect the state have done.

Raids on addresses of alleged IRA members were carried out on 9 August 1971, mainly because intelligence gathered by the RUC Special Branch and the Army was either completely wrong or totally outdated; hence, only a few activists were actually arrested. To further add to the ignominy, the IRA, which had clearly honed its intelligence capability, knew about the raids several days before they actually occurred. The policy of internment was a massive triumph for the IRA politically and served to bolster nationalist support on both sides of the border (Maloney, 2002) as supporters of the cause defended the underpinning grievances of the terrorist group (Martin, 2010).

The prime example here is that of Sinn Fein, who consistently articulated the nationalist cause of the extremists and became known as the 'political wing of the IRA'.

The IRA carried out many symbolic attacks on the British mainland, such as the 20-pound bomb fitted with a delayed timer on 16 October 1984 at the Grand Hotel, Brighton, which killed five members of the Conservative Party at their annual conference. Margaret Thatcher, the Prime Minister at the time, was extremely lucky to escape (Taylor, 1997). This was perhaps the nearest the IRA came to murdering a British Prime Minister, although on 7 February 1991 Prime Minister John Major and his Gulf War Cabinet survived a mortar attack by the IRA on Downing Street, which had been launched from a Ford transit van parked in Whitehall (Taylor, 1997).

Peace: the prize

By the early part of the 1990s and after John Major had replaced Margaret Thatcher as British Prime Minister, there were clear signs that both sides, British and republican, had realised that an impasse (stalemate) in the Troubles had been reached.

Informal contact had always been maintained between the IRA and the British Government via an MI6 (Secret Intelligence Service) operative later identified as Michael Oatley (Adams, 2003), who acted as a conduit between the two organisations and was better known by the codename 'The Mountain Climber'. This was despite consistent denials from British Government officials claiming that 'We don't talk to terrorists.' This was true in that direct negotiations were not taking place; however, indirectly they clearly were, albeit under the cloak of intelligence gathering.

Negotiations continued behind the scenes with several trusted parties on both sides becoming involved with the nationalist side led by Sinn Fein, often described as the 'political wing of the IRA'. Eventually, these efforts culminated in the Downing Street Declaration announced jointly by the British and Irish Governments on 15 December 1993 (Adams, 2003).

Although the scale of the subsequent discussions cannot be truly reflected here, this did lay the foundations for an all-party signing of a new political agreement on Good Friday in 1998 between both the British and Irish Governments.

Since this time, Northern Ireland has elected its own Assembly government sitting at Stormont Castle, Belfast, with members represented across the political spectrum working together, as opposed to direct rule from London, which was the case throughout the Troubles. At the height of the Troubles in the late 1970s and early 1980s, this could never have been perceived as feasible and illustrates the magnitude of the Good Friday Agreement.

Statistics for lives lost illustrate this point. From the start of the Troubles in 1969 until 1993, the year of the Downing Street Declaration, a total of 3,284 people lost their lives in the associated violence. Loyalist terrorist groups were responsible for 871 deaths, republican paramilitaries 829 and the British military 203 (Martin, 2010).

C H A P T E R   S U M M A R Y

This chapter has focused on nationalist extremist violence. Ireland has such a rich tapestry of history that it is almost impossible to know where to start and what to include in providing some context to the growth of terrorism and its implications for both population and government. The history of the Troubles is a legacy of that history and this chapter has been written from an introductory perspective to provide a credible base for further academic study into the fascinating and diverse island of Ireland and its people.

Life has returned to normal following the signing of the Good Friday Agreement. Organisations that played such a prominent role during the Troubles, such as the RUC, have been reformed and renamed the Police Service of Northern Ireland (PSNI). This is to reflect a new beginning in Northern Ireland and build on the principles of the Patten Report of 1999, which promoted a true, representative balance of Protestant and Catholic police officers, to reflect the community within Northern Ireland, unlike its forerunner, the RUC, and associated policing bodies such as the 'B' Specials, which were in essence Protestant organisations.

Sporadic nationalist violence continues to occur from time to time with the police and military, as symbols of the state, being the main targets. These outbreaks have been attributed to two particular nationalist splinter groups – the Continuity IRA and the Real IRA – which did not agree with the overall political peace process, led by Sinn Fein on the nationalist side. This will be developed further in the final chapter of this book.

If the overall goal of the republican terrorist violence is considered, the only conclusion that could be reached is that the campaign failed, in that Northern Ireland remains part of the UK. However, it is clear that the republican movement did enjoy some considerable support and, as the British authorities were unable to defeat them, a stalemate occurred. A solution needed to be reached through political discussions and Sinn Fein was seen as crucial to that process (Martin, 2010).

Sinn Fein played a pivotal role in the peace process and now fills some key political appointments within the Northern Ireland Assembly. That alone could be considered as progress and, furthermore, people from all sides of the community in Northern Ireland are no longer being killed in the terrorist war.

If Catholics are now placed on an equal footing with their Protestant neighbours, with equal access to democratic structures, employment and civil rights, the terrorist war from a nationalist perspective could be perceived to be a limited success.

REFERENCES

Adams, G (2003) *Hope and History: Making Peace in Ireland*. London: Brandon.

Boyle, K, Hadden, T and Hillyard, P (1975) *Law and State: The Case of Northern Ireland*. London: Robertson.

Caulfield, M (1995) *The Easter Rebellion*. Dublin: Gill and Macmillan.

Farrell, M (1976) *Northern Ireland: The Orange State*. London: Pluto Press.

Farrell, M (1986) *The Apparatus of Repression*. Derry: Field Day Theatre Company.

Foster, RF (1988) *Modern Ireland 1600–1972*. London: Penguin.

Maloney, E (2002) *A Secret History of the IRA*. London: Allen Lane.

Martin, G (2010) *Understanding Terrorism: Challenges, Perspectives and Issues*, 3rd edition. London: Sage.

O'Callaghan, S (1998) *The Informer.* London: Bantam Press.

Powell, J (2008) *Great Hatred, Little Room: Making Peace in Northern Ireland.* London: Bodley Head.

Taylor, P (1997) *Provos: The IRA and Sinn Fein.* London: Bloomsbury.

Townsend, C (1983) *Political Violence in Ireland: Government and Resistance Since 1848.* Oxford: Clarendon.

USEFUL WEBSITES

www.bbc.co.uk/northernireland/ashorthistory/archive/topic86.shtml (BBC – A Short History of Ireland)

www.constitution.org/eng/habcorpa.htm (Habeas Corpus Act 1679)

www.easter1916.net (Easter Rising 1916)

www.grandorangelodge.co.uk (The Grand Orange Lodge of Ireland)

www.libraryireland.com/articles/Eighteenth-Century-Ireland/Irish-Penal-Laws.php (Library Ireland – State of Ireland during the Eighteenth Century, Chapter 5 of *The British Empire in the Nineteenth Century* by Edgar Sanderson (1898))

LEGISLATION

Government of Ireland Act 1920

Habeas Corpus Act 1679

Suppression of Disturbances Act 1833

5 Countering the terrorist threat

Barrie Sheldon

CHAPTER OBJECTIVES

By the end of this chapter you should be able to:

- understand some of the options that are available to counter the terrorist threat;
- analyse the effectiveness of certain counter-terrorism measures.

Introduction

When a country is threatened or experiences terrorist acts, decisions are required by those responsible for national security (usually government) to take action to counter the terrorist threat and prevent further atrocities. There is a range of options available to state rulers and politicians and within this chapter these are highlighted and explored.

Many countries will take action in accordance with international, regional and national law, while others, who are not bound by such laws, may respond without regard to important issues such as the rule of law, human rights and civil liberties.

Martin (2009) explains counter-terrorism as proactive policies that seek to eliminate terrorist environments and groups, with the objective of saving lives by preventing and decreasing terrorist attacks. There are many options to be considered, from doing nothing, which in itself may frustrate a terrorist, to the use of force, such as going to war to eliminate the terrorist completely. Following the terrorist attack in New York (9/11) President George W Bush announced the global war against terrorism and proceeded to attack both Afghanistan and Iraq, the results of which are still having major implications for the Western world today.

REFLECTIVE TASK

Consider the actions taken by President George W Bush. Was he justified in taking these actions or were his responses premature and disproportionate in the circumstances?

This is not an easy question to answer and people will provide a range of views and perspectives to the debate based on factors such as personal belief and experience, culture or where located in the world. President Bush had to make a decision and history will tell us whether it was the right one.

The option of war is considered further below.

Counter-terrorism options

Figure 5.1 provides an overview (which is not exhaustive) of some of the methods that may be used to counter terrorism based on three options: the use of force, operations not requiring force and legalistic options.

The use of force

The use of force as a counter-terrorism response is a serious and drastic step to take, but is sometimes necessary to eradicate the terrorist threat and to suppress terrorist environments.

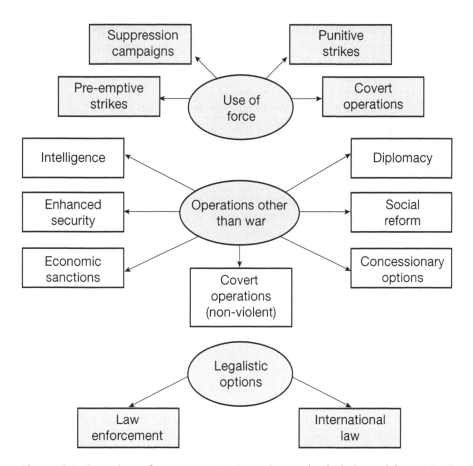

Figure 5.1 Overview of some counter-terrorist methods (adapted from Martin, 2009, pp463–5)

War is the ultimate option, where military or paramilitary units are deployed to incapacitate the terrorist using a range of tactics, including killing, capturing and destruction of property. The decision to use military force should not be taken lightly and should provide a legitimate and proportionate response to the threat posed. Operations can take place domestically or internationally and are governed by national and international law.

Just war doctrine

When engaging in war a number of moral and ethical issues need to be considered. The just war (*justum bellum*) doctrine provides a set of principles that aim to retain a plausible moral framework for war. It has two components: *jus ad bellum* (justice of war) – being able to show that a decision to go to war was just, was taken as a last resort, was declared by a proper authority, has a reasonable chance of success and is proportionate; and *jus in bello* (justice in war) – adhering to laws and rules of engagement (Moseley, 2009). If war is an option for a state, the just war doctrine is an important consideration in any decision-making process.

The UK is a member of the United Nations (UN) and is bound by rules set out within their charter, which states that a nation cannot plan and make war (Article 33). Where there is a dispute nations must exhaust all possible means of settlement and, even then, if settlement is not achieved, only the UN can authorise war (Ratner, 1992). Most countries in the world are members of the UN and the full list can be found online at www.un.org/en/members.

The Hague Conventions 1899 and 1907, Geneva Conventions 1929 and 1949, and the Nuremberg Principles 1950 are just a few examples of international laws that attempt to control the use of war by nations and set out rules of engagement.

PRACTICAL TASK

Find out more about the just war doctrine and apply it to the previous reflective task, considering specifically the declaration of war by the USA against Iraq in 2003, which was strongly suspected of developing WMDs. Make a list of your reasons for supporting the premise (or not) that this was in fact a 'just war'.

Domestic use of force

The military, police or other security forces can be deployed by states to tackle a domestic terrorist threat using force if necessary. Within the UK, security personnel are required to work within a legal framework that is designed to meet both the needs of national security and individual human rights, but this may not be the case in other countries with unstable regimes. The use of force can be problematic and have severe consequences, such as innocent casualties, sympathy and support for the terrorist group and escalation of violence. In extreme circumstances some nations can revert to state-sponsored terrorism (see Chapter 2).

Suppression campaigns

Suppression campaigns can be achieved by military and paramilitary operations targeting the terrorist, their bases and support mechanisms. They are uniquely adapted to the conditions of the terrorist environment and are usually of indeterminate duration, launched within a policy context of war or quasi war. The ultimate goal is to defeat the terrorist movement (Martin, 2009).

Pre-emptive strikes

When a threat of terrorism is imminent or suspected, a pre-emptive strike has the capability of catching the terrorist off guard and disrupting or preventing future attacks. Article 51 of the UN charter permits the use of pre-emptive strikes as a matter of self-defence when a nation is threatened. Following 9/11 President Bush stated within his foreign policy doctrine a willingness to take pre-emptive military action against 'rogue states' and terrorist groups before they attacked the USA or became an unmanageable future threat (Devanny, 2001). The invasion of Iraq in March 2003 is a good example of the doctrine being applied in practice to prevent the development and use of WMDs.

More recently, Iran has been identified as posing a potential nuclear threat to Israel. This is being monitored closely and should the threat escalate the possibility of pre-emptive strikes against Iran could become a reality.

CASE STUDY

Al-Kibar nuclear facility, Syria

On 6 September 2007 Israeli jets entered Syrian airspace and bombed a suspected nuclear facility at al-Kibar. Israel remained silent following the attack and Syria denied that the building destroyed was a nuclear facility. Post-attack analysis suggested a North Korean connection with the site – it mirrored a nuclear facility in Yongbyon, North Korea, North Korean personnel had been seen at the Syrian facility, and key materials were being smuggled via China and Europe by a North Korean company (Gartenstein-Ross and Goodman, 2009).

Since becoming an independent nation in 1948 Israel has been in a constant state of war. It has clashed with Syria on a number of occasions, which actively supports terrorist groups such as Hezbollah and the Palestinian Islamic Jihad, which remain a serious threat to Israel. The prospect of having a neighbour with a nuclear capability creates understandable national security concerns and the pre-emptive strike was an effective means of eradicating the potential threat.

Punitive strikes

A punitive strike is a retaliatory option rather than a preventive measure and is launched as a reprisal for a terrorist attack. The target should be symbolically and politically linked to the actual terrorist incident. The Palestinian conflict provides many examples of retaliatory action.

CASE STUDY

Israeli air strikes, Gaza strip

On Tuesday, 21 December 2010 Israel launched a series of air strikes in the Gaza strip in retaliation for a number of Palestinian rocket and mortar attacks that had taken place during the previous week. Seven targets were bombed and eight militants were wounded, provoking a further Palestinian rocket attack that resulted in the wounding of a 16-year-old Israeli girl. On the Saturday prior to the rocket and mortar attacks Israel had killed five Gaza militants.

Israeli military leaders claimed that the air strikes targeted a weapons factory and smuggling tunnels that were being used by militants to infiltrate Israel; however, the Palestinians claimed that a government-built dairy factory was hit.

(Teibel, 2010)

REFLECTIVE TASK

The Israeli conflict with the Palestinians has continued since 1948 and persists with no realistic solution to end the conflict. Consider the use of punitive strikes by the parties concerned and question whether their use is viable and effective as a counter-terrorism strategy.

Covert operations

Covert operations can be used to infiltrate, disrupt and destroy terrorist groups, with the use of special or conventional forces. Within a war scenario such as Afghanistan, Special Forces are very often the first troops on the ground to provide detailed environmental and target information for conventional forces. They have the capability of conducting independent surgical operations to neutralise terrorist leaders or destroy terrorist training camps. Operations may occur without the public ever being made aware and their impact is such that terrorist leaders need to consider threats from silent abduction and guided munitions (Wright, 2001).

In other scenarios Special Forces may be used to respond to hostage situations, conduct rendition operations and even commit assassinations. The two case studies below provide examples of the use of Special Forces.

CASE STUDY

Special Forces operations

Hostage rescue (Operation Nimrod)

On 30 April 1980 six Iranians armed with guns forced their way into the Iranian Embassy, Princes Gate, London. The Iranians were aligned to a terrorist group called the 'Democratic Revolutionary Front for Arabstan' and were protesting against the oppression of Khuzestan by the Iranian leader, Ayatollah Khomeini. They took 26 people hostage and demanded the release of 91 political prisoners in Iran and a plane to fly them and the hostages out of the UK. During the siege a hostage was killed and the Government authorised the use of force by the military to bring the siege to an end. Five days later Special Air Service (SAS) commandos stormed the embassy using explosives, stun grenades and firearms to end the siege. Five of the terrorists were killed and one was arrested; the hostages were freed but one was killed and two were injured.

Assassination

On 19 January 2009 Mahmoud al-Mabhouh (a Hamas military commander) was found dead in his hotel room in Dubai. It is strongly suspected that the Israeli secret service, Mossad, was responsible for the assassination. The team involved in the assassination were using false passports that included the stolen identity of six British citizens residing in Israel. Israel have not admitted to the attack nor denied their involvement; however, they are strongly suspected. Government deniability is commonly found in this type of operation.

The purpose of assassination is to remove the threat permanently; however, it is suggested that there is little evidence to support the supposition that assassination has provided a deterrent for the determined terrorist. The terrorist often operates within a supportive environment and, if terminally removed, is likely to be seen as a hero and elevated to martyrdom status. Martyrdom can invigorate terrorist support and recruitment (Martin, 2009).

Extraordinary rendition

Following 9/11 the Bush administration embarked on an extraordinary rendition programme that is both controversial and unconventional:

> *Extraordinary rendition is a process which allows the apprehension and extrajudicial transfer of a person suspected of terrorist activity from one country for arrest detention and/or interrogation to another country known to employ harsh interrogation techniques.*

(Murtza, 2010)

Extraordinary rendition was used by the USA prior to 9/11 and allowed the seizure of crime and terrorism suspects (sometimes by means of abduction) anywhere in the world for return to the USA to appear before a court of law. Since 9/11 the practice has been extended to allow seized suspects to be detained covertly and transported to allied countries for interrogation, where allegations of torture have been made (see the Binyam Mohamed case study in Chapter 8, pages 131–2).

On 4 November 2009 an Italian court in Milan convicted 23 Americans and two Italians of kidnapping an Egyptian terrorist suspect, Abu Omar, from a street in Milan in February 2003. This was the first conviction anywhere in the world against those involved in the USA extraordinary rendition programme. In January 2009 President Obama closed down secret US overseas prisons and ended the practice of using harsh interrogation techniques, but has retained powers allowing renditions, secret abductions and transfers of prisoners to allied countries (Miller, 2009).

REFLECTIVE TASK

Consider the use of assassination and extraordinary rendition and the implications for a state that chooses to adopt both as counter-terrorism measures. Are these types of action acceptable and how might the local population and other states react to their use? Consider specifically the rule of law, human rights and civil liberty issues, and argue for or against the use of assassination and extraordinary rendition as legitimate counter-terrorism measures.

The United Kingdom Special Forces (UKSF) were established in 1987 and commanded by the Director Special Forces with the rank of Major General. The units highlighted in Table 5.1 come under the command of the UKSF.

Table 5.1 Units under the command of UKSF

Unit	Duties
Special Air Service (SAS) Regiment	Has a counter-terrorism wing known as the 'Special Projects' team, which can respond quickly to a terrorist incident within the UK and globally.
18 (UKSF) Signals Regiment	Provides significant communications and intelligence support to operations, including interception, monitoring and analysis.
Special Boat Service (SBS)	Trained for maritime counter-terrorism operations and on stand-by to respond to the threat of terrorism on ferries, cruise chips, hovercrafts, oil tankers and rigs.
Special Reconnaissance Regiment (SRR)	Gathers intelligence and carries out surveillance operations in support of the war against terrorism.
Special Forces Support Group	Provides specialist infantry and specialised support to SAS and SBS operations, including domestic anti-terrorism support.
United Kingdom Special Forces (UKSF) Aviation	Provides flight support for UKSF operations using highly skilled pilots from all branches of the UK military.

Source: Compiled from Eliteukforces.info (2010)

The Police Service within the UK also has a number of specialist operational units that can provide covert services and have a firearms capability.

Operations not requiring force

There are many options to counter-terrorism that do not include the use of force and within this section we shall explore seven of these: covert operations, intelligence, enhanced security, economic sanctions, diplomacy, social reform and concessionary options.

Covert operations

Non-violent covert operations can be very effective in disrupting terrorist activity, using means such as infiltration, disinformation and cyber attacks.

Infiltration can be very effective but sometimes difficult owing to the secretive nature of many terrorist groups, close-knit relationships and loose cell-based structures. Infiltration was a tactic used with some success by security forces against the IRA in Northern Ireland. The IRA suspected advance warning (as a result of infiltration) had been given for a number of botched operations, such as the capture of a shipload of Libyan weaponry in 1987 and the taking out of an active service unit in Gibraltar in 1988. Weapons caches were found, trackers were planted on firearms, and IRA members were identified and assassinated by loyalists (James, 2003).

Disinformation has long been a military tactic and used to some effect. During the Second World War, prior to the invasion of Normandy in 1944, part of a deception plan (operation Bodyguard) was to mislead the Germans through disinformation that the attack would take place elsewhere and at a later time. Then Prime Minister Winston Churchill stated at a conference in Tehran a year before that *truth is so precious that she should always be attended by a bodyguard of lies* (Beelman, 2001, p1). Disinformation is a key option to be considered and applied in the war against terrorism.

The rapid development of information technology has contributed to globalisation and terrorists will utilise it accordingly to achieve their goals. The interception of digital information provides options such as the gathering of intelligence, thwarting operations, identifying group members, bringing terrorists to justice and severely disrupting terrorist financing.

Cyber warfare today is a serious option for any counter-terrorism strategy and is a tactic that can produce some excellent results. For example, it was reported in January 2011 that American and Israeli experts had designed a computer worm called 'Stuxnet', which was used to infect a uranium enrichment plant in Iran to reduce the nuclear threat against Israel. A leading computer security expert suggested that the use of Stuxnet was not simply about sending a message or proving a concept but about destroying targets with utmost determination in military style (Hider, 2011).

Intelligence

Intelligence plays a key role in all counter-terrorism strategies and can be collected by either overt or covert means. Chapter 8 deals exclusively with intelligence, explaining its function and how it is collected, processed and disseminated, identifying intelligence agencies and exploring some of the problems associated with it, such as information sharing.

Enhanced security

Target hardening is a key component of any crime-prevention strategy and terrorism is no exception. Certain actions can be taken to reduce the risk of terrorist attacks by simply making any potential terrorist target more difficult to attack.

Since 9/11 airport security has been tightened considerably with no access to the flight deck and additional security checks before entering the departure lounge. Terrorist events see states reacting quickly to prevent further instances of terrorism and the three examples below provide evidence of this.

CASE STUDY

Target-hardening tactics

The shoe bomber
Richard Reid (nicknamed the shoe bomber) boarded an American Airlines flight in Paris on 22 December 2001 en route to Miami. During the flight he attempted to detonate plastic explosives concealed in the sole of his shoe. There was sufficient explosive within the shoe to blow a large hole in the fuselage and cause the death of all passengers and crew. He was overpowered and detained before he could detonate the explosive and was later convicted in an American court in January 2003 for a series of terrorism-related offences, receiving a sentence of life imprisonment. Following his detention American airline passengers were required to remove their shoes for inspection prior to boarding a flight or entering the airport terminal.

Glasgow airport
On 30 June 2007 Bilal Abdulla and Kafeel Ahmed drove a burning Jeep Cherokee loaded with explosive material into the main terminal building at Glasgow airport in an attempted suicide bombing. The consequences could have been disastrous, with about 4,000 people in the building. Fortunately there were only a small number of casualties with no serious injury; however, Ahmed, who was the driver of the vehicle, died a number of weeks later from burns received during the attack. Abdulla was convicted at Woolwich

---

Crown Court on 16 December 2008 for conspiracy to cause murder and cause explosions, and received a 32-year jail sentence. As a result of the attack BAA Glasgow has invested £4 million in repairs, improvements to the forecourt and heightened airport security. In addition, 300 steel-encased bollards have been placed along the length of the terminal (Crichton, 2008). Similar security measures are now found at most UK airports.

Bombs disguised as drinks

In August 2006 a number of men were arrested in the London area for conspiracy to activate bombs disguised as drinks on aircraft. Three of the men, Abdulla Ahmed Ali, Tanvir Hussain and Assad Sarwar, were convicted on 7 September 2009 and three others, Ibrahim Savant, Arafat Waheed Khan and Waheed Zaman, were later convicted on 8 July 2010 following a number of retrials. All received substantial terms of imprisonment. The arrests sparked an immediate global security alert with restrictions (still enforced today) placed on the carrying of liquids in hand luggage.

Safer places

In July 2007 the UK government commissioned a review of how best to protect crowded places from terrorist attack. It was found that, although substantial work had been completed to increase levels of protective security, more was required to turn advice into action. The review highlighted the importance of engaging with a wide range of local partners, such as local authorities and local businesses, to implement counter-terrorist protective security advice (Home Office, 2009).

Find a copy of 'Safer Places: A Counter Terrorism Supplement' (an internet search will provide access to a pdf document). Read through the document and identify the range of protective measures that can be adopted to counter the terrorist threat.

Economic sanctions

Economic sanctions place restrictions on international trade and finance and can be considered as a potential counter-terrorism measure. Success factors include firm international cooperation, control of trade leaks and ensuring that the sanctioned regime actually suffers. This type of strategy has certain limitations and problems can occur, for example:

- *the people rather than the regime usually suffer;*
- *states involved in a coalition do not always remain firm;*
- *difficulties in controlling trade embargo leaks; and*
- *sanctioning policies becoming porous.*

(Martin, 2009, p487)

Diplomacy

Diplomacy is a non-coercive counter-terrorism option that opens up lines of communication to settle political disputes and grievances. Peace processes allow dialogue and negotiation with terrorist groups and terrorist states, and provide a good example of diplomacy in action. The peace process in Northern Ireland saw the political wing of the IRA, Sinn Fein, take a legitimate place in government (1998) and the cessation of terrorist operations; however, in contrast the Middle East peace talks have a history of failure, but diplomatic options continue to be utilised in seeking a solution to the conflict.

CASE STUDY

ETA

Chapter 1 (pages 6–7) highlighted how the Basque Fatherland and Liberty (ETA) terrorist group in Spain had attempted to seek political legitimacy with their Batasuna party, which was banned by the Spanish Supreme Court in 2003. On Monday, 10 January 2011 ETA announced a permanent ceasefire to end its 51-year violent campaign in Spain for an independent Basque nation. The Government responded by stating that the announcement was heavy on rhetoric and flimsy on detail (Elkin, 2011). Diplomacy continues as an option for the Spanish government despite previous setbacks and there is potential to end the conflict, provided both parties are willing to engage and follow a course similar to that witnessed in Northern Ireland.

REFLECTIVE TASK

Consider both the Middle East and Northern Ireland peace processes. Why has one succeeded but the other continues to fail?

Social reform

To resolve political conflicts that breed terrorism, social reform can relieve tension within communities and significantly reduce violence. Reforms may include enhancing economic conditions, improving living conditions, providing essential services, recognising and resolving grievances, and fair representation within the political process.

CASE STUDY

AQAP

Yemen has been identified as a base for an al-Qaeda subsidiary terrorist group known as al-Qaeda in the Arabian Peninsula (AQAP), which was believed responsible for two attacks targeted at the USA. On Christmas Day 2009 a Nigerian, Umar Farouk Abdulmutallab, attempted to detonate a homemade bomb concealed in his underwear on Northwest Flight 253 en route from Amsterdam to Detroit and AQAP claimed responsibility for the attack. On 29 October 2010 packages containing bombs in printer cartridges were found in cargo planes in Dubai and at East Midlands airport. The packages were addressed to a Chicago synagogue and originated in Yemen.

The American government is assisting the Yemeni President, Al Abdullah Saleh, in countering the terrorist threat within Yemen using a number of options that include social reform. American Secretary of State, Hillary Clinton, visited Yemen in January 2011 and encouraged leaders to speed up economic and political reforms to relieve social problems that she said helped create conditions that breed terrorism (Warrick, 2011).

Concessionary options

Concessionary options include negotiation and compromise with terrorists by negotiators rather than diplomats. The USA and many of its allies, including the UK, are committed to a policy of non-negotiation with terrorists; however, despite this policy there are many examples where states have negotiated with terrorists to bring about resolutions to terrorist activity. The problem of conceding to terrorist demands is the continuance of violence, encouragement to others to commit acts of terrorism and the state losing its credibility. The list below provides some examples of concessions that could be considered.

- *Payment of ransom money.*
- *Payment of bribe or protection money.*
- *Provision of weapons, food, material, technology or information.*
- *Release of imprisoned terrorists or terrorist supporters.*
- *Release of political prisoners, dissidents, extremists and spiritual fanatics.*
- *Provision of transport to another location.*
- *Provision of political asylum or amnesty within host country.*
- *Provision of legal services and public court forum to air their cause; and*
- *Provision of access to news media to broadcast their propaganda.*

(Adelman, 2010, no page)

Consider the premise that concessions simply reward extremist behaviour. Is a policy of non-negotiation feasible or do states need to be more flexible and be prepared to employ concessionary options?

Legalistic options

Legalistic options are concerned with the application of law and the use of law enforcement agencies to apprehend terrorists and process them through the Criminal Justice System (CJS). This involves investigation, arrest, questioning, charging, criminal trial and sentencing. Terrorist crimes are usually very serious and ultimately result in long terms of imprisonment, which incapacitates the terrorist and can act as a deterrent to others.

Law enforcement

The police are the primary law enforcement agency within the UK and work in conjunction with the Security Service (MI5) in relation to terrorist investigations. In addition to its law enforcement role, the Police Service is also responsible for the provision of specialised services such as firearms, civil protection, maintenance of public order, and civil contingency to deal with the aftermath of a terrorist attack.

Security is paramount and both the police and other law enforcement agencies provide protective services at strategic locations such as airports, ports, border crossings and critical infrastructure sites. For example, the UK Border Agency has a strategic objective of protecting UK borders and the national interest, and their activities include preventing drugs, weapons, terrorists and illegal immigrants reaching the UK (Home Office, 2010).

The role of the police in countering terrorism will be examined in more detail in subsequent chapters. Police structures, terrorist legislation and its application, intelligence capability, community engagement to tackle the problem of radicalisation, and protection of the national critical infrastructure will be explored.

Counter-terrorism operations are challenging and the police have to work within the rule of law, be aware of human rights issues, and ensure the safety of the public at all times.

CASE STUDY

Jean Charles de Menezes

On 21 July 2005 a number of explosive devices that had failed to detonate were found in London. One of these devices was found at Shepherd's Bush in a rucksack and, following a search of it, a South Bank gym card was found in the name of Hussain Osman, linking him to a block of flats in Scotia Road, London SW2.

The Metropolitan Police subsequently commenced Operation Theseus to locate and arrest those responsible for the failed bombs. The following day covert surveillance teams were deployed to two addresses in London, including Scotia Road. CCTV pictures had been obtained of the man responsible for the Shepherd's Bush attempt and these were in possession of the surveillance team who were required to watch the flats in Scotia Road and follow any person leaving.

At about 9.33 am Jean Charles de Menezes, a 27-year-old electrician, left the flats where he resided and was immediately followed by a police surveillance team. Within an hour

---

Menezes was dead, having been shot seven times in the head by police in a train carriage at Stockwell underground station.

A tragic and fatal mistake had been made and the later investigation completed by the Independent Police Complaints Commission (IPCC) highlighted a number of failings of the police operation. In November 2007 the Metropolitan Police were convicted of an offence under the Health and Safety at Work Act 1974 relating to the death, but no blame was attached to the leader of the operation, Commander Cressida Dick.

Conflicting messages had been received from the surveillance team regarding the identity of Menezes and the IPCC investigation found that no positive identification had been made between Menezes and the CCTV pictures showing Osman; however, this was not clear within the police control room where key decisions were being made about the threat Menezes posed and the possibility that he was a suicide bomber. The IPCC raised the following concern:

> There was no threat assessment and the risk assessments undertaken for this operation did not consider the risk of misidentification or uncertainty regarding the identification of a suspect. The assessment did not consider a suspect leaving the premises before firearms resources were in place.

> *(IPCC, 2007, p163)*

Following 9/11 the Metropolitan Police introduced Operation Kratos, which considered a range of options to deal with the threat of a suicide bomber. The ultimate sanction and last resort is the killing of the bomber before the explosive device can be activated. Those involved in the police operation resulting in the death of Jean Charles de Menezes considered him to be a threat at a time when tensions were high (i.e. 7/7 bombings and 21/7 failed bombings).

Consider the options available to remove the threat of a suicide bomber to ensure safety of the public. Is a 'shoot to kill' policy appropriate and how do we ensure that sufficient safeguards are in place to avoid another tragic mistake? Your considerations should include the rule of law, human rights, police accountability and government responsibility.

Decision making is a key skill for a police officer both in the field and when managing operations. Training, experience, robust policies and procedures, integrity and accurate and timely intelligence all contribute to the decision-making process. Police counter-terrorist operations require careful planning and execution, effective leadership and an ability to respond appropriately to what can sometimes be a fast-moving scenario where life-and-death situations arise.

In some cases the police face the dilemma of not knowing when to strike. An early arrest of terrorist suspects may compromise the collection of sufficient evidence to support a successful prosecution, but failure to arrest may result in loss of life and police confidence.

C H A P T E R   S U M M A R Y

Within this chapter a range of options have been considered to counter the terrorist threat, from the ultimate sanction of war, to non-violent and conciliatory options. Where terrorism is a threat, government is expected to provide a response to seek out the terrorist, prevent further attacks and reduce terrorist opportunities. The 9/11 attacks acted as a catalyst for Western governments to review and implement counter-terrorism policies and the UK was no exception. In the next chapter the UK counter-terrorism strategy (CONTEST) will be examined and the range of counter-terrorist options utilised will be highlighted.

REFERENCES

Adelman, Kenneth (2010) Counterterrorism: Diplomatic and Intelligence Operations. Megalinks in Criminal Justice. Available online at http://drtomoconnor.com/3400/3400lect08.htm (accessed 13 January 2011).

Beelman, Maud S (2001) The Dangers of Disinformation in the War on Terrorism. *Neiman Reports*, Winter 2001, Harvard College, Cambridge, MA. Available online at www.nieman.harvard.edu/reports/article/101451/The-Dangers-of-Disinformation-in-the-War-on-Terrorism.aspx (accessed 10 January 2011).

Crichton, Torcuil (2008) Glasgow Airport Terror Attack: Bomber Found Guilty. *Scotland Herald*, 16 December. Available online at www.heraldscotland.com/glasgow-airport-terror-attack-bomber-found-guilty-1.897576 (accessed 11 January 2011).

Devanny, Joe (2001) Pre-emptive Action, Doctrine of [US]. International Debate Education Association (IDEA). Available online at www.idebate.org/debatabase/topic_details.php?topicID=283 (accessed 6 January 2011).

Eliteukforces.info (2010) British Special Forces and Elite Units. Available online at www.eliteukforces.info (accessed 7 January 2011).

Elkin, Mike (2011) Basque Separatists Eta Declare a 'Permanent' End to Violence. *Independent*, 11 January. Available online at www.independent.co.uk/news/world/europe/basque-separatists-eta-declare-a-permanent-end-to-violence-2181127.html (accessed 11 January 2011).

Gartenstein-Ross, Daveed and Goodman, Joshua D (2009) The Attack on Syria's al-Kabir Nuclear Facility. *In Focus Quarterly*, 3(1), Spring. Available online at www.jewishpolicycenter.org/826/the-attack-on-syrias-al-kibar-nuclear-facility (accessed 6 January 2011).

Hider, James (2011) Computer Virus that Halted Iran's Nuclear Plans 'Devised by US and Israeli Experts' – Cyber Warfare. *The Times*, 17 January.

Home Office (2009) *Safer Places: A Counter Terrorism Supplement.* London: Home Office.

Home Office (2010) *UK Border Agency Annual Report and Accounts 2009–10.* London: The Stationery Office.

IPCC (Independent Police Complaints Commission) (2007) *Stockwell One: Investigation into the Shooting of Jean Charles de Menezes at Stockwell Underground Station on 22 July 2005.* London: IPCC.

James, Steve (2003) The 'Steak Knife' Affair and Britain's Dirty War in Northern Ireland. World Socialist Web Site, 9 August. Available online at www.wsws.org/articles/2003/aug2003/irel-a09.shtml (accessed 10 January 2011).

Martin, Gus (2009) *Understanding Terrorism: Challenges, Perspectives and Issues*, 3rd edition. London: Sage.

Miller, Greg (2009) Obama Preserves Renditions as Counter Terrorism Tool. *Los Angeles Times*, 1 February. Available online at http://articles.latimes.com/2009/feb/01/nation/na-rendition1 (accessed 7 January 2011).

Moseley, Alexander (2009) Just War Theory, in *Internet Encyclopedia of Philosophy*. Available online at www.iep.utm.edu/justwar (accessed 5 January 2011).

Murtza, Sahra (2010) Extraordinary Rendition. Law, Crime & Justice @ Suite101, 19 September. Available online at www.suite101.com/content/extraordinary-rendition-a286784 (accessed 7 January 2011).

Ratner, Michael (1992) International Law and War Crimes. The Commission of Inquiry for the International War Crimes Tribunal. Available online at http://deoxy.org/wc/wc-ilaw.htm (accessed 5 January 2011).

Teibel, Amy (2010) Israel Steps Up Retaliatory Attacks On Gaza. *Minnesota Star Tribune*, 21 December. Available online at www.startribune.com/world/112288504.html?elr=KArks:DCiUBcy7hUiD3aPc:_Yyc:aULPQL7PQLanchO7DiUr (accessed 6 January 2011).

Warrick, Joby (2011) In Yemen, Clinton Urges Social Reform. *Washington Post*, 12 January. Available online at www.washingtonpost.com/wp-dyn/content/article/2011/01/11/AR2011011107142.html (accessed 12 January 2011).

Wright, Ian (2001) Q & A Covert Operations. *BBC News*, 3 October. Available online at http://news.bbc.co.uk/1/hi/uk/1577794.stm (accessed 7 January 2011).

LEGISLATION

Health and Safety at Work Act 1974

6   9/11 and the UK response

Barrie Sheldon

CHAPTER OBJECTIVES

By the end of this chapter you should be able to:

- describe the terrorist attacks in New York (11 September 2001), London (7 and 21 July 2005) and Mumbai (26 November 2008) and understand their implications for countering the terrorist threat;
- outline the development of the UK counter-terrorism strategy (CONTEST);
- analyse the impact and effectiveness of UK counter-terrorism policy.

Introduction

The impact of the terror attack in New York on Tuesday, 11 September 2001 (9/11) provided the stimulus for the worldwide war on terror and for many countries to review and reconsider the effectiveness of their counter-terrorism strategies. This chapter will explore the events of 9/11, identifying the lessons learned and how it contributed to the development of the UK counter-terrorism strategy (CONTEST). It will briefly explore each element of the strategy (Pursue, Prevent, Protect and Prepare) and look at other events that have contributed to further reviews of the strategy, such as the London bombings and attempted bombings in July 2005, and the Mumbai terrorist attack in November 2008. It will pose the question as to whether the strategy is effective and set the scene for subsequent chapters that will explore elements of the strategy in more detail, identifying a number of problems, some of which impact on human rights.

Al-Qaeda attacks America

The date Tuesday 11 September 2001 is firmly etched on the minds of millions of people worldwide who watched in utter disbelief as jet aircraft that had been hijacked by al-Qaeda (AQ) terrorists crashed into the twin towers of the World Trade Center, New York, and the Pentagon, Washington, killing thousands of people. A further aircraft destined for Washington crashed into a field in Pennsylvania after the terrorists were thwarted by passengers from achieving their goal of attacking the White House (official residence and workplace of the President of the USA).

The attacks were audacious, meticulously planned and provided a spectacular success for the AQ terrorist group.

The mechanics of the plot have been examined in infinitesimal detail. The tragic events themselves have been analysed from every conceivable angle. Currently, we are far too close to them to place them in any kind of context, and they remain, for most commentators, unprecedented and unique.

(Burke, 2007, p235)

Table 6.1 provides a timeline of events on that fateful day.

Table 6.1 Time line of events, 11 September 2001

0600	Mohamed Atta and Abdul Aziz al Omari fly from Portland airport, Maine, to Boston's Logan international airport, Massachusetts.
0645–0740	Atta and Omari join Satam al Suqami, Wail al Shehri and Waleed al Shehri at Boston and board American Airlines flight 11 (AA11) to Los Angeles, California. In another terminal at Boston, Marwin al Shehhi, Fayez Banihammad, Mohand al Shehri, Ahmed al Ghamdi and Hamza al Ghamdi board United Airlines flight 175 (UA175) to Los Angeles.
0715–0735	At Dulles international airport, Virginia, Khalid al Mihdhar, Majed Moqed, Hani Hanjour, Nawaf al Hazmi and Salem al Hazmi board American Airlines flight 77 (AA77) to Los Angeles.
0739–0748	At Newark Liberty international airport, New Jersey, Saeed al Ghamdi, Ahmed al Nami, Ahmad al Haznawi and Ziad Jarrah board United Airlines flight 93 (UA93) to Los Angeles.
0759	AA11 takes off from Boston.
0814	AA11 last contact with air traffic controllers.
0814	UA175 takes off from Boston.
0819	AA11 passenger reports emergency aboard the flight; cockpit is not answering, someone is stabbed in business class, two flight attendants have been stabbed; passenger thinks mace has been sprayed and passengers are struggling to breathe.
0820	AA77 takes off from Washington.
0842	UA93 takes off from Newark.
0842–0846	UA175 terrorists take control of aircraft with use of knives, mace and threat of a bomb on board. It is reported that flight crew have been stabbed and both pilots killed.
0846	AA11 crashes into the north tower of the World Trade Center, New York.
0851–0854	AA77 terrorists take control of aircraft with use of knives and box cutters and move passengers to rear of plane.
0903	UA175 crashes into the south tower of the World Trade Center, New York.
0928	UA93 terrorists take control of aircraft with use of knives and threat of a bomb on board. It is reported that a passenger has been stabbed and two people are lying on the floor of the cabin, injured or dead. Passengers moved to rear of aircraft.
0937	AA77 crashes into the Pentagon, Washington.
0957	UA93 passengers decide to overpower terrorists.
1002	UA93 terrorists decide to abort plan (believed to be crashing of aircraft into the White House, Washington) and crash plane into an empty field in Shanksville, Pennsylvania, about 20 minutes away from Washington.

Source: Adapted from Zelikow et al. (2004)

The terrorists

The USA quickly attributed the blame for the attacks on AQ and named Osama bin Laden as the mastermind behind them. Bin Laden, who evaded capture for many years but was killed by American special forces in Abbottabad, Pakistan, on 1 May 2011, made statements following the attack that were supportive rather than claiming responsibility for them. The following is taken from a transcript of a statement made by bin Laden broadcast by Al Jazeera TV, Qatar, on 7 October 2001:

> There is America, hit by God in one of its softest spots. Its greatest buildings were destroyed, thank God for that. There is America, full of fear from its north to its south, from its west to its east. Thank God for that.

(bin Laden, 2001)

Ten days later President George W Bush addressed a joint session of Congress, where he said that evidence pointed to AQ being responsible for the attack. He highlighted al-Qaeda's links with the Taliban in Afghanistan and accused them of sponsoring, sheltering and supplying terrorists. He made a number of demands of the Taliban, including the permanent closure of terrorist training camps and the delivery of AQ leaders to the USA authorities (CNN, 2001).

Following an extensive investigation by the Federal Bureau of Investigation (FBI) and other law enforcement, security and intelligence agencies, evidence was provided to a National Commission about the role of the AQ leadership in planning the attacks and how the 19 terrorists were recruited, trained and organised to carry them out. The evidence reflected assertions made by various 9/11 conspirators and captured AQ members following interrogation. The investigation team admitted that there were some inconsistencies, but had attempted to corroborate the evidence provided and made judgement calls, based on the weight and credibility of the evidence obtained (Zelikow, 2004).

One of the key organisers of the attack was Khalid Sheikh Mohammed, who was arrested in Pakistan in March 2003 and later detained at Guantanamo Bay. In March 2007 the Pentagon announced that, during interrogation, Mohammed had claimed that he was the mastermind behind the attacks and said *I was responsible for the operation from A to Z* (*BBC News*, 2007).

PRACTICAL TASK

Find out more about the evidence against AQ being responsible for the 9/11 attacks and consider the culpability of Osama bin Laden. Can we be certain that he was directly responsible for orchestrating the planning, recruiting, training, financing and logistical support required?

To assist with this task the evidence against AQ and Osama bin Laden can be found within the National Commission archive (see below). The Commission's twelfth public hearing, held on Wednesday, 16 June 2004, listened to the evidence available. The evidence presented is available in both written and video format at: http://govinfo.library.unt.edu/911/archive/hearing12/index.htm

USA response

The USA response was swift and dramatic. The day following the attacks President Bush announced a 'war on terror' and, following the Taliban's later refusal to hand over Osama bin Laden and other AQ leaders, the USA, supported by the UK, attacked the heart of Kandahar, Afghanistan, with a series of air strikes during the night of 7 October 2001.

Within days a government cabinet post was created for an office of homeland security to oversee and coordinate a comprehensive national strategy to safeguard the USA against the threat of terrorism. It soon became apparent that more than a hundred different government organisations were responsible for national security and that a single unified security structure was required.

New terrorist legislation was made available within weeks. In October the Uniting and Strengthening America by Providing Appropriate Tools Required to Intercept and Obstruct Terrorism Act of 2001 ('USA Patriot Act') provided a range of enhanced surveillance and investigatory powers for law enforcement agencies. The Act contained a number of controversial powers, such as roving wiretaps and secret searches of records, and was considered by some to be a serious threat to civil liberties.

> *From the USA PATRIOT Act's over-broad definition of domestic terrorism, to the FBI's new powers of search and surveillance, to the indefinite detention of both citizens and non-citizens without formal charges, the principles of free speech, due process, and equal protection under the law have been seriously undermined.*
>
> (CCR, 2002, summary)

REFLECTIVE TASK

Consider whether the USA Patriot Act of 2001 was drafted too quickly. The Act granted sweeping new powers to law enforcement agencies and was passed with little or no Congressional debate. Having announced the war on terror there was an urgency to tackle the problem of terrorism, but was sufficient consideration given to the balance between national security and civil liberties?

On 25 November 2002 the Homeland and Security Act established a Department of Homeland Security (DHS). The primary mission of the DHS included preventing terrorist attacks; reducing the vulnerability of the USA to terrorism; and minimising damage and assisting in the recovery from terrorist attacks (section 101). The Act also provided for the rationalisation of USA security and federal agencies.

Two days later the President created a National Commission on Terrorist Attacks Upon the United States (the 9/11 Commission) with a remit to investigate facts and circumstances relating to the attacks, including those related to law enforcement and intelligence agencies, border control, financing of terrorists, commercial aviation, congressional oversight and resource allocation, and other areas determined relevant by the Commission (Zelikow et al., 2004).

The completed report was published in July 2004 and made a series of recommendations to enhance the USA capability to reduce the terrorist threat, and to respond more effectively to terrorist incidents.

PRACTICAL TASK

Get hold of a copy of the 9/11 Commission report and find out about the recommendations made. Consider how the recommendations have informed policy, practice and procedure within the USA and whether they have contributed to (a) making the USA and the world a safer place, (b) the erosion of human rights and (c) providing an effective counter-terrorism capability.

UK response

The news of the 9/11 attacks spread quickly and many people around the world watched in horror as live television pictures showed the planes crashing into the World Trade Center and its later collapse. Within the UK the Government held an emergency civil contingencies meeting (COBRA – Cabinet Office Briefing Room A). London was declared a 'no fly' zone and special security measures were introduced at airports and certain public buildings. Then Prime Minister Tony Blair addressed the nation, stating that what had occurred in New York was not a battle between the USA and terrorism, but between the free democratic world and terrorism (Hewitt, 2008, p30).

Domestically the UK had produced a Terrorism Act in 2000 which provided a range of powers to meet immediate needs and concerns. The initial focus following the attacks was foreign policy and assisting the USA in the pursuit of Osama bin Laden and AQ in Afghanistan. However, because of the increasing threat to the UK from international terrorism and the changing nature of terrorist attacks, the Government developed a countering international terrorism strategy (CONTEST) in 2003.

The aim of the strategy was to reduce the risk from international terrorism so that people could go about their daily lives freely and with confidence (Home Office, 2006). A revised strategy published in July 2011 removed international terrorism from the aims, broadening the scope of the strategy to cover all forms of terrorism. CONTEST is divided into four principal strands: Pursue, Prevent, Protect and Prepare.

Pursue

Pursue is concerned with reducing the terrorist threat domestically and to UK interests overseas by disrupting operations and pursuing both the terrorists and those who sponsor them. This is achieved through developing effective intelligence systems, introducing new legislation, bringing terrorists to justice, and enhancing international cooperation to gather intelligence and disrupt terrorists outside the UK more effectively.

Chapter 7 will explore the range of terrorist legislation introduced since 2000 and examine its impact, particularly from a civil liberties perspective. Chapter 8 will discuss how the UK has developed its intelligence capability and highlight a number of problems relating to communication and information sharing.

Prevent

Radicalisation of individuals is identified as a key factor associated with the growing problem of international terrorism and this strand is aimed at tackling disadvantage, supporting reform by confronting inequality and discrimination, deterring those who facilitate and encourage terrorism, and challenging extremist ideology and beliefs.

Chapter 9 will explore issues related to radicalisation and question whether the strategy effectively deals with the problem or contributes to incidents of hate crime and community division.

Protect and Prepare

There is a need to put certain protection measures in place to deter and prevent terrorism. Borders, key installations such as energy, water and transport systems, and crowded places are all areas requiring effective counter-terrorism measures.

Terrorist attacks are inevitable no matter what precautions are taken and it is equally important to ensure that any emergency response is well planned and organised, and is able to deal effectively with the aftermath. The Prepare strategy concerns the identification of risks and assessing their impact; building the capability to respond to an attack effectively; and improving responses from lessons learned.

Chapter 10 will explore some of the protective measures adopted and assess their impact and effectiveness. The chapter also explores the role of the emergency services, the multi-agency approach, and how we are preparing for worst-case scenarios such as the use of chemical, biological, radiological and nuclear (CBRN) weapons.

London, 7 July 2005

Following 9/11 the Islamic jihadist terrorist threat remained a big concern for the Western world, with governments preparing for the possibility of another terrorist atrocity. The UK was no exception and the threat in Europe was very real, particularly when, on the morning of Thursday, 11 March 2004, a terrorist group later linked to al-Qaeda detonated 13 explosive devices on commuter trains in Madrid, Spain. A total of 191 people were killed and 1,841 injured in what was the most devastating act of insurgent terrorism in Western Europe and the second most lethal attack (the most lethal was the bombing of Pan Am flight 103 over Lockerbie in December 1988, which killed 259 people).

In one analysis of the Madrid attacks it was suggested that the attack was not only evidence of jihadist terrorism in transition but also illustrated the changing nature of the threat being posed. The attacks were not planned, prepared or executed by al-Qaeda alone; the network involved was a complex, composite source of threat where individuals from different groups and organisations converged. It also highlighted the choice of transport systems as a soft target for the terrorist, the preference for improvised explosive devices and the propensity for suicide (Reinares, 2010).

The Director General of the Security Service (MI5), Dame Eliza Manningham-Buller, while making a speech to business leaders in Birmingham on 8 November 2004, warned of the terrorist threat to the UK. She said that there was a serious and sustained threat of terrorist attacks, that al-Qaeda retained the capability of mounting attacks on Western interests, that al-Qaeda had inspired other groups and networks, and that the threat was real, was here and affected us all (Manningham-Buller, 2004).

Sir Ian Blair, the Commissioner of the Metropolitan Police, speaking on the BBC news programme *Breakfast with Frost* on 17 April 2005, made a statement purporting that there was a real clarity that al-Qaeda affiliates were targeting the UK and that they were operating in a sense of very loose-knit conspiracies (Woolf, 2005).

The question was not if, but when, a terrorist attack would take place within the UK. The message coming from politicians and those responsible for national security was quite clear – an attack was highly likely. The security services were busy identifying many potential UK terrorists and carrying out a series of operations to disrupt and bring to justice those involved in terrorist activity; however, inevitably a group slipped through the net and on 7 July 2005 the London transport system was attacked. Table 6.2 shows a timeline of events.

This was the first time suicide bombers had been deployed within the UK and the impact of this event sent a shockwave throughout the nation. Within the previous 24 hours the UK had been celebrating the news that the Olympic Games would be coming to London in 2012.

Table 6.2 Time line of events, 7 July 2005

0649	Four suicide bombers, Shehzad Tanweer, Mohammad Sidique Khan, Hasib Hussain and Germaine Lindsay, meet in a car park at Luton railway station. They are in possession of two vehicles later found to contain explosives and a 9mm handgun. They are seen moving property between the two car boots and each puts on a rucksack containing the bombs.
0725	The four men board a train at Luton to King's Cross, London.
0823	The four men arrive at King's Cross and a few minutes later are witnessed hugging each other then splitting up to access the London Underground rail system. Three catastrophic explosions occur within the Underground system.
0849	Eastbound Circle Line train, Liverpool Street – seconds after the train leaves the station towards Aldgate, smoke is seen billowing from the tunnel. Tanweer has detonated his bomb, killing 8 (including Tanweer) and injuring 171.
0850	Westbound Circle Line train, Edgware Road – shortly after train leaves the station towards Paddington, Khan detonates his bomb, killing 7 (including Khan) and injuring 163. Piccadilly Line train between King's Cross and Russell Square – Lindsay detonates his bomb, killing 27 (including Lindsay) and injuring over 340.
0854	Hussain seen leaving King's Cross Underground station on to Euston Road.
0924	Hussain seen walking towards Gray's Inn Road where it is believed he boarded a number 91 bus travelling from King's Cross to Euston, where he switched to a number 30 bus travelling to Old Street.
0947	Tavistock Square – while sitting on the upper deck of the bus Hussain detonates his bomb, killing 14 (including Hussain) and injuring over 110.

Source: Adapted from Keith (2010)

The terrorists

The four men responsible for the attack were connected to the Islamic faith, were indoctrinated with extremist beliefs and, during the post-attack investigation, were linked to al-Qaeda (see Chapter 1, page 15). Brief profiles of the four men are provided in Table 6.3.

What drove these four young men to commit such an act of terrorism and how serious was the threat from other individuals and groups within the UK? Radicalisation was identified as a key issue following 9/11 and the Prevent strand of the UK counter-terrorism strategy reflected the need to tackle the problem effectively.

Just 14 days after the devastation another team of bombers attacked London, but fortunately, owing to their ineptness at constructing a viable explosive device, the operation failed. On 21 July 2005 five men attempted to detonate the devices at three Underground locations (between Stockwell and the Oval; between Oxford Circus and Warren Street; and between Latimer Road and Shepherd's Bush) and on a bus in Hackney Road. Four of the men, Muktar Ibrahim, Yassin Omar, Ramzi Mohammed and Hussain Osman, were convicted of conspiracy to murder at Woolwich Crown Court and on Wednesday, 11 July 2007 were sentenced to life imprisonment. The fifth man, Manfo Kwaku Asiedu, was later convicted of conspiracy to cause explosions and sentenced to 33 years' imprisonment at Woolwich Crown Court in November 2007 following a retrial.

Table 6.3 Profiles of the 7/7 terrorists

Name	Age	Ethnicity	Religion	Home	Status	Occupation	Attacked
Mohammad Sidique Khan	30	Second-generation British citizen of Pakistani origin	Islam	Dewsbury, West Yorkshire	Married with one child	Classroom assistant	Tube train, Edgware Road
Shehzad Tanweer	22	Second-generation British citizen of Pakistani origin	Islam	Beeston, Leeds, West Yorkshire	Single, residing with parents	Student; Sports Science graduate	Tube train, Aldgate
Germaine Lindsay	19	Jamaican-born British resident	Islam	Aylesbury, Bucks	Married with one child	Unemployed carpet fitter	Tube train, Russell Square
Hasib Hussain	18	Second-generation British citizen of Pakistani origin	Islam	Holbeck, Leeds, West Yorkshire	Single, residing with parents	Student	Bus, Tavistock Square

Source: Adapted from House of Commons (2006)

UK response

The aftermath of the attacks seriously challenged the emergency services, who were not fully prepared for an incident of this magnitude. Following the emergency response a number of official reports and enquiries were completed to provide a clear understanding of the events prior to, during and after the bombings. This was important to highlight lessons learned and develop new counter-terrorism strategies.

The list below provides an overview of some of the key reports published following the attacks.

- May 2006 – House of Commons: *Report of the Official Account of the Bombings in London on 7 July 2005.*

- May 2006 – Intelligence and Security Committee: *Report into the London Terrorist Attacks on 7 July 2005.*

- June 2006 – London Assembly: *Report of the 7 July Review Committee* (Volumes 1–3).

- September 2006 – London Resilience Forum report on emergency planning: *Looking Back, Moving Forward – The Multi Agency Debrief.*

- August 2007 – 7 July Review Committee of the London Assembly follow-up report (Volume 4).

- May 2009 – Intelligence and Security Committee: *Could 7/7 Have Been Prevented?*

- May 2011 – *Coroner's Inquests into the London Bombings of 7 July 2005* by the Right Honourable Lady Justice Hallett DBE.

PRACTICAL TASK

All of these documents are publicly available and can easily be found with an internet search (see links provided under 'Useful websites' at the end of the chapter). Download the reports and find out what recommendations were made within each to enhance and develop an effective counter-terrorism response.

Counter-terrorism structures

The Government directs and supports the counter-terrorism strategy through the Home Office. In May 2007 the Labour Government took a decision to split Home Office responsibility in two to tackle the problems associated with terrorism more effectively. At this time the Government had been beset with a number of problems relating to the release of foreign prisoners, a backlog of asylum claims, inmates escaping from open jails, failure to log details of foreign convictions, and overcrowding of prisons. Countering terrorism was a national priority and these issues became a distraction for the Home Secretary, John Reid, compromising his ability to focus effectively on the terrorism issues (Shaw, 2007). A Ministry of Justice was introduced which took on the responsibility for prisons, probation and the courts, and the new Home Office became responsible for security, policing, counter-terrorism and immigration.

Within the Home Office is the Office for Security and Counter-Terrorism (OSCT). The OSCT provides the strategic direction to counter the threat from international terrorism. Its primary objective is to protect the public from terrorism by working with others to develop and deliver the UK counter-terrorism strategy – CONTEST (Home Office, 2011).

Government's counter-terrorism structure

The structure can be presented as four strands.

1. *COBRA – immediately convened in the aftermath of an attack and chaired by either the Prime Minister or Home Secretary. A Commonly Recognised Information Pattern (CRIP) is produced that ensures that after an attack all of those engaged in counter-terrorism activity are sharing information and are working to the same information.*

2. *The Ministerial Committee on National Security, International Relations and Development (NSID), chaired by the Prime Minister and responsible for counter-terrorism policy.*

3. *A weekly security meeting chaired by the Home Secretary and attended by representatives from the intelligence services, police and key government departments, to tactically coordinate counter-terrorism strategy, policy and communications, and the sharing of intelligence prior to a terrorist attack.*

4. *The immediate operational response provided by the police service which appoints a 'Gold' commander responsible for setting the strategic direction of the operations.*

(House of Commons, 2010, p5)

Intelligence structures

Chapter 8 will provide both a diagram and a description of intelligence agencies that provide support for the counter-terrorism strategy (see page 119).

Policing structures

The Association of Chief Police Officers (ACPO), in partnership with government and the Association of Police Authorities (APA), lead and coordinate the direction and development of the Police Service within the UK (see Figure 6.1). ACPO is split into a number of business areas, one of which is Terrorism and Allied Matters (TAM), whose work is aligned with the four strands of CONTEST. The ACPO (TAM) committee is responsible for providing a bridge between government direction on counter-terrorism and its operational implementation (Staniforth, 2009).

SO15 is the Metropolitan Police Counter Terrorism Command (CTC), which was introduced in October 2006, bringing together the former anti-terrorist and Special Branch departments. It was introduced to provide a more effective capability and capacity to meet ongoing and future threats of terrorism. The command brings together intelligence analysis and development for investigations, and operational support activity (Metropolitan Police, 2011).

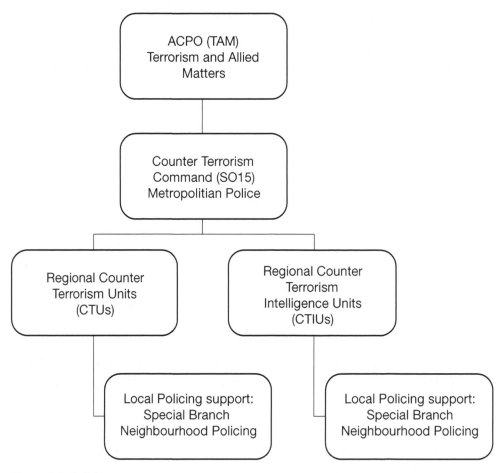

Figure 6.1 Policing structures

Go to the Metropolitan Police website and find the link 'Counter Terrorism'. Access the Counter Terrorism Command section and find out what SO15 is responsible for.

SO15 is supported by four Counter Terrorism Units (CTUs) based in Leeds, Manchester, Birmingham and Thames Valley. The four CTUs are further supported by four regionally based Counter Terrorism Intelligence Units (CTIUs) – East Midlands, Eastern, Wales and South West. Scotland also has a CTIU and the Police Service of Northern Ireland has a CTU capability within its Crime Operations Branch.

The CTUs are responsible for gathering intelligence and evidence to prevent and disrupt terrorist activity. Intelligence is gathered on a regional basis to provide a national perspective and contribute to a more effective and coordinated counter-terrorism response. The units are staffed by policing experts providing a range of services, including intelligence analysis and financial investigation, and by forensic specialists, hi-tech investigators and community contact teams (Staniforth, 2009).

Locally the Police Service has Special Branch departments that work in conjunction with the Security Service (MI5), CTUs and CTIUs. The primary role of the Special Branch is related to intelligence gathering, analysis and dissemination and it assists MI5 in carrying out its statutory duties under the Security Services Act 1989. This includes protection against threats of terrorism, sabotage and the proliferation of WMDs.

There are currently 3,600 neighbourhood policing teams across the UK serving local communities (NPIA, 2011). Close contact with communities is vital to obtain information that may contribute to countering the terrorism threat, and the success of local policing is critical in identifying those concerned with terrorism, and the reporting of suspicious activity. The role of local policing in countering the terrorism threat is discussed further in Chapter 9.

Mumbai, 26 November 2008

The attack in Mumbai introduced new challenges for security forces and law enforcement agencies, and forced another rethink on counter-terrorism strategies to tackle this type of event effectively.

> *The operational modus operandi of this terrorist attack constitutes a major shift in the traditional terrorist tactics of using suicide operatives and planted explosive devices, to the execution of a well planned 'commando' type military assault using automatic weapons, hand grenades and urban combat tactics, intended to inflict the maximum number of casualties.*

(NYPD, 2008, p4)

Overview of events

On the evening of Wednesday, 26 November 2008 at least ten terrorists armed with bombs, grenades and firearms arrived in Mumbai in a fishing boat that they had stolen and in which they had killed the five crew members. At 2120 hours a series of attacks commenced, targeting both Indian nationals and foreigners at various locations throughout the city, including:

- Chhatrapati railway station (one of world's busiest stations);
- Nariman House (home of a Jewish orthodox outreach group);
- Leopold's restaurant (popular with foreigners);
- Oberoi hotel (5-star hotel);
- Taj Mahal Palace and Tower hotel (popular with the elite);
- Times of India newspaper offices;
- Bombay Municipal Corporation (civic body that governs Mumbai);
- Cama hospital (south Mumbai);
- GT hospital (city centre);
- Vidhan Sabha (India's legislative assembly).

(Adapted from *CBS News*, 2008)

The media reported 172 fatalities (including 15 police officers) and 239 injuries (NYPD, 2008).

The only known surviving attacker told police that his group trained for months in camps operated by a banned Pakistani militant group, learning close-combat techniques, explosives training and other tactics for their three-day siege (*CBS News*, 2008).

The terrorists

The terrorists were linked to Lashkar-e-Taiba (LeT) (Army of the Pure), a terrorist group based in Pakistan that seeks to drive out Indian security forces from Kashmir. Since 2001 the group's primary focus has been on liberating Kashmir and engaging in a wider war against India. In the past the group had provided training and logistical support to al-Qaeda and other jihadist groups in Pakistan but were weakened by the war on terror. Their role and relevance within the jihadi movement diminished, but the Mumbai attacks were seen as a 'game changer' for LeT and marked the group's emergence on the global jihadi stage (Tankel, 2009).

PRACTICAL TASK

Access one of the websites that provides information about terrorist groups (e.g. www.cdi.org/terrorism/lt.cfm). Find out more about the terrorist group Lashkar-e-Taiba and their connections with the Soviet invasion of Afghanistan and al-Qaeda.

UK response

The nature of the attacks brought new problems to those responsible for developing effective counter-terrorism measures and further action was required. The National Counter Terrorism Security Office (NaCTSO) provided protective security guidance for hotels and restaurants, and arranged a number of exercises designed to simulate a terrorist attack (project ARGUS). The exercises were based around night-time economy, businesses, airports and railway terminal scenarios to prompt discussion, and to identify measures service providers can take to prevent, handle and recover from terrorist attacks (Home Office, 2009).

The Police Service also responded by enhancing firearms training and increasing the number of police officers trained. Baroness Neville-Jones also announced that ministers were actively taking part in exercises to improve understanding and response (*The Telegraph*, 2011).

Assessing the effectiveness of a counter-terrorism strategy

It is too early to assess the effectiveness of the UK counter-terrorism strategy but we do know that it is comprehensive, and that the Government, supported by the security services and other agencies, is actively involved in putting policy into practice.

The Government is willing to make changes when necessary and learn lessons from terrorist attacks, as seen following 7/7 and other subsequent terrorist attacks. Academic literature is limited and in a 2006 study the authors highlight the problem:

> *we discovered that there is an almost complete absence of evaluation research on counter-terrorism strategies. From over 20,000 studies we located on terrorism, we found only seven which contained moderately rigorous evaluations of counter-terrorism programs. We conclude that there is little scientific knowledge about the effectiveness of most counter-terrorism interventions.*

(Lum et al., 2006, p3)

PRACTICAL TASK

Write down a list of issues that could be considered when assessing the effectiveness of counter-terrorism measures.

In 2009 and 2011 CONTEST was reviewed and updated. The 2009 strategy provides details of key achievements since 2003, when introducing each of the four strands (Pursue, Prevent, Protect and Prepare), that could be used to consider the effectiveness of the approaches adopted; however, this is a governmental perspective. Performance is also assessed through a series of outcome measures (now scrapped by the Government) set out in annex 'A' (Home Office, 2009).

In subsequent chapters, which will explore the four CONTEST strands, issues relating to civil and human rights, freedom and security, racism, discrimination, community cohesion and civil peace will be highlighted, all of which can be considered when evaluating the effectiveness of counter-terrorism measures.

C H A P T E R   S U M M A R Y

The 9/11 terrorist attacks introduced the world to a new era of terrorism, provoked a global war on terror and caused many states to review and introduce more robust counter-terrorism strategies.

The UK introduced a counter-terrorism strategy (CONTEST) in 2003 and, following further terrorist atrocities such as those in Madrid, London and Mumbai, revised strategies were introduced by government in 2009 and 2011.

CONTEST is made up of four strands (Pursue, Prevent, Protect and Prepare), each of which provides a series of objectives that contribute to the overall aim of the strategy, which is to reduce the risk to the UK and its interests overseas from terrorism so that people can go about their daily lives freely and with confidence.

With any strategy there is a need to assess its effectiveness and some examples of government performance measures and a range of issues are provided for consideration. Assessing the effectiveness of an element of CONTEST can be used as a potential assignment topic and should be considered while working through subsequent chapters relating to the four strands.

REFERENCES

BBC News (2007) Key 9/11 Suspect 'Admits Guilt'. Available online at http://news.bbc.co.uk/1/hi/world/americas/6452573.stm (accessed 16 March 2011).

bin Laden, Osama (2001) Osama bin Laden Speeches. Translation of video-taped statement broadcast on Al Jazeera TV, 7 October. Available online at www.september11news.com/OsamaSpeeches.htm (accessed 16 March 2011).

Burke, Jason (2007) *Al Qaeda.* London: Penguin Books.

CBS News (2008) Mumbai Terror Timeline. Available online at www.cbsnews.com/elements/2008/12/01/in_depth_world/timeline4640856.shtml (accessed 23 February 2011).

CCR (Center for Constitutional Rights) (2002) The State of Civil Liberties in the US One Year After 9/11. Derechos/Equipo Nizkor. Available online at www.derechos.org/nizkor/excep/ccr.html (accessed 16 March 2011).

CNN (Cable News Network) (2001) Transcript of President Bush's Address. Available online at http://articles.cnn.com/2001-09-20/us/gen.bush.transcript_1_joint-session-national-anthem-citizens?_s=PM:US (accessed 15 September 2011).

Hewitt, Steve (2008) *The British War on Terror.* London: Continuum.

Home Office (2006) *Countering International Terrorism: The United Kingdom's Strategy.* Norwich: The Stationery Office.

Home Office (2009) *Pursue Prevent Protect Prepare: The United Kingdom's Strategy for Countering International Terrorism.* Norwich: The Stationery Office.

Home Office (2011) Office for Security and Counter Terrorism. Available online at www.homeoffice.gov.uk/counter-terrorism/OSCT (accessed 22 March 2011).

House of Commons (2006) *Report of the Official Account of the Bombings in London on 7th July 2005.* London: The Stationery Office.

House of Commons (2010) *Home Office's Response to Terrorist Attacks: Home Affairs Committee Sixth Report of Session 2009–10.* London: The Stationery Office.

Keith, Hugo QC (2010) *Hearing Transcript from the Coroner's Inquests into the London Bombings, 7th July 2005.* Available online at http://7julyinquests.independent.gov.uk/hearing_transcripts/11102010am.htm (accessed 23 February 2011).

Lum, Cynthia, Kennedy, Leslie W and Sherley, Alison J (2006) *The Effectiveness of Counter Terrorism Strategies.* Available online at www.rutgerscps.org/publications/Lum_Terrorism_Review.pdf (accessed 1/5/11).

Manningham-Buller, Dame Eliza (2004) Speech by the Director General of the Security Service at CBI Annual Conference Birmingham on 8 November 2004. Available online at www.mi5.gov.uk/output/director-generals-speech-to-the-cbi-annual-conference-2004.html (accessed 21 March 2011).

Metropolitan Police (2011) Specialist Operations – Counter Terrorism Command. Available online at www.met.police.uk/so/counter_terrorism.htm (accessed 8 April 2011).

NPIA (National Policing Improvement Agency) (2011) Local Policing. Available online at www.neighbourhoodpolicing.co.uk/neighbourhood_policing.aspx (accessed 8 April 2011).

NYPD (New York Police Department) (2008) *Mumbai Attack Analysis.* New York: NYPD Intelligence Division. Available online at http://info.publicintelligence.net/nypdmumbaireport.pdf (accessed 23 February 2011).

Reinares, Fernando (2010) The Madrid Bombings and Global Jihadism. *Survival*, 52(2), April–May: 83–104.

Shaw, Danny (2007) Terrorism Focus for New-look Home Office. *BBC News*, 29 March. Available online at http://news.bbc.co.uk/1/hi/uk/6507523.stm (accessed 22 March 2011).

Staniforth, Andrew (2009) *Blackstone's Counter Terrorism Handbook.* Oxford: Oxford University Press.

Tankel, Stephen (2009) *Lashkar-e-Taiba: From 9/11 to Mumbai.* London: International Centre for the Study of Radicalisation and Political Violence (ICSR). Available online at www.icsr.info/news/attachments/1240846916ICSRTankelReport.pdf (accessed 28 February 2011).

The Telegraph (2011) Baroness Neville-Jones: British Police in Training for Mumbai-style Attack. *The Telegraph*, 15 March. Available online at www.telegraph.co.uk/news/uknews/terrorism-in-the-uk/8383097/Baroness-Neville-Jones-British-police-in-training-for-Mumbai-style-attack.html (accessed 1 May 2011).

Woolf, Marie (2005) Met Chief Under Fire for Intervening in Debate on ID Cards. *The Independent*, 18 April. Available online at www.independent.co.uk/news/uk/politics/met-chief-under-fire-for-intervening-in-debate-on-id-cards-491349.html (accessed 21 March 2011).

Zelikow, Philip (2004) *Transcript of Proceedings: Twelfth Public Hearing of the National Commission on Terrorist Attacks upon the United States, June 16, 2004.* Available online at http://govinfo.library.unt.edu/911/archive/hearing12/9-11Commission_Hearing_2004-06-16.pdf (accessed 16 March 2011).

Zelikow, Philip, Jenkins, Bonnie D and May, Ernest R (2004) *The 9/11 Commission Report.* National Commission on Terrorist Attacks upon the United States. New York: WW Norton.

USEFUL WEBSITES

Information on the 7/7 attacks

http://7julyinquests.independent.gov.uk/docs/orders/rule43-report.pdf (*Coroner's Inquests into the London Bombings of 7 July 2005*)

www.cabinetoffice.gov.uk/resource-library/intelligence-and-security-committee-special-ad-hoc-reports (Intelligence and Security Committee report: *Could 7/7 Have Been Prevented?*; also: *Report into the London Terrorist Attacks on 7 July 2005*)

www.iwar.org.uk/homesec/resources/7-7/london-assembly-report.htm (London Assembly: *Report of the 7 July Review Committee* (Volumes 1–3); also: http://legacy.london.gov.uk/assembly/reports/7july/follow-up-report.pdf (7 July Review Committee of the London Assembly's follow-up report (Volume 4)) www.londonprepared.gov.uk/downloads/lookingbackmovingforward.pdf (London Resilience Forum report on emergency planning: *Looking Back, Moving Forward*)

www.official-documents.gov.uk/document/hc0506/hc10/1087/1087.asp (*Report of the Official Account of the Bombings in London on 7 July 2005*)

Other resources

http://news.bbc.co.uk/hi/english/static/in_depth/americas/2001/day_of_terror (*BBC News* special site for 9/11)

http://news.bbc.co.uk/1/hi/in_depth/uk/2005/london_explosions/default.stm (*BBC News* special site for 7/7 and 21/7)

http://news.bbc.co.uk/1/hi/in_depth/south_asia/2008/mumbai_attacks/default.stm (*BBC News* special site for the Mumbai attack, November 2008)

www.homeoffice.gov.uk/counter-terrorism (Home Office Counter Terrorism website)

www.washingtonpost.com/wp-srv/nation/911report/911reportbychapter.html (the 9/11 Commission report)

Homeland Security Act 2002 (Public law: 107-296: 25.11.02)

National Commission on Terrorist Attacks Upon the United States 2002 (Public law: 107-306: 27.11.02)

Security Services Act 1989

Uniting and Strengthening America by Providing Appropriate Tools Required to Intercept and Obstruct Terrorism Act of 2001 (Public law 107-56: 26.10.2001)

7 Legislative development

Chris Blake

CHAPTER OBJECTIVES

By the end of this chapter you should be able to:

- outline the key legislation concerned with terrorism and counter-terrorism;
- outline some of the legal procedures used to investigate and punish those who commit terrorist acts and political violence;
- debate the tensions between the proportionality of legislation, maintaining national security and human rights;
- debate the issues around proscribing an organisation.

Introduction

In many Western countries, global terrorism has led to an extensive expansion of the criminal law dealing with forms of risk, a development that poses new questions about the constitutional limits of criminal law. This chapter examines the scope of criminal law in relation to anti-terrorist legislation and how a fair reconciliation between individual freedom and collective security can take place.

Discussions are primarily concerned with twenty-first-century legislation that governs state powers and procedures, particularly those within the Terrorism Act 2000. The reader is encouraged to reflect on policy decisions that affect not only a limited number of individuals but also societal attitudes towards fundamental issues of the day. Such are their importance that they represent something more than a due process. And so the recent and continuing debate(s) over terrorism will take place in a wider context of how British traditions of freedom are faring in the current security climate; for example, through an examination of detention without charge, stop and search powers, control orders and deportation.

The framework of international law, established from 1948 onwards, was intended to give states sufficient flexibility to respond to genuine threats. Since 2001, however, it could be argued that the contemporary threat from terrorism is of an unprecedented and exceptional nature. For example, groups such as al-Qaeda have become truly international in character, have access to more dangerous technologies of killing, including 'dirty bombs', utilise highly sophisticated communication technologies to carry out attacks and to evade law enforcement measures, have individuals who employ tactics such as suicide bombing, which require different approaches on the part of law enforcement personnel, and/or have ill-defined or unrealisable demands that make negotiation difficult.

Legalistic responses are both law enforcement and law-related approaches that apply the norms of criminal justice and legal procedures to investigate and punish those who commit acts of political violence. Legislation, criminal prosecutions and incarceration are typical policy measures. In dealing with terrorism, Martin (2009) suggests that legal protocols exist to promote and implement formal and informal international treaties and laws, while others have been implemented as matters of domestic policy, such as Homeland Security measures required to harden targets, deter attacks and thwart conspiracies. Internal security requires the extensive use of non-military security personnel, such as customs officials, law enforcement agencies and immigration authorities. But in an era of 'new terrorism' and international counter-terrorist warfare, international cooperation at the operational level has become a central priority for policy makers and, by its very nature, international law expects and demands international cooperation to create a semblance of formality and consistency in global counter-terrorist efforts. Thus, counter-terrorist laws attempt to criminalise terrorist behaviour by declaring, for example, certain behaviours to be criminal terrorism or by enhancing current laws such as those that punish murder. The overall objective, however, of any legalistic response is to promote the rule of law and regular legal proceedings, which includes counter-terrorist laws and international law. The following are given by Martin (2009) as examples of these responses.

- Law enforcement, which involves the use of criminal investigative techniques in the prosecution of suspected terrorists.

- International law, which involves parties who are subject to international agreement and which denies refuge or sanctuary for terrorist behaviour and/or brings them before international tribunals.

International law enforcement cooperation, in particular, provides global access to extensive criminal justice systems that have well-established institutions (such as prisons) for use against terrorists. These institutions can effectively incapacitate terrorists by ending their ability to engage in violence or propaganda, disrupt terrorist conspiracies and destabilise terrorist networks. But following the UK response to the events of 9/11, Chandler (2002) suggests that the gap between 'justice' and what is 'legal' has led to the degradation of international law rather than to its development. And it's difficult to argue with his conclusion that:

> *International Law is no longer accepted as a legitimate curb on the use of force while the coercive intervention by Western Powers against other states is increasingly legitimised through the framework of 'International Justice'.*

> (2002, p158)

The fragility of international order is thus doubly revealed, not only in the ability of small groups to strike terror in powerful societies but also in those societies with a weak attachment to human rights values.

REFLECTIVE TASK

Research the Achille Lauro Operation, which involved the hijacking of an Italian cruise ship by Palestinian terrorists in 1985. The terrorists were transported to Port Said, Egypt, and then flown out of the country to an intended place of safety. While en route, they were intercepted by American warplanes and forced to land in Sicily. The terrorists were eventually tried before an Italian court.

Examine the circumstances of the case and the final outcomes, paying particular attention to the disposal methods used and the so-called Italian 'repentance laws'. Consider why tensions were high during the initial stand-off and whether comments by the judge were appropriate and/or within the context of a political environment in Italy that granted the Palestinian Liberation Organisation diplomatic status.

Legislation as a counter-terrorism measure?

Since the attacks on New York, Madrid and London, most Western democracies can be considered as potential terrorist targets, which causes both a deep sense of unease within the population and the need for heightened security. The UK's initial response saw the introduction of legislation with preventive and security-related goals in mind. The primary objective was to allow earlier government intervention by criminalising preparatory acts in advance of terror attacks. The resulting interference into individuals' freedoms was justified by the supposed security provided by the new offence definitions against future attacks. But in a democracy there need to be clear limits on state power as, without this, the ability for early intervention in the run-up to crime can result in criminal punishment for 'mere thoughts'. Furthermore, the penalisation of behaviour well in advance of an attack can raise issues of legitimacy. For example, should the possession of articles that are actually harmless in isolation become punishable if the intention exists to use them for an attack? This debate is further complicated by the fact that, in Anglo-American literature, the debate about the legitimisation of (anti-terrorism) criminal law is seen primarily as a philosophical question (Kiesel, 2011). New risks, therefore, present questions about the legitimacy and the functional limits of criminal law, and highlight the tensions between security and individual freedom. The balance between collective security and individual freedom has to be carefully struck under the ever-changing and constantly evolving threat of international terrorism.

UK anti-terrorism legislation has attracted significant interest and debate from various sectors, including Parliament, the media and competing lobby groups. This is fuelled by what is sometimes the oversimplistic analysis of key issues around the proportionality of legislation, national security and human rights. On the one side are those who argue for effective state measures to ensure the safety of individuals, even if this means surrendering a modest amount of freedom. Robinson (2002) describes the overall speed with which UK human rights provisions have been set aside in the interests of national security as 'instructive' and highlights the aggressive way in which this has been done.

Since the 9/11 bombings many of the UK anti-terrorist measures have been based on the continued threat to fundamental rights and freedoms. But human rights considerations should not be neglected because of the imperatives of national security and public safety. This is a point well made by those who, while accepting the state's duty to protect public safety, believe in fundamental rights and freedoms irrespective of the threat. It has been argued that, where legislation is drafted too quickly, there is inadequate scrutiny and that problems subsequently arise. Indeed, ill-thought-out legislation can actually alienate and disenfranchise communities, resulting in a climate of fear and suspicion, a point referred to by the International Commission of Jurists (2009), which warned of the corrosive effect of open-ended departures from ordinary procedures, and recommended the regular inspection of legislation to ensure that the *Tests initially met still prevail, and . . . that no unintended consequences have arisen* (2009, p47).

Review of UK legislation and contemporary issues

Since 2000 five major pieces of terrorism legislation have been introduced in the UK: the Terrorism Act 2000 (TA 2000), the Anti-terrorism, Crime and Security Act 2001 (ATCSA), the Prevention of Terrorism Act 2005 (PTA 2005), the Terrorism Act 2006 (TA 2006) and the Counter-Terrorism Act 2008 (CTA).

The Terrorism Act 2000

Initial parliamentary scrutiny of the TA 2000 was virtually abandoned, although the Government did accept concerns expressed in the second reading of the Bill, to the extent of agreeing to an annual report to Parliament (Commons Hansard Debates, 2000).

The Act came into force on 19 February 2001, retaining most of the special powers and offences adopted under the Prevention of Terrorism (Temporary Provisions) Act 1989 (PTA 1989) and the Northern Ireland (Emergency Provisions) Act 1996 (EPA). Perhaps most significantly, these powers were applied to a much wider range of groups, including Irish splinter groups opposed to the peace process, 'international terrorist' groups, and the threat of violence by a wide and disparate range of domestic and single-issue groups such as animal rights and environmental activists.

The PTA 1989 and EPA contained a number of criminal offences relating to membership of, or support for, 'proscribed organisations'. The offences included making contributions of money and other property towards acts of terrorism or the resources of proscribed organisations; assisting in the retention or control of terrorist funds; displaying support in public for a proscribed organisation; or wearing a hood, mask or other means of concealing identity in public. In particular, it was an offence to belong or profess to belong to a proscribed organisation. The TA went on to merge separate lists of proscribed organisations and extended the ambit of 'proscription' to include organisations concerned with both international and domestic terrorism.

The Act itself contained some key hallmarks: it was permanent and there was no pretence made that temporary, emergency measures were otherwise required; its main provisions applied equally across the UK, which is arguably more satisfactory than passing Northern Ireland legislation and then transferring it to Great Britain, although this erodes the principle that special powers should be as narrow as possible, that is, if the threat is greater in one locality it justifies the introduction of further powers confined to that locality.

Pre-charge detention of terrorist suspects

Unlike other criminal investigations where the normal period of detention without charge should not exceed 24 hours (although in some cases the maximum period, with extensions, can be as long as 96 hours), Schedule 8 of the TA 2000 (s41) allows for the arrest and detention of suspected terrorists and for incremental extensions of detention without charge for up to 28 days. The original maximum period of detention of seven days was first extended to a maximum of 14 days by the Criminal Justice Act 2003 (s306) and then to 28 days by the TA 2006 (s23).

Arguments for extended detention seem to focus on practical issues around the investigation of suspected terrorist cases, where it is not unusual for arrests to occur earlier than would normally be the case. The gathering of evidence can also take considerable time and effort due to the numbers of people who are often engaged in a terrorist network and because of the nature of the evidence required. For example, the TA 2006 provides that the review officer may extend detention if he or she is satisfied that it is necessary pending the result of an examination or analysis of any relevant evidence or an examination or analysis of anything that may result in relevant evidence being obtained. An examination or analysis would include a DNA test. Where there is an overseas aspect to the investigation there will be a need to secure and preserve evidence from foreign jurisdictions, which tend to have different law enforcement and judicial procedures (s24). It is also widely argued that suspected terrorists need to be detained during the post-arrest phase of the investigation on public safety grounds.

Detention versus civil rights

While the debate on pre-charge detention has focused on the maximum period of detention pre-charge, there has also been concern whether Schedule 8 of the TA 2000 is compatible with the right to liberty under Article 5 of the European Convention on Human Rights (ECHR). The *Review of Counter-terrorism and Security Powers* (Home Office, 2011a, p9) cites two principal reasons.

- *Suspects are not told the basis on which they are being detained in sufficient detail in order to allow them properly to challenge their continuing detention without charge.*

- *There is insufficient judicial control over decisions to hold a suspect in pre-charge detention.*

These points were considered in the case of *Sher and others* v *Chief Constable of Greater Manchester Police* [2010], where Justices Laws and Coulson held that detention procedures were entirely in accordance with Article 5 and that the minimum level of disclosure in control order cases didn't apply to pre-charge detention cases. This was partly on the basis that the provisions of Schedule 8 already provide for the individual to be told of the basis for their detention.

Within the context of security and counter-terrorism, opponents and supporters of pre-charge detention have long debated the merits, or otherwise, of this sensitive and controversial power. This, and the court's judgment in the Sher case, contributed to the announcement of a *Review of Counter-terrorism and Security Powers* in July 2010 (Home Office, 2011a). Commissioned by the Home Office, the review was set up to examine the effectiveness, proportionality and necessity of powers and measures in meeting inter-national and domestic human rights obligations. The review found that just 11 individuals had been held for more than 14 days in pre-charge detention. Nine were arrested in Operation Overt, the 2006 transatlantic airline plot, one in Operation Gingerbread, a 2006 Manchester-based case, and one in Operation Seagram, the 2007 London Haymarket and Glasgow airport attacks. Six of these 11 people were held for the maximum 27–28 days; three were charged and three released without charge. The review heard arguments from opponents of the powers that some of these people could have been charged earlier, and that not all those charged post-14 days were subsequently convicted (Home Office, 2011a).

The review concluded that, in some areas, UK counter-terrorism and security powers were neither proportionate nor necessary and so made a number of recommendations aimed at restoring *Public confidence in counter-terrorism and security legislation (and) civil liberties while enabling the police and security services to protect the public effectively* (Home Office, 2011a, p5).

One of the recommendations was that the maximum period of pre-charge detention for terrorist suspects should be 14 days, and that this limit should be reflected on the face of the primary legislation. But it was also recognised that there may be urgent situations where more than 14 days' pre-charge detention is considered necessary and that such situations should be catered for by the use of emergency legislation, which would enable Parliament to increase the maximum period to 28 days, if and when required. These and other proposals are contained within the current draft Detention of Terrorist Suspects

(Temporary Extension) and Protection of Freedoms Bills, which were both presented before the UK Parliament in February 2011. The Bills will be extensively debated by Parliament and progress implementing the review's findings is to be set out in the Home Office's published structural reform plans.

REFLECTIVE TASK

Professor Clive Walker has argued that detention for terror suspects should be limited to 14 days. Presenting evidence to the joint Committee on the Draft Detention of Terrorist Suspects (Temporary Extension) Bills on 4 April 2011, he argued that there are sufficient legal measures and extra funding for the police, security services and prosecutors to give confidence that liberty should not be put at further risk.

Do you agree with the 14 days proposal or should there be an emergency power that the police and security services can use, when necessary? You may find the 'Democracy Live' web link useful in your deliberations: http://news.bbc.co.uk/democracylive/hi/house_ of_commons/newsid_9447000/9447200.stm.

The need to retain the power to stop and search without reasonable suspicion

Following a decrease in Northern Ireland terrorism, Lord Lloyd of Berwick reported on the need for specific, UK counter-terrorism legislation (Lloyd, 1996). He observed that a decision to give the police a power to stop and search at random in any permanent counter-terrorism legislation was not to be taken lightly, albeit there was evidence that a number of terrorists had been intercepted by alert officers on patrol. He said that there was also reason to believe that terrorists were deterred to some extent by the prospect of police road checks and the consequent risk that they would be intercepted. The report recommended the indefinite extension of the Northern Ireland powers to the rest of the UK (Lloyd, 1996). It also recommended that the Government develop an official list of organisations proscribed as terrorist – a key mechanism used by states to condemn acts of terrorism. The report was part of a legislative process that led to the TA 2000, which was intended to modernise and strengthen terrorism law. The Act provides the police with wide discretion as to how, when and against whom to use these powers, some of which have already been discussed.

Police officers now have the power to stop and search individuals under a range of legislation. Section 1 of the Police and Criminal Evidence Act 1984 allows an officer to stop and search a person or vehicle to look for stolen or prohibited items. Section 60 of the Criminal Justice and Public Order Act 1994 allows a senior officer to authorise the stop and search of persons and vehicles where there is good reason to believe that to do so would help to prevent incidents involving serious violence or that persons are carrying dangerous instruments or offensive weapons. But the actual police power to stop and search at random and where expedient to prevent acts of terrorism was first introduced as a response to the bombing campaign between 1992 and 1994 in and around London. The Criminal Justice and Public Order Act 1994 (s81) inserted a new section – 13A – into the PTA 1989, but without any requirement that the Secretary of State confirm the authorisation.

The Prevention of Terrorism (Additional Powers) Act 1996 created an additional, separate power to stop and search pedestrians, under section 13B of the 1989 Act.

One significant change was the creation of new stop and search powers provided under sections 44–47 of the Act. Section 44 authorises police officers to stop and search vehicles, persons within vehicles and pedestrians if the authorising officer considers it expedient for the purposes of preventing acts of terrorism. The powers operate within a defined geographical area, but they do not require any grounds for believing or suspecting that the person stopped is involved in terrorist activity. A Code of Practice (Police and Criminal Evidence Act 1984, para. 1.1) for the exercise by police officers of statutory powers of stop and search requires that such powers be *used fairly, responsibly, and with respect to people being searched*. It requires that the power under section 44 of the 2000 Act *must not be used to stop and search for reasons unconnected with terrorism* and that the power should be used *to search only for articles which could be used for terrorist purposes* (para. 2.24). It is quite clear that failure to use the powers in the proper manner reduces their effectiveness.

The operation of section 44 stop and search

While section 44 powers have provided benefits in a range of counter-terrorism operations and situations, its utility reflects the very broad way in which the legislation is framed. In particular, the absence of a requirement for any suspicion has led to concerns about its misuse, in terms of both the authorisation procedures and the number of individual stops and searches. Lord Carlile has expressed concern over variations in the use of stop and search, particularly where authorisations are perceived to be needed in some force areas, and in relation to some sites, but not others with strikingly similar risk profiles (2010, para. 184). He has suggested that there is little evidence that using the power has the potential to prevent an act of terrorism as compared with other statutory powers of stop and search. (Carlile, para. 185). Commenting on the *Gillan and Quinton v UK* [2010] case, he argues that section 44 in its present form needs to be replaced (Carlile, 2010, para. 268). The plaintiffs in this case had been on their way to a demonstration close to an arms fair when they had been stopped by police who used powers under the TA 2000, sections 44–47. One was riding a bicycle and carrying a rucksack and the other, a journalist, was stopped and searched by a police officer and ordered to stop filming in spite of the fact that she showed her press cards. The court held that the use of section 44 powers had been contrary to the ECHR, Article 8:

> *The Court considers that the powers of authorisation and confirmation as well as those of stop and search under sections 44 and 45 of the 2000 Act are neither sufficiently circumscribed nor subject to adequate legal safeguards against abuse. They are not, therefore, 'in accordance with the law' and it follows that there has been a violation of Article 8 of the Convention.*
>
> (Gillan and Quinton v UK [2010])

The broader issues in this case were considered by the review (Home Office, 2011a) together with concerns over the excessive and disproportionate use of section 44. In January 2011 the Government published the following specific recommendations regarding section 44.

i. *The test for authorisation should be where a senior police officer reasonably suspects that an act of terrorism will take place . . . and should only be made where the powers are considered 'necessary', rather than the current requirement of merely 'expedient' to prevent such an act.*

ii. *The maximum period of an authorisation should be reduced from the current maximum of 28 days to 14 days.*

iii. *The authorisation may only last for as long as is necessary and may only cover a geographical area as wide as necessary to address the threat. The duration of the authorisation and the extent of the police force area . . . must be justified by the need to prevent a suspected act of terrorism.*

iv. *The purposes for which the search may be conducted should be narrowed to looking for evidence that the individual is a terrorist or that the vehicle is being used for purposes of terrorism rather than for articles which may be used in connection with terrorism.*

v. *The Secretary of State should be able to narrow the geographical extent of the authorisation (as well being able to shorten the period or to cancel or refuse to confirm it as at present).*

(Home Office, 2011a, p18)

ACPO has since introduced some key measures aimed at reducing the use of section 44. These include publishing updated guidance and measures to ensure an enhanced level of effectiveness and scrutiny in the processing of section 44 authorisations. The Metropolitan Police has said that, in future, it intends to use section 43 of the TA 2000, which states that an officer should have reasonable suspicion that someone is involved in terrorist activity before they can be stopped. The exceptions are around important landmarks such as Parliament, key government buildings and Buckingham Palace, which are believed to be of heightened interest to terrorists because of their 'iconic' status. Section 44 powers will also be used where intelligence suggests the need to prevent and deter terrorist activity (Metropolitan Police, 2009).

Significant progress is being made in refining the use of stop and search powers and this would seem to be supported by data relating to avoiding discrimination on the grounds of race. Ministry of Justice recorded figures (Home Office, 2011b) show that a total of 45,932 stops and searches were made in Great Britain under section 44 of the TA 2000 in the year ending 30 September 2010, a 77 per cent fall on the previous 12 months. The number of stops and searches in the second quarter of 2010/11 (666) was 98 per cent below the same quarter in 2009/10.

PRACTICAL TASK

ACPO emphasises, in its Practice Advice on Stop and Search Powers (2006), community involvement under section 44, since it will increase confidence, reassure the public and encourage the flow of intelligence (p12).

PRACTICAL TASK *continued*

Consider what, if any, progress has been made to provide this reassurance. The Home Affairs Committee, Terrorism and Community Relations, 2004–05 report considers how the threat of international terrorism has affected relations between communities in this country and may be useful in your research. It can be accessed at: www.publications. parliament.uk/pa/cm200405/cmselect/cmhaff/165/165.pdf.

The Anti-terrorism, Crime and Security Act 2001

This Act received Royal Assent on 14 December 2001 as a response to the events of 9/11. The Act was wide in scope, including additional powers for the police, along with measures relating to information sharing and to the security of airports and laboratories. Among the most controversial measures was the (potentially) indefinite detention without charge of foreign nationals suspected of involvement with al-Qaeda and associated terrorist networks, but who could not be prosecuted or deported. Further controversy was caused by measures that allowed public bodies to disclose information obtained in pursuit of their own functions to assist criminal investigations and proceedings, both in the UK and abroad. The enactment of Part 4 required derogation from the right to liberty under the European Convention on Human Rights.

The Prevention of Terrorism Act 2005

The PTA 2005 was introduced in response to a Law Lords ruling in December 2004, which reversed a decision of the Court of Appeal that had upheld the right of the Secretary of State to detain suspected terrorists without trial under emergency counter-terrorism powers. The Lords ruled that the detention without trial of the 'Belmarsh Eight' under Part IV of the Anti-terrorism, Crime and Security Act 2001 had been incompatible with European and, thus, domestic human rights laws. The Government had claimed that the men represented a security threat, but rules covering secret intelligence meant it was unable to prosecute them. Lawyers successfully argued that the men's imprisonment breached Articles 5 and 14 of the ECHR.

Control orders

The PTA 2005 introduced 'control orders', which were designed to address the threat from a small number of people suspected of being engaged in terrorist activities. They are part of the UK counter-terrorism strategy (CONTEST) and are intended to provide a combination of control measures by matching the circumstances of a particular case.

There are two distinct species of control order – derogating and non-derogating. A derogating order is one that imposes obligations incompatible with the right to liberty under Article 5 of the ECHR – a 'derogation obligation'. This must be justified by reference to a designation order under the Human Rights Act 1998 (HRA) (s14(1)) and can only be done at the time of a national emergency. It requires an application to the court by the Home Secretary.

Non-derogating control orders can impose conditions short of the deprivation of liberty under Article 5 and are limited to 12 months' duration. If the Home Secretary wishes to renew a control order there is no automatic referral to a full judicial review, but the individual can apply to the court for a further judicial review if he or she wishes.

Under section 2(1) of the PTA 2005 the Secretary of State can make a control order if two conditions are satisfied. The first is that he or she has reasonable grounds for suspecting that the individual is, or has been, involved in terrorism-related activities. The second is that an order is necessary for purposes connected with protecting members of the public from a risk of terrorism. Control orders can place a number of restrictions on suspects' activities, including curfews, restrictions on access to associates and communications. Suspects can be required to reside at a specific address, which can involve relocation. They can be subjected to a 16-hour curfew, must wear an electronic tag and must report regularly to the police. They can be banned from meeting named individuals and from using mobile phones or the internet and are usually confined to a tight area around their home.

Because only reasonable grounds are required for suspecting terrorism-related activities, this means that the facts have to be examined through the eyes of the Secretary of State in the light of the information available. The information will usually consist of confidential material obtained from intelligence sources and, with over 200 partner services around the world operating what is known as the 'control principle', the state will often be reluctant to disclose that information, or its origins. The 'control principle' means that whoever first discovers the intelligence has the right to control how it is used, who else can use it and what action can be taken, a point taken up in October 2010 by Sir John Sawers, head of MI6:

> *Intelligence and security agencies have to make sure that (those) secrets do not become the property of those who are threatening our country; we have to protect our partner's secrets.*

> (*The Guardian*, 2010)

Control order powers remain contentious, primarily because they are imposed in the early stages of an investigation, prior to charge and generally with some reliance on closed material. In ordinary criminal cases a charge would first be required before such strict conditions can be imposed. Clearly, there is a tension here between basic rights of freedom and the state's obligation to protect its citizens from terrorism. The security services, on the one hand, have long argued that control orders are an important, practical means of fighting terrorism. Opponents, on the other, have argued that control orders represent a breach of basic principles of common law and due process. Put simply, the state must prove its case before removing someone's liberty. A second issue is the extent to which terror suspects should understand the case against them. But there is a small cohort of individuals, currently fewer than a dozen, who cannot be prosecuted. The reasons, often rehearsed, include the protection of home and foreign intelligence sources, and the secrecy of technical surveillance methods. And yet, knowing the case against you is a basic requirement under Article 6 of the ECHR!

PRACTICAL TASK

Research the House of Lords decision in Secretary of State v AF and others *[2009] UKHL 28, 3 WLR 74. This case led to a repeal of the detention powers provided by the Anti-terrorism, Crime and Security Act 2001, Part 4, and replaced them with control orders in March 2005. Decide what merit there is in the argument that* control orders remain a largely effective necessity for a small number of cases, in the absence of a viable alternative for those few instances *(Carlile, 2010, para. 37).*

Evidence obtained by the counter-terrorism and security powers review suggests that the current control orders system act as an *impediment to prosecution* and that any replacement scheme needs, as a primary aim, *to encourage and to facilitate the gathering of evidence, and to diminish any obstruction of justice, leading to prosecution and conviction* (Home Office, 2011a, p9). The Government's commitment to replace control orders with a more focused and less intrusive system of terrorism prevention and investigation measures lies within the provisions of the Terrorism Prevention and Investigation Measures Bill (2010–2011).

The Bill abolishes the existing system of control orders for terrorism suspects and replaces it with a new regime – the Terrorism Prevention and Investigation Measures, or T-Pims. New measures will have a maximum time limit of two years, after which further measures can only be imposed if there is evidence of an individual's further engagement in terrorism. There will also be a more stringent test than for existing control orders. Lengthy curfews will be replaced by a more flexible overnight residence requirement and relocation to another part of the country without consent will be scrapped.

The Terrorism Act 2006

The TA 2006 was drafted after the 7 July 2005 London bombings and commenced on 13 April 2006. It provides a statutory basis for the independent review of the legislation and significantly extends police powers in terrorist investigations, creates new terrorism offences and amends existing ones. There was immense disagreement over the creation of a new offence involving the 'glorification' of terror and a new maximum detention period of 90 days. Some argued that the former would damage legitimate freedom of speech and that the new offence could see the Irish Taoiseach prosecuted in the UK for celebrating the Easter Rising. The measure was drafted out of the legislation and is now included in the wider offence of 'encouragement'. This is committed if a person makes a statement that is likely to be understood by some, or all, members of the public to whom it is published as a 'direct or indirect encouragement to them' to commit, prepare or instigate acts of terrorism. The 90-day detention proposal was defeated after severe criticisms, particularly by the House of Commons Home Affairs Committee. This saw the existing period extended from 14 to 28 days.

The Act is divided into three parts.

Part 1 – creates new criminal offences relating to the encouragement of acts of terrorism (s1) and to the dissemination of terrorist publications (s2). It also creates offences relating to the preparation of terrorist acts (s5) and terrorist training (s6).

Part 2 – miscellaneous provisions – amends the grounds on which the Secretary of State is empowered to proscribe organisations (s21), a process through which a proscribed organisation may be identified by another name. It also extends the period of detention of terrorist suspects (s23). Other provisions include powers to search premises and seize terrorist publications (s28) and powers to stop and search under section 44 of the TA 2000 (ss29–30).

Part 3 – supplemental provisions – provides for the oversight and review of terrorism legislation (s36) through an independent annual review to Parliament and replaces section 126 of the TA 2000.

The Counter-Terrorism Act 2008

The CTA extends the existing legislation and introduces new powers to gather and share information to counter terrorism; to make further provision about the detention and questioning of terrorist suspects, and the prosecution and punishment of terrorist offences; to impose notification requirements on persons convicted of such offences; and to confer further powers to act against terrorist financing. The theme for the Act appears to be *early intervention* which is motivated by the *very different nature and scale* of the terrorist threat (Commons Hansard Debates, 2008, cols 647, 653).

The original Bill included a number of controversial provisions, most notably the 'reserve power', which called for the extension of pre-charge detention from 28 to 42 days. Despite large-scale, cross-party opposition, these proposals were initially accepted, though were later dropped after an in-depth scrutiny of the legislation that lasted for some 17 months.

The main provisions of the Act permit:

- the taking of fingerprints and DNA samples from individuals subject to control orders for use in terrorism investigations;
- the post-charge questioning of terrorist suspects and the drawing of adverse inferences by a refusal to say something if later relied on in court;
- extended sentences for offenders convicted of offences with a terrorist connection;
- the police to request monitoring information from convicted terrorists and to prevent them from foreign travel;
- the use of intercept material in specified proceedings;
- the inclusion of 'racial bias' within the meaning of 'terrorism';
- action on suspected money laundering or terrorist financing transactions in countries outside the European Economic Area;
- entry by force if necessary, to search the premises of individuals subject to control orders who are reasonably suspected of having absconded or of failing to grant access.

C H A P T E R   S U M M A R Y

This chapter has explored the nature and impact of UK terrorism legislation and a number of issues arising from what some argue is a 'new' security environment. It introduced new policy and frames theoretical questions in a 'new' era of terrorism where the enormity and scale of the problem cannot be overstated. The contention that a dichotomy exists between freedom and security has been evidenced, and it has been established that legislation involves more than simply selecting from different policy options. The legislative process is laden with political and social considerations, in both an international and a national, domestic context, and sometimes with unwelcome consequences.

REFERENCES

ACPO (Association of Chief Police Officers) (2006) *Practice Advice on Stop and Search Powers.* The Wyboston: National Centre for Policing Excellence.

Carlile of Berriew, Lord (2010) *Report on the Operation in 2009 of the Terrorism Act 2000 and of Part 1 of the Terrorism Act 2006.* London: HMSO.

Chandler, D (2002) *From Kosovo to Kabul: Human Rights and International Intervention.* London: Pluto Press.

Commons Hansard Debates (2000) 15 March. Available online at www.publications.parliament.uk/pa/cm199900/cmhansrd/vo000315/debtext/00315-20.htm#00315-20_spnew4 (accessed 15 March 2011).

Commons Hansard Debates (2008) 1 April. Available online at www.publications.parliament.uk/pa/cm200708/cmhansrd/cm080401/debtext/80401-0007.htm#08040156000001 (accessed 17 April 2011).

The Guardian (2010) Speech by Sir John Sawers, 28 October. Available online at www.guardian.co.uk/uk/2010/oct/28/sir-john-sawers-speech-full-text (accessed 3 March 2011).

Home Office (2011a) *Review of Counter-Terrorism and Security Powers: Review Findings and Recommendations* (Cm 8004). London: The Stationery Office.

Home Office (2011b) *Operation of Police Powers under the Terrorism Act 2000 and Subsequent Legislation: Arrests, Outcomes and Stop & Searches: Quarterly Update to September 2010.* London: Home Office.

International Commission of Jurists (2009) *Assessing Damage, Urging Action: Terrorism, Counter Terrorism and Human Rights.* Available online at http://ejp.icj.org/IMG/EJP-Report.pdf (accessed 12 January 2011).

Kiesel, S (2011) *Limits of Criminal Law in Terrorism Legislation.* PhD thesis, Ein Institut der Max-Planck-Gesellschaft, Germany.

Lloyd, AJL (Chairman) (1996) *Enquiry into Legislation against Terrorism* (Cm 3420). London: HMSO.

Martin, G (2009) *Understanding Terrorism: Challenges, Perspectives and Issues.* London: Sage.

Metropolitan Police (2009) Section 44, Terrorism Act 2000: Tactical Use Review, 7 May. Available online at www.mpa.gov.uk/committees/sop/2009/090507/10/?qu=Section%2044%20Terrorism%20Act%202000%20-%20tactical%20use%20review&sc=2&ht= (accessed 15 March 2011).

Robinson, M (2002) After September 11th: Human Rights are Still as Important as Ever. *International Herald Tribune*, 21 June 2002.

http://news.bbc.co.uk/1/hi/uk_politics/8583643.stm (*BBC News*: Review All Anti-terrorism Laws, Say MPs)

www.archive.official-documents.co.uk/document/cm41/4178/4178.htm (Home Office: *Legislation Against Terrorism* (Cm 4178))

www.guardian.co.uk/commentisfree/libertycentral/2009/jan/22/explainer-terrorism-legislation (*The Guardian*: Explainer: Terrorism Legislation)

www.homeoffice.gov.uk/media-centre/news/28-day-detention (Home Office: Review of Pre-charge Detention)

www.iengage.org.uk/component/content/article/784-muslim-communities-perceive-counter-terrorism-legislation-to-be-unfair-unjust-and-discriminatory (Engage: Muslim Communities Perceive Counter-terrorism Legislation as 'Unfair, Unjust and Discriminatory')

www.libdemvoice.org/antiterrorism-legislation-news-emerges-of-likely-reforms-22242.html (Liberal Democrat Voice: Anti-terrorism Legislation: News Emerges of Likely Reforms)

www.liberty-human-rights.org.uk/human-rights/terrorism/overview-of-terrorism-legislation/index.php (Liberty: Overview of Terrorism Legislation)

Gillan and others v *United Kingdom* [2010] ECHR 4158/04

Secretary of State v *AF and others* [2009] UKHL 28, 3 WLR 74

Sher and others v *Chief Constable of Greater Manchester Police* [2010] EWHC 1859 (Admin) [2011] 2 All ER 364

Anti-terrorism, Crime and Security Act 2001

Counter-Terrorism Act 2008

Criminal Justice and Public Order Act 1994

Human Rights Act 1998

Northern Ireland (Emergency Provisions) Act 1996

Police and Criminal Evidence Act 1984

Prevention of Terrorism Act 2005

Prevention of Terrorism (Additional Powers) Act 1996

Prevention of Terrorism (Temporary Provisions) Act 1989

Terrorism Act 2000

Terrorism Act 2006

Terrorism Prevention and Investigation Measures [HC] Bill (2010–2011) [193]

8 Developments in intelligence

Rachael Strzelecki

CHAPTER OBJECTIVES

By the end of this chapter you should be able to:

- understand definitions of intelligence, forms of intelligence and its uses;
- outline UK intelligence agencies, intelligence structures and their specific roles in counter-terrorism;
- describe European intelligence agencies and their specific roles in counter-terrorism;
- analyse some of the difficulties that UK and international government intelligence agencies face in relation to countering terrorism effectively.

Introduction

Terrorists operate in secret. Intelligence is vital to detect and disrupt their activities.

(Home Office, 2009)

You have already seen in Chapter 5 that, following a review of events leading to the 9/11 terrorist attacks in New York, a significant problem was highlighted in the management and sharing of intelligence between agencies. This resulted in the UK Government also reviewing its intelligence capability and a number of changes were introduced to provide a more effective intelligence response in order to counter terrorism.

This chapter considers various definitions of intelligence and explores the nature and development of intelligence structures within the UK and Europe. It discusses a number of problems that might contribute to intelligence failures, highlights the importance of effective intelligence sharing, and also considers some issues relating to civil liberties.

The 9/11 attacks in New York highlighted intelligence failings and, in 2003, as a result of the Homeland Security Act 2002, a Department of Homeland Security (DHS) was established within the USA. The main aim of the DHS is to protect the USA from terrorist attacks and its intelligence capability provides a focal point for all terrorist-related intelligence. In June 2003 the UK introduced a Joint Terrorism Analysis Centre (JTAC), situated at MI5 headquarters in London, whose remit is to analyse and assess intelligence related to international terrorism. Despite these developments the effectiveness of intelligence collection and management was further questioned following the bombings in London on 7 July 2005 (7/7).

In April 2006, following publication of the Serious Organised Crime and Police Act 2005, the Serious Organised Crime Agency (SOCA) was set up, drawing together various agencies within the UK, including the National Crime Squad, the National Criminal Intelligence Service (NCIS), HM Revenue and Customs, and Immigration Services. Although SOCA has a mandate to tackle organised crime, there are clear links between organised crime and terrorism. A good example of this is in Colombia, where the terrorist group, the Revolutionary Armed Forces of Colombia (FARC), engages in the cocaine trade to finance itself (Grabosky and Stohl, 2010).

REFLECTIVE TASK

Although SOCA does not have a direct counter-terrorism mandate, consider how, as an organisation, it assists the UK against threats of terrorism. To assist with this task refer to the SOCA yearly threat assessment that can be found on their website: www.soca. gov.uk/threats.

Other key developments such as the introduction of Counter Terrorism Units (CTUs) within the UK are explored later in the chapter.

Defining intelligence

Although there have been some significant intelligence-related events and the creation of many intelligence agencies, there is still no one single definition of intelligence. Similarly, academics have not been able to come up with a workable definition; rather, they conceptualise the idea of intelligence in different capacities of *criminal, crime, community and contextual intelligence* (Innes et al., 2005, p44).

Before launching into a discussion on intelligence it is imperative that you have a conceptual understanding of 'information' and 'intelligence' and are able to differentiate between them. The word 'information' comes from the Latin *informare*, which means 'give form to' (Barabba and Zaltman, 1990). Information is mainly viewed as a collection of facts and, in terms of law enforcement, it can be deemed as raw data. It is more difficult to pinpoint a single definition for 'intelligence' as different agencies and personnel think of it in different ways, according to their operational duty or academic studies. Definitions of intelligence over the years have been fashioned around the changes and developments in government. The earliest recordings relate to espionage and military intelligence compiled and published in *The Art of War* by Sun Tzu in 500 BC. At the turn of the nineteenth century intelligence was devalued by Carl von Clausewitz, who said that it *added to the fog of war* (Warner, 2002, p1). By the end of the nineteenth century intelligence was being utilised on a grand scale to aid tactics in wars and negotiations.

The following are some examples of definitions of intelligence.

> *Information that has been subject to a defined evaluation and risk assessment process in order to assist with police decision making.*
>
> (ACPO, 2005, p13)

> *Information gathered from anywhere in the world that involves threats to the US, its people, property or interests; the development, proliferation or use of weapons of mass destruction; or any other matters bearing on US national homeland security.*
>
> (CIA, 2009, p6)

> *Information that is gathered clandestinely through eavesdropping or other data collection methods.*
>
> (Riley et al., 2006, p2)

> *Intelligence can be viewed in three ways:*
>
> - *as a process where the information has been requested, put through an intelligence cycle and disseminated to the customer;*
>
> - *it can be defined as a product; and*
>
> - *it can be viewed as a service or institution.*
>
> (Lowenthal, 2002, p22)

PRACTICAL TASK

Consider the value and nature of 'intelligence' and how this might differ from the value and nature of 'information'. Draw up a simple chart to show the differences.

ACPO published a National Intelligence Model (NIM) in 2000 and the definition provided above is one that police officers need to understand, particularly those who are engaged in intelligence provision.

Intelligence forms and structures

There are usually two main sectors (civilian and military) responsible for managing the intelligence process. Intelligence comes in various forms and is exploited by intelligence agencies and organisations. Within the UK a number of agencies and organisations are responsible for the collection, analysis and dissemination of intelligence.

United Kingdom

> *Our intelligence agencies have their crucial part to play in detecting threats and preventing them from turning into carnage on our streets.*
>
> (Cameron and Clegg, 2010, p5)

The coalition Government introduced its first National Security Strategy in October 2010. The strategy was developed by the National Security Council, which is responsible for assessing UK security risks and advising the Government on security priorities. A number of 'highest priority' risks were identified that included international terrorism, the threat of weapons of mass destruction (chemical, biological, radiological, nuclear – CBRN), domestic terrorism (Northern Ireland), and the considerable growing threat of cyber terrorism.

Figure 8.1 depicts UK agencies and organisations that play a key role in supporting national security priorities and each one is examined below.

Intelligence and Security Committee
Section 10(1) of the Intelligence Services Act 1994 provided a statutory mandate for the ISC, whose role is to examine the expenditure, administration and policy of MI6, MI5 and GCHQ. The ISC is based within the Cabinet Office and in March 2010 it identified the need for a stronger independence from the Government to carry out more effectively its statutory remit of holding agencies and other bodies with an intelligence role to account (ISC, 2010).

Joint Intelligence Committee
The JIC is part of the Government's Cabinet Office and is responsible for providing the UK intelligence requirement based on the priorities set out within the National Security

Figure 8.1 UK intelligence agencies and organisations

Strategy, and to provide intelligence assessments to ministers. The primary collection agencies for this intelligence are MI6 and GCHQ, whose functions are set out in the Intelligence Services Act 1994. MI5 also contributes and its functions are set out within the Security Service Acts 1989 and 1996.

Secret Intelligence Service

MI6 provides the UK Government with a global covert capability to promote and defend the national security and well-being of the UK (Cabinet Office, 2009). It collects secret intelligence and hosts covert operations overseas. The intelligence is collected from both human and technical sources, and MI6 works in conjunction with a range of foreign intelligence and security services. Its main partnerships are with MI5, GCHQ, the Ministry of Defence (MOD), HM Revenue and Customs, and UK law enforcement agencies.

REFLECTIVE TASK

In October 2010 the head of MI6, Sir John Sawers, spoke publicly for the first time, highlighting some of the difficulties around information sharing and the use of torture. In relation to torture, he said it was illegal and abhorrent under any circumstances and we have nothing whatsoever to do with it (The Guardian, 2010).

Consider whether torture can ever be a legitimate means of obtaining information when national security is at stake. List arguments both for and against as you reflect on the statement made by Sir John Sawers.

Security Service

MI5 is responsible for protecting the UK against threats to national security and has a number of aims, including specific terrorist-related responsibilities:

- *to frustrate terrorism;*
- *to frustrate procurement by proliferating countries of material, technology or expertise relating to weapons of mass destruction;*
- *to watch out for new or re-emerging types of threats;*
- *to protect government's sensitive information and assets and the Critical National Infrastructure (CNI).*

(Security Service, 2009a, no page)

In the mid-1990s its capacity was expanded to include the Special Branch (police) and the National Criminal Intelligence Service (which was replaced by SOCA in 2006). The main function of MI5 is to protect the economic well-being of the UK and its national security. It supports law enforcement agencies in preventing and detecting serious crime and collects and disseminates intelligence, investigates and assesses threats, and works with others to counter them. MI5's principal activity is the fight against terrorism, which includes both international and domestic terrorism relating to Northern Ireland, and the provision of protective security in the support of these tasks (Security Service, 2009a).

Commenting on the challenge facing MI5 in protecting the UK against terrorism, the Director General of MI5, addressing security professionals in September 2010 stated:

> Every day hundreds of officers are involved in this intense struggle, identifying and investigating people suspected of being, or known to be, involved in terrorism or the infrastructure that makes terrorism possible.
>
> *(Evans, 2010, no page)*

In August 2010 it was suggested that MI5 was failing to gather intelligence to tackle new republican dissidents in Northern Ireland (Booth, 2010).

Consider the importance of intelligence in assessing the terrorist threat and identifying security priorities. Where should the focus be (domestic or international terrorism?) and is it reasonable to suggest that terrorism is 100 per cent preventable?

For further information and perspectives on these issues explore the MI5 website: www.mi5.gov.uk.

Government Communications Headquarters

The Government Code and Cipher School was first established in 1919, becoming formally known as the Government Communications Headquarters (GCHQ) in 1946. Historically this department has spent time breaking codes and developing cryptography (hiding information). It now deals with vast amounts of intelligence being received through information and communications technology (ICT) systems.

GCHQ's main aim is to provide intelligence, protect information and inform relevant UK policy to keep society safe and successful in the internet age. It works in close partnership with both MI5 and MI6. While the primary customer for GCHQ intelligence products is the MOD, it also works with the Foreign and Commonwealth Office and local law enforcement agencies (Cabinet Office, 2009).

Joint Terrorism Analysis Centre

JTAC was established in 2003 and is responsible for the analysis and assessment of international terrorism. It works closely with the MI5 international counter-terrorism branch, whose primary role is to manage investigations concerning terrorist activity within the UK. This enables JTAC to analyse and assess the extent of the international terrorist threat within the UK.

JTAC's main roles are to:

- *analyse and assess all intelligence relating to international terrorism both within the UK and overseas;*
- *position the threat levels for the country;*

- *issue warnings of threats and other related terrorist subjects;*

- *produce comprehensive reports on crime trends, terrorist networks and their capabilities for attack.*

(Security Service, 2009b, no page)

Defence Intelligence Staff

Military intelligence is specifically focused towards planned operations. It makes use of both strategic and tactical intelligence gathered from its own civilian population as well as from foreign enemies. An integral role of the MOD is to collect and analyse defence intelligence to support government policy making, military operations and crisis management. It also contributes to the work of the JIC.

DIS provides a central assessment process for all incoming military intelligence.

PRACTICAL TASK

The Army, Navy and RAF all contribute to defence intelligence. Access the MOD website at www.mod.uk/DefenceInternet/Home and find the links for the three armed services. What methods does each use to support intelligence collection?

Police Service

In 1883 the Metropolitan Police introduced a Special Branch following a series of terrorist attacks by the Irish Fenian movement. During the 1960s provincial police forces introduced their own Special Branch departments and their main remit today is to acquire and develop intelligence to protect the public from national security threats, such as terrorism and other extremist activity. They also contribute to the challenge of promoting community safety and cohesion (Home Office, 2004). In 2006 the Metropolitan Police integrated their Special Branch and Anti-terrorist Branch to create a Counter Terrorism Command (CTC) unit in 2006 (known as SO15).

PRACTICAL TASK

Complete an internet search for the Special Branch Guidelines 2004 and download the document. Identify and explore the various functions of Special Branch (pp6–9) that relate directly to counter-terrorism. Establish how intelligence is collected, who is targeted, how intelligence is used and the role of Special Branch in security at ports and in countering extremism.

In Chapter 6 the current counter-terrorism structure was highlighted (see pages 92–3) and the role of the Counter Terrorism Units (CTUs) and Counter Terrorism Intelligence Units (CTIUs) was discussed.

The CTIUs have a primary intelligence function, whereas the CTUs have a much wider remit that includes investigation, disruption and prosecution. The next chapter explores further how the counter-terrorism teams work with the community as part of the 'Rich Picture' programme to obtain intelligence and information on issues related to violent extremist activity.

Outside England, units with an intelligence capability include:

- Major Crime and Terrorism Investigation Unit (Scotland);

- Welsh Extremism and Counter Terrorism Unit (Wales);

- Crime Operations Branch (Police Service of Northern Ireland).

The Police Service also has a number of Counter Terrorism and Extremism Liaison Officers based overseas in foreign law enforcement agencies and UK Missions. Part of their remit is to exchange police counter-terrorism and extremism intelligence (Home Office, 2009).

REFLECTIVE TASK

Consider why a new intelligence structure was introduced by the UK Government following 7/7 and reflect on how it contributes to national security.

Intelligence-led policing

Throughout the 1990s the notion of intelligence-led policing gained momentum and was used to deal more effectively with increases in both volume crime and organised crime. The NIM was introduced in 2000 and given statutory authority by the Police Reform Act 2002. The model operates at three levels: local, cross-border and national/international (levels 1, 2 and 3 respectively). Level 1 is important for the targeting and collection of local intelligence relating to terrorism; however, the major implications for terrorism are at level 3 where specialised resources and dedicated teams are required.

The NIM provides a core business model for policing, using a tasking and coordination process at strategic and tactical levels. This is designed to ensure that resources are used effectively to target organisational priorities and current threats. It can be very effective when used in partnership with other agencies to tackle terrorism. However, owing to the number of individual police forces within the UK and the number of other law enforcement and intelligence agencies, collaboration can be fragmented and limited, restricting the potential of the NIM (Field, 2009).

Association of Chief Police Officers

The ACPO business group, Terrorism and Allied Matters (TAM), responsible for dealing with terrorism, extremism and associated matters, was briefly explored in Chapter 6. Part of the group's remit is to tackle domestic extremism and this is achieved through the structure shown in Figure 8.2.

The NCDE is the national lead on domestic extremism and is comprised of the three units (see Figure 8.2) that work collaboratively to coordinate the police response. Intelligence used by the NCDE is owned by the police force that collected it. The National Public Order Intelligence Unit (NPIOU) coordinates the intelligence collected, which is then used to develop a national picture and to advise the Police Service accordingly.

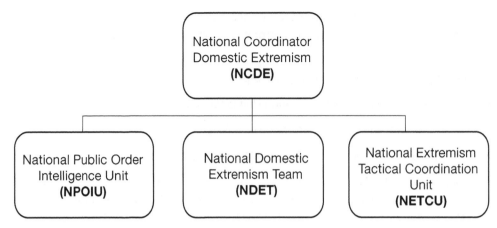

Figure 8.2 Domestic extremism structure

For further information on the structure and role of these groups, go to www.acpo. police.uk/ncde.

Police intelligence and privacy
The Police Service and other security organisations are responsible for the collection and management of vast amounts of intelligence. Current rules, regulations or statutory controls for intelligence gathering, analysis, dissemination and retention include the Human Rights Act 1998, the Data Protection Act 1998 and the Regulation of Investigatory Powers Act 2000. However, can we safely assume that sufficient control is in place and that the balance between national security and civil liberties is properly aligned? Consider the following two case studies.

CASE STUDY

National security or civil liberties?

Automatic Number Plate Recognition
ANPR was first developed in 1976 by the Police Scientific Development Branch. It provides mass surveillance using optical character recognition to read vehicle registration marks. ANPR is used widely by the Police Service and during the 1980s it was used in support of counter-terrorism initiatives.

Today's ANPR technology is smaller, faster, more reliable and relatively inexpensive, and the Police Service quickly recognised the potential of the technology, not only for tackling terrorism but also for the prevention and detection of crime and reducing road casualties. The Government has provided substantial funding to develop the use of ANPR and a national ANPR data centre now sits at Hendon alongside the Police National Computer (PNC). The database stores the millions of vehicle registration numbers recorded on a daily basis from a network of cameras situated throughout the UK. The stored data can be useful for both intelligence and evidence for post-incident investigation, and to support work in tackling terrorism and organised crime.

Statistics provided by the National Police Improvement Agency (NPIA) revealed that, during a seven-day period (3–9 June 2010) data was captured from 4,045 cameras and that there were 7.6 billion 'read records' on the database, which could be retained for a maximum of two years (NPIA, 2010).

The database is not without controversy and public concerns relating to privacy issues, and the security and accuracy of data, have been raised by the media and civil liberty organisations.

Safer Birmingham Project

The 'Safer Birmingham Project', which involved members of West Midlands Police, Birmingham City Council and other agencies, received £3 million Government funding to assist with tackling terrorism. Under 'Project Champion', a system of over 200 cameras (including covert cameras) was set up in a number of city wards, including the densely populated, predominantly Muslim areas of Washwood Heath and Sparkbrook.

The funding had been provided by ACPO TAM, granted for projects designed to deter or prevent terrorism, or help to prosecute those responsible for terrorism. A few local councillors had been briefed about the cameras but believed they were being used to tackle antisocial behaviour, drug dealing and vehicle crime (Lewis, 2010).

The Guardian *newspaper published the story (June 2010) following an investigation and reported:* Police sources said the initiative was the first of its kind in the UK that sought to monitor a population seen as being 'at risk' of extremism.

The action has caused both widespread public concern and a lack of trust and confidence in policing in the areas concerned.

Explore these two case studies and identify relevant human rights and privacy issues. Where does the balance lie between national security needs and civil liberties, and how can public trust and confidence be effectively achieved?

Europe

Most countries within Europe have their own national intelligence agencies and some examples are provided in Table 8.1.

The European Police Agency (Europol), Joint Situation Centre (SitCen) and the European Union Satellite Centre (SatCen) are EU agencies that provide intelligence services and play an important role in tackling the problem of domestic and international terrorism.

Table 8.1 Mainland European national intelligence agencies

Country	Agency	Status
Belgium	State Security Service (SE or SV)	Civilian agency
Denmark	Security Intelligence Service (PET)	Part of Danish Police
France	Directorate of Territorial Surveillance (DST)	Part of Police Nationale
Germany	Federal Department for Constitutional Protection (BfV)	Civilian agency
Italy	Internal Information and Security Agency (AISI)	Civilian agency
Netherlands	General Intelligence and Security Service (AIVD)	Civilian agency
Sweden	National Security RPS/SAK Service (Säpo)	Part of Swedish National Police

Source: Gregory (2008, p48)

European Police Agency

Europol, based in the Hague in the Netherlands, is the EU law enforcement and criminal intelligence agency that became fully operational in 1999. Its role is to gather, analyse and disseminate information and to coordinate operations related to international serious crime and terrorism in support of EU member states and other non-EU partners.

It provides an annual European Organised Crime Threat Assessment (OCTA) and a European Terrorism Situation and Trend Report (TE-SAT). The TE-SAT describes and analyses terrorist attacks and activities, and also identifies terrorist trends from information provided by EU member states, some third states and open sources (Europol, 2010).

PRACTICAL TASK

Look at Table 8.2, taken from the 2010 TE-SAT report, and consider whether it is information or intelligence.

Table 8.2 Number of failed, foiled or successfully executed attacks in 2009 per Member State

Member State	Islamist	Separatist	Left-wing	Right-wing	Single-issue	Not specified	Total 2009
Austria	0	0	0	0	1	5	6
France	0	89	0	0	1	5	95
Greece	0	0	15	0	0	0	15
Hungary	0	0	0	4	0	0	4
Italy	1	0	2	0	0	0	3
Spain	0	148	23	0	0	0	171
Total:	1	237	40	4	2	10	294

Source: Europol, 2010, p12)

The TE-SAT report is an unclassified document that does not contain any confidential information. It is used as a reporting mechanism for the Terrorism Working Group of the Council of the EU to the European Parliament. It does not provide a complete picture and it is interesting to note that certain quantitative data is not available from the UK because it does not meet statistical criteria required for the report. It is an information report containing facts and some analysis, and provides important information for policy makers responsible for setting security priorities and developing counter-terrorism strategies.

To access the latest TE-SAT report, go to the Europol website: www.europol.europa.eu.

Joint Situation Centre

SitCen is based in Brussels, Belgium, and has been part of the EU European External Action Service (EEAS) since July 2009. It is directly accountable to the High Representative for Foreign Affairs and Security Policy. The centre monitors and assesses events in relation to terrorism and the proliferation of WMDs. Its initial remit was the analysis of trends in countries outside the EU, but post-9/11 this was extended to monitoring and assessing terrorist threats within the EU. SitCen is divided into three main units:

- *Civilian Intelligence Cell with intelligence staff working on political and counter-terrorism intelligence;*

- *General Operations Unit, which provides operational support, research and non-intelligence analysis;*

- *Communications Unit, which deals with security in relation to communication.*

(Clarke, 2005, no page)

European Union Satellite Centre

SatCen was founded in 1992 and became an EU agency in 2002. It is situated near Madrid, Spain, and provides intelligence products resulting from the analysis of satellite imagery and collateral data, including aerial imagery and related services. Its priorities are based on the European Security Strategy, which includes terrorism and the proliferation of WMDs.

United States

The USA has a comprehensive range of intelligence services that are an integral part of combating the terrorism threat. Their 2010 National Security Strategy highlights the continuing challenge to better integrate the intelligence community; enhance the capability of intelligence community members; strengthen partnerships with foreign intelligence services; and sustain strong ties with close allies (White House, 2010).

To find out more about US and other global intelligence agencies, go to www.loyola.edu/departments/academics/political-science/strategic-intelligence/index.html.

Interpol

On a global basis the foremost intelligence agency is the International Criminal Police Organisation (Interpol), which is based in Lyon, France, with a membership of 188 countries. It supports member countries by collecting, storing, analysing and exchanging information about suspected terrorist groups and individuals. It coordinates the circulation of terrorist alerts and warnings to the law enforcement agencies of member countries and, following the 9/11 attacks, it has introduced a 'Fusion Task Force', which has a clear intelligence mandate to:

- *identify active terrorist groups and their membership;*

- *solicit, collect and share information and intelligence;*

- *provide analytical support;*

- *enhance the capacity of member countries to address threats of terrorism and organised crime.*

(Interpol, 2010, no page)

Intelligence failures

In the aftermath of a terrorist attack, a review or enquiry usually reports on events, and will identify any lessons to be learned. This text has highlighted the reported failure of a number of intelligence agencies following the 9/11 and 7/7 bombings (see pages 7–8 and 11). The following task provides additional context.

REFLECTIVE TASK

Find out more about the 9/11 and 7/7 terror attacks in New York and London, and consider whether there are any similarities between the suggested intelligence failings. Refer to The 9/11 Commission Report *(pp71–107 and 407–18), and the ISC* Report into the London Terrorist Attacks on 7 July 2005 *(pp5–16), both of which are readily available online. A further report by the ISC in 2009,* Could 7/7 Have Been Prevented, *provides an updated and more critical review of intelligence at the time of the 7/7 attacks.*

In the report on the 7/7 attacks you will have found that intelligence was available to MI5 in respect of two of the bombers (Khan and Tanweer) from a previous operation (Crevice). An initial report recognised the priority of other MI5 investigations at that time and the restriction of resource limitations. It also suggests that the decision not to give a greater investigative priority to the two individuals was understandable (ISC, 2006).

So is it fair to criticise intelligence-gathering agencies every time there is a terrorist attack? Field (2009) suggests that 7/7 highlighted the fragmented nature of the intelligence system, making it difficult for agencies to share and integrate information, and that a lack of communication led to missed intelligence. The list below (not exhaustive) highlights some of the problems that intelligence agencies face:

- institutional barriers;

- economic restrictions;

- legal restrictions;

- security risks;

- integration of technology systems;

- information sharing.

Institutional barriers

Each intelligence agency has its own priorities and specific roles to play when dealing with the terrorist threat. A disjointed and inconsistent approach has the potential for intelligence failures and the challenge for government is to ensure a coordinated and effective approach. Consider the roles of MI5 and the Police Service; one has a clear national security intelligence mandate, while the other has a much wider remit to investigate crime, make arrests and take suspects to trial. Different priorities, objectives and roles may hinder effective intelligence collection, analysis and dissemination.

Economic restrictions

The use of covert methods to obtain intelligence is very costly and resource-intensive. Intelligence agencies do not have an open-ended budget and need to prioritise their investigations. The directed surveillance of a number of suspects requires a large team of specially trained officers. Listening and tracking devices and other covert equipment can be expensive, and very often requires a considerable back-room support team.

CASE STUDY

MI5 prioritisation

MI5 prioritises its targets as essential (people suspected of a direct involvement in or knowledge of terrorist attack planning), desirable and other. In 2004 MI5 could only provide a 6 per cent cover for the known terrorist threat, therefore effective prioritisation of suspects was critical. Over 60 per cent of MI5 target cover was described as inadequate or nil and 52 per cent of the 'essential' category had no cover at all. Prioritisation was necessary within the essential group owing to limited resources, so the desirable and other categories were, in essence, abandoned (ISC, 2010).

Khan and Tanweer (see above) were believed to have been on the periphery of Operation Crevice, which later resulted in the conviction of five men in 2007 for conspiracy to cause explosions. At the time of their arrest they were found in possession of 600kg of fertiliser intended for bomb-making (see http://news.bbc.co.uk/1/shared/spl/hi/guides/457000/457032/html/nn1page6.stm for the full story).

Khan and Tanweer were heard discussing financial fraud, rather than planning an actual terrorist attack, and would only have been classified within the desirable category. If MI5 were expected to complete further intelligence work on those in the desirable category, it was crudely estimated that this would require several hundred thousand officers as opposed to the 3,500 that MI5 had at their disposal at the time (ISC, 2010).

Legal restrictions

The Human Rights Act 1998 protects the rights and freedoms of individuals from interference by the state. It includes rights of life, prohibition of torture, liberty and security, a fair trial, and respect for private and family life (Articles 2, 3, 5, 6 and 8). The security services cannot carry out any directed or intrusive surveillance on an individual without lawful authority, and they have to justify any interference of rights by evidencing necessity, proportionality and non-discrimination before an authority is granted for any interference. This is a statutory requirement provided by the Regulation of Investigatory Powers Act 2000. Although certain intelligence may be available about certain individuals, it may be insufficient to allow security services to develop it through covert operations and more traditional methods of intelligence gathering may be required.

Security risks

Intelligence agencies have a responsibility for the security of secret and confidential information, together with a duty of care for individuals who have provided information. If an intelligence source is compromised or specialised techniques to obtain intelligence are revealed, consequences may be severe, such as putting a life at risk, the loss of potential evidence, the loss of public confidence and endangering the viability of future operations. Trust and confidence between intelligence agencies is paramount and an open and accessible intelligence network with robust and secure processes is required. Without this, intelligence failures are likely.

Integration of technology systems

Joined-up intelligence is an ideal that would make collection, analysis and dissemination more effective, and ensure that key links are made to facilitate more effective investigation. Failures of intelligence systems were clearly highlighted following the murder of two schoolgirls in Soham in 2002. The Bichard report noted that the police national intelligence strategy first introduced in 1994 had been abandoned in 2000 (Bichard, 2004). Bichard's first recommendation was that the Home Office provide a national intelligence system for England and Wales (one for Scotland was already in place at this time). A national police intelligence system (IMPACT) has now been introduced but at time of writing in 2010 was still not fully developed.

SCOPE is a secure web-based communication system linking the main intelligence agencies (MI6, MI5 and GCHQ) and both enables and enhances information sharing. It became operational in 2007 but plans to extend it to the wider intelligence community were scrapped by the Government the following year. This was severely criticised by the ISC (2010); however, an alternative solution called Collaboration in the Intelligence Community (CLiC) is to be introduced as a replacement.

Other intelligence databases are being used by the intelligence community. A fragmented approach can contribute to intelligence failures. There are no easy solutions and replacement technology is very expensive, but both the police and the security services are working towards a more integrated approach that will enhance the sharing of intelligence.

Information sharing

The 9/11 Commission cited breakdowns in information sharing and the failure to fuse pertinent intelligence (i.e., 'connecting the dots') as key factors in the failure to prevent the 9/11 attacks.

(Randol, 2009, p1)

Due to the complex nature of global, national and regional intelligence structures, information sharing can be a serious challenge to governments. In order to protect a country from terror attacks, effective sharing of intelligence between agencies is paramount. Since the suggested intelligence failings of 9/11 and 7/7, steps have been taken within the USA and the UK to improve structures, relationships and communication between law enforcement, security services and intelligence agencies.

CASE STUDY

Binyam Mohamed

Binyam Mohamed was born in Ethiopia in 1978 and came to the UK in 1994 seeking asylum. His initial application was rejected, but in 2000 he was given exceptional leave to remain in the country for a further four years. He converted to Islam in 2001 and travelled to both Pakistan and Afghanistan. The USA believed he had taken part in firearms and explosives training with al-Qaeda and had fought in Afghanistan against Northern Alliance Forces. He was arrested in Pakistan in 2002 and later detained in both Morocco and Afghanistan, before being transferred to Guantanamo Bay, Cuba, in September 2004. It was at Guantanamo that he alleged he had been subjected to torture. In 2007 the UK requested that some of the Guantanamo detainees be returned to Britain, but the USA was unwilling to release Mohamed. In 2008 his lawyers commenced legal proceedings, referring to the torture claims and requesting the disclosure of US intelligence reports that referred to the torture. The court refused disclosure, highlighting a threat to US intelligence sharing with the UK (BBC News, 2010).

The case was heard in the Court of Appeal in February 2010 (EWCA Civ 65) where disclosure was allowed. This was based on the fact that the intelligence was already in the

---

public domain following a district court hearing in Columbia, USA. The court went on to recognise and discuss two key principles: first, that justice should be open and that the court should publish the reasons for its decisions; and, second, that material should not generally be published if there is a serious risk to national security (p262).

REFLECTIVE TASK

Find out more about the above case and consider its wider implications for the sharing of intelligence. The following links will give you access to the full Court of Appeal decision and a BBC report that includes a video of David Miliband (Foreign Secretary) addressing the House of Commons about the case:

- *www.bailii.org/ew/cases/EWCA/Civ/2010/65.html*

- *http://news.bbc.co.uk/1/hi/uk/8507852.stm.*

C H A P T E R   S U M M A R Y

Intelligence plays a key role in any counter-terrorism strategy and there is an array of intelligence agencies and organisations both within the UK and in other countries.

Recent major terrorist attacks have highlighted intelligence failings; however, this chapter has provided evidence of the considerable challenge that intelligence agencies face today. It has also shown how the UK Government has taken steps to enhance intelligence processes and structures. It is reasonable to suggest that no matter how robust any intelligence response is, terrorists will continue to succeed, but this success will be diminished through the continuous development of our intelligence capability. It is therefore suggested that it is the limitations of our intelligence systems, rather than its failures, that have contributed to some of the major terrorist attacks.

It has also been established that obtaining the right balance between national security needs and civil liberties is difficult to achieve and that careful consideration needs to be given to the process of intelligence gathering.

An analysis of the development and effectiveness of current intelligence processes and structures, and the range of problems that exist, provides a good basis for an assignment topic. There is much academic material available regarding terrorism and intelligence, and further reading and research is recommended.

ACPO (Association of Chief Police Officers) (2005) National Intelligence Model. Available online at http://tulliallan.police.uk/workingparties/nim/documents/NIMManual(New05InteractiveManual).pdf (accessed 28 October 2010).

Barabba, V and Zaltman, G (1990) *Hearing the Voice of the Market*. Cambridge, MA: Harvard Business School Press.

BBC News (2010) Profile: Binyam Mohamed. *BBC News*, 12 February. Available online at http://news.bbc.co.uk/1/hi/uk/7906381.stm (accessed 26 November 2010).

Bichard, Sir Michael (2004) *Bichard Inquiry Report*. London: The Stationery Office.

Booth, Robert (2010) MI5 Intelligence-gathering 'Failing to Tackle New Republican Dissidents'. *The Guardian*, 16 August. Available online at www.guardian.co.uk/uk/2010/aug/16/mi5-intelligence-gathering-northern-ireland (accessed 23 November 2010).

Cabinet Office (2009) Intelligence Agencies. Available online at www.cabinetoffice.gov.uk/intelligence-security-resilience/national-security.aspx (accessed 12 August 2010).

Cameron, David and Clegg, Nick (2010) Foreword, in *A Strong Britain in an Age of Uncertainty: National Security Strategy*. Norwich: The Stationery Office.

CIA (Central Intelligence Agency) (2009) *National Intelligence: A Consumer's Guide*. Available online at www.dni.gov/reports/IC_Consumers_Guide_2009.pdf (accessed 28 October 2010).

Clarke, C (2005) Home Secretary Statement on Joint Situation Centre (SitCen), 25 June.

Europol (2010) *TE-SAT 2010: EU Terrorism Situation and Trend Report*. Available online at www.europol.europa.eu/publications/EU_Terrorism_Situation_and_Trend_Report_TE-SAT/Tesat2010.pdf (accessed 23 November 2010).

Evans, Jonathan (2010) The Threat to National Security Address, given to the Worshipful Company of Security Professionals,16 September. Available online at www.mi5.gov.uk/output/the-threat-to-national-security.html (accessed 16 September 2011).

Field, Antony (2009) Tracking Terrorist Networks: Problems of Intelligence Sharing within the UK Intelligence Community. *Cambridge Journal Review of International Studies*, 35(4): 997–1009.

Grabosky, Peter and Stohl, Michael (2010) *Crime and Terrorism*. London: Sage.

Gregory, F (2008) The Police and the Intelligence Services, in Harfield, C, MacVean, A, Grieve, J and Phillips, D (eds) *The Handbook of Intelligent Policing* (pp47–61). Oxford: Oxford University Press.

The Guardian (2010) MI6: Open Secrets. *The Guardian*, 29 October. Available online at www.guardian.co.uk/commentisfree/2010/oct/29/mi6-national-security-editorial (accessed 29 October 2010).

Home Office (2004) *Guidelines on Special Branch Work in the United Kingdom*. London: HMSO.

Home Office (2009) *Pursue Prevent Protect Prepare: The United Kingdom's Strategy for Countering International Terrorism*. Norwich: The Stationery Office.

Innes, M, Fielding, N and Cope, N (2005) The Appliance of Science? The Theory and Practice of Crime Intelligence Analysis. *British Journal of Criminology*, 45(1): 39–57.

ISC (Intelligence and Security Committee) (2006) *Report into the London Terrorist Attacks on 7 July 2005*. Norwich: The Stationery Office.

ISC (Intelligence and Security Committee) (2010) *Annual Report 2009–2010*. Norwich: The Stationery Office.

Interpol (2010) Fusion Task Force: Operational Investigative Support. Available online at http://interpol .int/public/FusionTaskForce/default.asp (accessed 28 August 2010).

Lewis, Paul (2010) Birmingham Stops Camera Surveillance in Muslim Areas. *The Guardian*, 17 June. Available online at www.guardian.co.uk/uk/2010/jun/17/birmingham-stops-spy-cameras-project (accessed 26 November 2010).

Lowenthal, M (2002) *Intelligence: From Secrets to Policy*. Washington, DC: CQ Press.

NPIA (National Police Improvement Agency) (2010) Freedom of Information. Letter sent to HMP Britain, 15 June. Available online at www.whatdotheyknow.com/request/36663/response/91833/attach/ 2/NRSB99%200111%20100610%20draft%20response%2047217.pdf (accessed 26 November 2010).

Randol, Mark A (2009) *Terrorism Information Sharing and the Nationwide Suspicious Activity Report Initiative: Background and Issues for Congress.* Washington, DC: Congressional Research Service.

Riley, J, Treverton, G and Wilson, J (2006) State and Local Intelligence in the War on Terrorism. Cambridge, MA: The Rand Corporation.

Security Service (2009a) Objectives and Values. Available online at www.mi5.gov.uk/output/ objectives-and-values.html (accessed 16 September 2011).

Security Service (2009b) Joint Terrorism Analysis Centre. Available online at www.mi5.gov.uk/output/ joint-terrorism-analysis-centre.html (accessed 22 October 2010).

Sun Tzu (1963) *The Art of War* (reprint). New York: Oxford University Press.

Warner, M (2002) Wanted: A Definition of Intelligence. *Studies in Intelligence*, 46(3): 15–23.

White House (2010) *National Security Strategy.* Washington, DC: White House. Available online at www.whitehouse.gov/sites/default/files/rss_viewer/national_security_strategy.pdf (accessed 25 November 2010).

USEFUL WEBSITES

www.acpo.police.uk/ncde (National Coordinator Domestic Extremism)

www.cia.gov (US Central Intelligence Agency)

www.dhs.gov/index.shtm (US Department of Homeland Security)

www.europol.europa.eu (Europol)

www.eusc.org (EU Satellite Centre)

www.fbi.gov (US Federal Bureau of Investigation)

www.gchq.gov.uk (Government Communications Headquarters)

www.gmp.police.uk/mainsite/pages/ctu.htm (Counter Terrorism Unit (North West))

www.interpol.int (Interpol)

www.loyola.edu/departments/academics/political-science/strategic-intelligence/index.html (Strategic Intelligence (Comprehensive list of worldwide intelligence links))

www.met.police.uk/so/counter_terrorism.htm (SO15 (Metropolitan Police))

www.mi5.gov.uk (Secret Service – MI5)

www.mi5.gov.uk/output/joint-terrorism-analysis-centre.html (Joint Terrorism Analysis Centre)

www.mod.uk/DefenceInternet/AboutDefence/WhatWeDo/SecurityandIntelligence/DIS (Defence Intelligence Staff)

www.sis.gov.uk/output/sis-home-welcome.html (Secret Intelligence Service – MI6)

www.soca.gov.uk (Serious Organised Crime Agency)

CASES

The Queen on the application of Binyam Mohamed (Respondent) and the Secretary of State for Foreign and Commonwealth Affairs (Appellant) [2010] EWCA Civ 65

LEGISLATION

Criminal Justice and Police Act 2001

Data Protection Act 1998

Homeland Security Act 2002

Human Rights Act 1998

Intelligence Services Act 1994

Police Reform Act 2002

Regulation of Investigatory Powers Act 2000

Security Service Act 1989

Security Service Act 1996

Serious Organised Crime and Police Act 2005

9 Violent extremism

Peter Williams

CHAPTER OBJECTIVES

By the end of this chapter you should be able to:

- understand key influences within the Islamic world;
- outline the process of radicalisation;
- understand how radicalisation has manifested itself within the UK context;
- describe strategies that have been implemented to prevent violent extremism;
- analyse whether the problem is being resolved or is leading to community fragmentation and the potential for hate crime.

Introduction

The issues surrounding radicalisation and violent extremism have presented new challenges for the security services in the UK, particularly the Police Service in respect of its leading role in preventing violent extremism (PVE). Prior to 9/11 and the overall global recognition of the threat from Islamic extremists, little was known about this most sensitive of community engagement activity that the Police Service has had to engage with. The vast majority of Muslims throughout the world condemn this aspect of the Islamic faith and it is a very small minority who engage, or encourage others to do so, in either radicalisation or the further step of violent extremism.

This chapter examines the roots of this strain of Islam and how that ideology and events in other areas of the world have manifested themselves in contemporary Britain. In respect of the UK there is another feature that emphasises the poignancy of this issue and that is this country's historic links with Pakistan in particular and the Indian sub-continent in general.

Pakistan has become the centre for operations of al-Qaeda (Hewitt, 2008) and shares a long border with Afghanistan, the home of the *Taliban*. Again, it should be stressed that most citizens of Pakistan who are resident in the UK and UK citizens who have ethnic ties to Pakistan, or anywhere else on the Indian sub-continent, have no sympathies at all with this extremist minority.

Later, the chapter discusses measures that are in place to counter effectively the influence of radicalisation and minimise its effect. The chapter also comments on the success or otherwise of these counter-measures and assesses whether they are divisive or conducive to community cohesion.

Origins of radicalisation

The roots of radicalisation and extremism date back many centuries to the emergence of the Islamic faith and, to appreciate fully the contemporary situation and the motivation of those who have been exposed to radicalisation, it is necessary to understand these origins. This will also explain the ideology and motivation of terrorist groups such as al-Qaeda and those loosely connected to Islamic extremism.

Islam is a far more politically motivated religion than others and, as a consequence, is more likely to adopt legitimate political issues when addressing grievances (Burke, 2003). This function of the religion also triggers a specific element of power for Islam throughout the Islamic world.

While this section examines the earliest beginnings of the Islamic faith, it must be stressed that the Islamic religion is neither violent nor extreme; far from it. Any radicalisation or extremism that has manifested itself over the centuries is as a result of conflicting interpretations of texts and events that occurred in the Islamic world. This is known as the *tafseer* – the study of the commentary on the Qur'an (Husain, 2007). Some of these key influences will be explored.

Muslims, the followers of Islam, believe that their Holy Book, the Qur'an, is the true word of God or Allah. The Prophet Mohammed was chosen to receive the spoken word of God, which ultimately became the Qur'an, and as a consequence it is pure and unchangeable. This is an important contrast with the New Testament in the Bible, which was written by others regarding the ministry of Jesus Christ during his life. The Qur'an is what is known as a 'revealed text' (Burke, 2003) in that it is the true word of God or Allah as spoken to the Prophet Mohammed.

Muslims believe that Mohammed was the last in a line of prophets, which includes both Moses and Jesus, to reveal the word of God to mankind. The society that Mohammed grew up in, which is now within Saudi Arabia, was completely hierarchical in nature, with inequality, violence, greed and sectarianism featuring prominently within it. This latter issue was highlighted to Mohammed by the polytheism (worship of more than one god) that was widely practised at this time. Inter-tribal warring was also occurring within Arabian society during this period, which left it divided and weak compared with the superpowers of that time – the Persians and the Romans (Burke, 2003).

The situation that Mohammed faced when he started his ministry could be summarised as a society that was characterised by a hedonistic elite ruling class, contrasted lower down the social scale with one that was beset with inequality and violent inter-faction fighting, which effectively weakened the whole of the community. Injustice within society was everywhere and this was particularly abhorrent to Mohammed, who by his later years had established a society recognised by Muslims for its justice. Justice and injustice are powerful motivating factors within Islam and both have clear economic, political and social ramifications (Burke, 2003).

The message from Mohammed the Prophet was simply that the only authority was God or Allah as it is denoted within Islam, and this presented a challenge to the ruling Arabian class, based in Mecca. Muslims only worship Allah and Allah alone; they do not worship Mohammed or the Qur'an and this is a fundamental principle of Islam, reflecting both the pre-eminence and unity of God. Again, there is a difference here between Islam and Christianity in that Christians worship both God and Jesus Christ as the Son of God; Muslims do not worship Mohammed. This singular body within the Islamic religion is known as *tauhid* and again, although a theological concept, reflects a wider political ideology. There is a wide body of belief within Islam, which included that of Osama bin Laden, that this concept should form part of the political expediency via the removal of divisions, national or otherwise, and the coming together of the *umma*, or the wider Muslim community (Burke, 2003).

The issue of *divisions* within the Islamic world cannot be overestimated for Muslims and can be traced directly to the situation that pertained within seventh-century Arabian society at the commencement of Mohammed's time as messenger. In addition to the Qur'an, there is a series of texts called the *hadith* or *hadeeth*, which were compiled by the followers of Mohammed based on the sayings (Husain, 2007) and behaviour of the Prophet, which is known as the *Sunna*. Islamic law, or *Sharia*, is based on the Qur'an and the Sunna (Rehman, 2010).

Given the iniquitous and violent society that the Prophet was initially faced with, within a relatively short period of time tranquillity began to establish itself across a growing Islamic world, not merely confined to the Arabian peninsula, but also west across northern Africa and down into southern Asia, which mirrors the Islamic world as we know it today.

The first Muslims, the forefathers of Islam or the *Salaf* (Burleigh, 2009), witnessed this developing and rapid success, and this has been tangible proof to Muslims ever since that strictly observing the writings of the Qur'an and following the examples as demonstrated by the Prophet will guarantee a just and peaceable society, together with the associated cultural, military and political supremacy of the Islamic world (Burke, 2003). Therefore, the texts and the examples set by the very first generations of Muslims provide almost a template of authenticity and pure Islamic society to contemporary followers and, in the context of the political element within Islam, are an extremely powerful resource. For some, the ideology of the *Salafists* is considered to be one of the key causes of violent extremism (Baker, 2008).

It is in situations like this that Muslims can justifiably claim that Islam is first and foremost a peaceful religion and that the Qur'an teaches a passive approach to living, which during the lifetime of Mohammed brought peace and stability to what had been a violent society.

The original texts of the Qur'an and the texts gathered by the followers of Mohammed – the hadith – are considered to be 'closed', in that they are metaphorically speaking set in stone. Another feature of these texts is that they are also flexible by offering prima facie solutions to all situations and this further illustrates how Islam is always politically engaged, as it allows non-conformist groups within the Islamic world to appeal to the purity of this earlier society and religious-political order, based upon the true and bona fide reading of the Qur'an (Burke, 2003).

To apply this ideology to practice, it means that there is a clear answer, based on the theology of the Qur'an and an associated programme for action, for any political issue. If the problem elements are addressed and dealt with, a fair and just society will be formulated (Burke, 2003).

The Qur'an dates from the seventh century and its teachings are being applied in the twenty-first century, which leaves it open to criticism that it is applying medieval solutions to contemporary problems that could not have been envisaged at the time. For Muslims, this has been addressed by the interpretation of both the Qur'an and the Sunna via the aforementioned process of tafseer, or exegesis (Husain, 2007) – the critical explanation of a text, in this case a religious one. Muslims are encouraged by this in the knowledge that Mohammed overtly welcomed reasoned argument, which led to a consensus ruling over the issues that were not specifically referred to in the Qur'an. This process is known as the *ijtihad*, which means 'the effort to interpret' and comes from the same root within Arabic as *jihad* (Burke, 2003). Although the religion does not recognise clergy with official powers in this regard, a body of specialists emerged who are known as the *ulema*,'the learned' (Burke, 2003). This perhaps goes some way to understanding how so-called 'radical' Muslim clergy within modern-day Islam have been able to preach their message with some authority and appeal to a small minority within the faith.

Like any religion (and Christianity is no exception to these internal fissures, for example with the ordination of women), Islam has witnessed numerous reformist movements proffering the message of a return to the Qur'an and the Prophet's teachings.

Sunni and Shi'a

One of these involves the split between *Sunni* and *Shi'a* branches of Islam, which occurred within a century of the death of the Prophet. The Shi'as argue that only a direct descendant of the Prophet should be appointed as *caliph*, the leader of the umma, and to do otherwise is a corruption of the Message. As Islam has a clear and distinct political element and schisms such as this have a social and political component to them, many academics argue that this was based on the ethnic divisions between the Persians, now known as Iranians, and the Arabs (Burke, 2003).

This has some clear resonance today and, in recent times, the most famous Shi'a leader was Ayatollah (term for a leading Shi'a scholar) Ruhollah Khomeni of Iran, who came to power in 1979 in an Islamic revolution. Furthermore, Western press and intelligence often cite Iranian support for beleaguered Shi'a minorities in countries such as Iraq, where until recently the ruling party led by Saddam Hussein was Sunni-dominated, and 80 per cent of the world's Muslims are Sunni (Burleigh, 2009). There are numerous other examples of this that cannot be explored here.

Sword verses

While the earliest writings in the Qur'an were very much associated with pacifism and were delivered between AD 610 and 623, urging peace and spreading the message accordingly, verses added later, when Mohammed was well established as the Prophet of Islam, commanded a fight against unbelievers: *fight and slay the pagans wherever ye find them and seize them, beleaguer them and lie in wait for them* (Burke, 2003, p31). These are known as the 'Sword' verses of the Qur'an; for some within Islam, such as the contemporary radicals, they supersede the peaceful and original verses. At first appearance the above seems fairly unequivocal; however, there are verses in the Qur'an that support freedom of religion and freedom of expression (Rehman, 2010).

Jihad

Often associated with the 'Sword' verses is the word *jihad*, which actually means 'strain, effort, struggle or striving'. This is a response to tyranny, or *zulm*', which is the opposite of justice (Burke, 2003), a key ideological objective within Islam. Jihad is a word we often hear associated with radical Islam nowadays and conjures up images of Taliban fighters. Again, this has been open to interpretation historically, based on various readings of the Qur'an set in a political context, and there are defensive and offensive elements in the contemporary understanding of jihad (Burke, 2003).

In respect of the contemporary radicals, such as we have witnessed with Osama bin Laden and other proponents of jihad in an offensive context, their ideology is influenced by Syed Qutb, an Egyptian writing in the early 1960s who is seen as the main visionary of modern Sunni Islamic radicalisation and an ardent anti-Westerner (Husain, 2007).

It is worth reflecting on this word 'jihad' and its many meanings. For example, the struggle to be a good Muslim in a material world full of trial and temptation is jihad. It is incorrect to see jihad as a means of attaining a specific worldly goal and this is critical in understanding why acts such as suicide bombings occur. Acts of jihad are demonstrations of faith for God by an individual. The short-term aims or adversaries are irrelevant, as jihad is part of a wider cosmic struggle and victory may be centuries or thousands of years away; it is the importance of the act, not the results. Jihad is an eternal process of demonstrating faith that should be performed by all Muslims at all times (Burke, 2003).

As identified within this chapter so far in respect of the 'flexibility' of key Islamic texts, for example the application of seventh-century writings in the Qur'an and the hadith to twenty-first-century contexts, jihad is transferable to any geographic or political situation.

The issue of justice has been a key feature so far in this historic overview of Islamic theology and radical thought. It is worth exploring further as it may provide some insight as to why individuals become radicalised and resort to extremism.

Osama bin Laden consistently referred to the 'humiliation' of the umma, the wider Muslim community. The objective is not world domination but world leadership by the umma, reflecting the political, cultural, military and social ascendancy of Muslims between the time of Mohammed and the Renaissance in Europe. Clearly, this has not happened in a contemporary world and this thwarted aspiration and sense of injustice is crucial in motivating substantial revolutionary political action – not absolute deprivation (Burke, 2003), but what we call *relative deprivation*.

Relative deprivation

The concept of relative deprivation is a key element within contemporary criminological theory known as Left Realism. It is the perceived level of deprivation within a specific social group that an individual is identified with, in relation to other social groups (Blake et al., 2010) and draws heavily on Strain Theory, written by Robert Merton in 1938 (Blake et al., 2010), who at the time was writing about *strains* within American society, brought about by economic inequality and racism.

In the case of Muslims, especially poignant in a globalised world with immediate media and internet access, where they can see other social groups are being more favourably rewarded or are more dominant either politically, militarily, economically or culturally, a sense of injustice is likely to occur and perhaps a motivating one towards radicalisation and ultimately extremism in an attempt to right the perceived wrong.

1979: A significant year

The year 1979 was critical in the Middle East, with the Islamic revolution in Iran; in December of the same year the Soviet Union invaded Afghanistan and finally abandoned the invasion in February 1989 after 15,000 Soviet troops had lost their lives (Rumsfeld, 2011). It was a humiliating defeat for the Soviets who believed that their military was invincible; however, they had been defeated by the *Mujahidin* (holy warriors), who were aggrieved by this invasion of an Islamic country and answered the call from across the Muslim world to join the *Mujahidin* and defeat the aggressor.

This emboldened the Islamic fighters, who would have been aware of the following from a chapter (*sura*) in the Qur'an: *Many a small band has, by God's grace, vanquished a mighty army. God is with those who endure with fortitude* (Burke, 2003, p36).

Unsurprisingly, bin Laden referred to this in his many media broadcasts to the wider world and this ideology, based on writings in the Qur'an, is obviously both motivating and instilling a sense of invincibility into the Taliban fighters in Afghanistan in the contemporary conflict, and is congruent with the issue of justice/injustice that is prominent within Islam.

Following the Soviet withdrawal, Saudi Arabia and Pakistan funded roads, hospitals and religious schools known as *madrassas* and, in the case of Pakistan in particular, cultivated Afghanistan's Pashtun warlords (Rumsfeld, 2011).

Matters that appeared to be fairly innocuous at the time, after Afghanistan was largely left to its own devices, have emerged as major motivating factors in radicalisation and extremism within Muslim youths in particular and the UK has witnessed this first hand.

Support framework for radicalisation

Parts of Pakistan have become incubators for radical Islamic extremism and the UK, with its close historical and cultural links, has been a victim to some of the extremist ideology that has emanated from within Pakistan's borders.

Following the Soviet exit from Afghanistan, with which Pakistan shares an 850-mile border known as the Durand Line, drawn up in an 1893 agreement, many members of al-Qaeda (AQ) relocated to the mountain areas of this border region, especially the semi-autonomous Federally Administered Tribal Areas (FATA), situated in the North West Frontier Province (NWFP). This is home to some 3.2 million, mostly tribal, people and constitutes the seven main tribes. The FATA is organised into seven tribal 'agencies' – Khyber, Bajaur, Mohmand, Orakzai, Kurram, and North and South Waziristan (Musharraf, 2006) (see Figure 9.1).

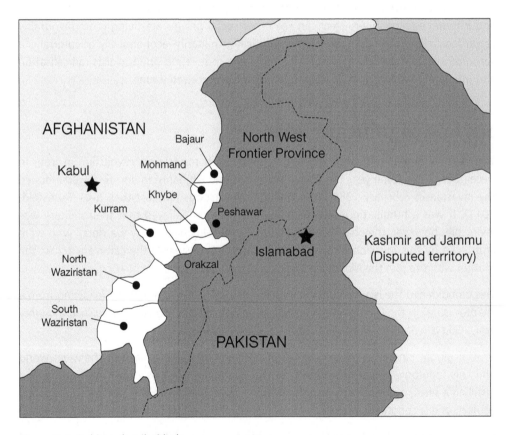

Figure 9.1 Pakistan's tribal belt

PRACTICAL TASK

The Durand Line perhaps has more significance now than at any other time since its inception. Complete an internet search into the emergence of the Durand Line and answer the following questions.

1. Who is it named after?

2. Who was he?

3. What nationality was he?

4. Which year was the agreement signed?

5. Between which countries was it agreed?

(See Appendix A on page 190 for answers.)

Although the Taliban are from Afghanistan, they emanate from the same ethnic stock as the Pakistani Pathans (Musharraf, 2006), a cultural bond that must strengthen any ideological link between them.

The first anti-terrorism operation (Tora Bora) in this area post-9/11, launched by the USA with the cooperation of Pakistan, netted 240 AQ fighters, fleeing the initial American efforts in Afghanistan (Musharraf, 2006).

Following 9/11, new terrorist groups aligned to the AQ political ideology began to emerge and form alliances, largely within the FATA. One of these is Tehrik-e-Taliban Pakistan (TTP), formed on 14 December 2007 (Gunaratna and Iqbal, 2011). This group had a direct input into the London 7/7 bombings and the TTP's main spokesman, Maulvi Omar, confirmed in August 2008 that the operation was planned from Bajaur Agency in the FATA (Gunaratna and Iqbal, 2011). FATA has become the centre of global terrorism which, given the ethnic links between the UK and Pakistan, constitutes considerable concern to UK authorities.

Key to spreading the AQ message to the masses are the madrassas (Hamilton and Rimsa, 2007). Madrassas are religious schools and were formed in the mid-nineteenth century by the tradition within Islam that bases its belief on a very strict interpretation of the Qur'an, reveres the aforementioned ulema, 'the learned', and acknowledges the latter's adjudication in textual interpretation. Students at madrassas are known as *taliban*, which is a Persian plural of the Arabic word *talib*, meaning a seeker of knowledge or student. In 1879 there were 12 madrassas; by 1967 there were almost a thousand in Pakistan, many in the Pashtun areas of the NWFP and, during the 1980s, almost 400,000 young males were being educated in Pakistan by the Deobandi tradition within Islam (Burke, 2003).

State education within Pakistan often suffers from lack of funding for crucial basic elements such as teachers and buildings. Madrassas became an attractive alternative offering both free education and accommodation, mainly to the masses, who make up those who are economically marginalised and those failed by the modern Pakistan state, although teaching methods were fairly rudimentary and based on rote learning. They catered mainly for the impoverished rural classes and those attending madrassas in the NWFP were drawn from villages with a population of under 10,000. Following on from the Soviet withdrawal from Afghanistan, and with Islamic militants clearly buoyed by those events, the recruits to the wider Islamic militancy were clearly coming from the poorer social classes (Burke, 2003).

The sheer numbers of young men that had attended the madrassas had an immediate impact on militants further afield via the narrow, dogmatic and narrow perception of Islam and the world that is readily identified within the modern militant (Burke, 2003).

AQ recruits at local mosques and madrassas (Hamilton and Rimsa, 2007) and, for some, madrassas are the key to spreading AQ's message to the masses and provide a source for economic aid in addition to providing a 'hearts and minds' campaign. Mosques are crucial too and, according to a 1999 report by the Islamic Council of America, 80 per cent of 3,000 mosques across the USA were controlled by extremists (Hamilton and Rimsa, 2007).

As part of their response to 9/11, the Government of Pakistan recognised that there was a problem with some of the 14,000 madrassas across their country and tacitly acknowledged that some of them were involved in terrorism and extremism. As an initial response, the Government implemented a normal curriculum specified by the education board with the Government only funding madrassas that complied with this policy direction; however, it appeared that some 20 per cent of madrassas were still in the hands of extremists (Musharraf, 2006).

In February 2011 an undercover report by the UK Channel 4 television programme, *Dispatches*, secretly filmed teachers and older pupils teaching boys as young as six to deride UK values and preaching religious intolerance at a Deobandi school in Birmingham, and at an after-school madrassa at Keighley in West Yorkshire. About 700 of the UK's 1,500 mosques are aligned to the Deobandi tradition, which produces about 80 per cent of UK-trained Muslim clerics (Norfolk, 2011).

The 7/7 bombings involved UK citizens with definitive links to the FATA in Pakistan. In addition, the thwarted London attack of July 2005 and the attack on Glasgow airport in 2007 were perpetrated by Muslims resident and predominantly born in the UK (Thomas, 2010).

Other events that have occurred over the past ten years in the UK strongly suggest that there is a generation of Muslim youths who are disenfranchised from mainstream UK values, and the violent disturbances in Oldham, Burnley and Bradford in 2001 (Thomas, 2010) underpin that assertion and give considerable succour to the concepts of relative deprivation and Strain Theory within criminology (Blake et al., 2010). Events in Pakistan and the wider Muslim world are no longer a million miles away and need to be viewed with immediacy and in real time.

To the disenfranchised and the economically marginalised Muslim youth in the UK, the message of radicalisation as proffered by legitimate and respected institutions such as mosques and madrassas *may* offer a credible alternative to many of the apparently insurmountable grievances within the Islamic world, as well as a virtuous resolution to perceived injustice and discrimination within the UK and its role in the contemporary globalised world.

Following the disturbances in Oldham, Burnley and Bradford in 2001 a number of official reports, notably by Professor Cantle and Lord Ouseley, expressed views as to why these events occurred. Other academic papers focusing on the disturbances have since been published and are available online. Carry out some research, read some of the reports/ papers and consider why the findings suggested that an atmosphere was being generated that contributed to the development of radicalisation within communities.

Steps to radicalisation

Before considering how individuals become radicalised, it is prudent to consider some definitions of what radicalisation is or what it leads to.

'Radicalisation' is defined as *the process by which people adopt an interpretation of religious, political and ideological belief that ultimately leads them to legitimising the use of violence* (Staniforth, 2010, p31). Also, *radicalisation refers to the process or processes, whereby individuals or groups come to approve of and ultimately participate in the use of violence for political aims* (International Centre for the Study of Radicalisation and Political Violence, 2009, p10, cited in Archetti, 2010).

Terrorism is the ultimate consequence of the radicalization process (Silber and Bhatt, 2007, p16). The authors are senior intelligence analysts with the New York Police Department (NYPD) and undertook research in this area. They provide a four-step model for radicalisation that is discussed later in the chapter.

CASE STUDY

Canada

In Toronto, in June 2006, 17 young Muslim males, all Canadian citizens, were charged with offences under the Anti-Terrorism Act and later became known as the 'Toronto 17'. They were due to receive a shipment of three tonnes of ammonium nitrate at a warehouse north of Toronto; fortunately the Royal Canadian Mounted Police (RCMP) national investigators had intercepted the delivery and the biggest North American terrorist operation since 9/11 was successfully thwarted (Bell, 2007).

For AQ, Canada is an attractive venue, with long borders and coastlines that offer multiple points of entry, together with ease of travel into the USA, especially with a Canadian passport. Furthermore, there are many potential targets with numerous American-owned corporations, and Canadian immigration laws have historically been favourable towards political refugees. Between 2001 and 2007, 15,000 persons falling into this category have arrived in Canada, including 2,500 from states that sponsor terrorism or are subject to domestic terrorism (Hamilton and Rimsa, 2007).

Some of the allegations against the 'Toronto 17' shocked Canadians: a training camp in the Canadian woods; plots to blow up the Toronto Stock Exchange and the headquarters of the Canadian Secret Intelligence Service (CSIS) in Toronto; and plans to storm the Parliament building and take high-profile hostages, including the Prime Minister, and threaten to behead them unless Canada withdrew its troops from Afghanistan (Bell, 2007).

A declassified CSIS report revealed that a 'high percentage' of Islamic extremists in Canada now are Canadian-born and had become radicalised there; this was homegrown terrorism, which has evolved considerably, especially since 9/11 (Bell, 2007).

REFLECTIVE TASK

Go online to http://news.bbc.co.uk/1/hi/world/americas/5044560.stm, which provides a BBC report regarding the 'Toronto 17'. Read the news article, reflect on what has been covered in the chapter so far, and consider why the Toronto 17 became radicalised and chose the path of violent extremism.

A model for radicalisation

Table 8.1 provides a four-stage model for the radicalisation process and the authors suggest that, if an individual passes through all four stages, the likelihood is that a terrorist act will occur (Silber and Bhatt, 2007).

Table 9.1 Stages of radicalisation

Stage 1	Pre-radicalisation
Stage 2	Self-identification
Stage 3	Indoctrination
Stage 4	Jihadisation

Source: Silber and Bhatt (2007, p19)

It is not possible within the parameters of this chapter to look at each stage in detail; however, it is highly recommended that the document published by Silber and Bhatt (2007) is accessed and considered (see 'Useful websites'). Some key points will be briefly discussed and will act as a precursor to the next section of the chapter.

In Stage 2 (Self-identification) the following practices *may* be an indicator that an individual has embarked on the road to radicalisation, but has not yet arrived at the final destination:

- rejection of one's former life; mixing with like-minded individuals;
- joining a group that follows a particular strain of Islam;
- giving up cigarettes, alcohol, gambling and other 'Western' leisure pursuits;
- wearing traditional Islamic dress or growing a beard;
- becoming involved in social activism and community issues.

The NYPD model is merely an aide-memoire for those involved in counter-terrorism and disruption of pre-radicalisation activities. The model retains considerable credibility, although applying the theory to practical situations is likely to be far more difficult.

It is to that task that we now turn, focusing on the Prevent strand of the UK counter-terrorism strategy (CONTEST).

Preventing radicalisation and violent extremism

The Prevent strand is concerned with the causes of violent extremism and the vulnerability of those who may be attracted to it, and is perceived to be a long-term and community-based activity (Bettison, 2009).

At first glance, it may not be fully appreciated as to why the Police Service is directly involved in this type of activity; however, parallels are drawn with the successful drugs education programmes that police operate with other agencies, addressing the demand side of the problem. This is an extremely sensitive area in which to operate and the ACPO Prevent strategy has been formulated to guard against insensitive operational policing activity in pursuing terrorists, in order that tensions with police in minority communities are avoided (Bettison, 2009).

While that may be the overall intention, other measures designed at defeating terrorist activity have been implemented that have had the opposite response from ethnic communities and they will be discussed later in the chapter. This is a lesson that the Police Service overall should have taken on board from their experiences during and after the 1981 inner-city disturbances and the subsequent reports from Scarman in 1981 and Macpherson in 1999.

During the 30 years that have passed since the 1981 disturbances, mainly afflicting inner-city areas with ethnic minorities, it has taken copious amounts of hard work and good will on both sides of the equation to rebuild police legitimacy and community confidence.

One of the more recent successful initiatives is the move towards neighbourhood policing, which involves some 3,500 neighbourhood teams across England and Wales. It is these teams that primarily deliver the Prevent strategy. Operational police officers have received briefings in this area, including how the key role of neighbourhood policing contributes to the strategy.

Neighbourhood policing is delivered in partnership with other key agencies, such as the local authorities, schools, youth workers and community groups. The Prevent strategy is no exception and calls upon a multi-agency approach in order to identify radicalisation and, if necessary, put in place measures designed to prevent it. In practice, when an individual is highlighted as being at risk, a multi-agency case conference is arranged and is structured on a basis similar to that convened under the child-protection system. It is a forum where all agencies freely consider the evidence, the options available and the most appropriate action to address the problem. Neighbourhood policing teams play a key role and need to engender the confidence of those within the community.

Mainly, the interventions are not police or judicial ones, but lead rather to counselling, mentoring or challenge, which incorporates school, parents or mosque and community representatives (Bettison, 2009). This work is taken up by what has become known as Project Channel, designed to support people at risk of being manipulated into participating in terrorism (Roberts, 2009). Neighbourhood policing relies heavily on community engagement and this Prevent role could be considered by the onlooker as 'Neighbourhood Policing Plus' (Bettison, 2009).

REFLECTIVE TASK

Neighbourhood policing is clearly a key function in preventing violent extremism by building links with the community and working together with other partners.

Consider what other agencies or partners are crucial in this role, and how they can contribute to reducing the problem of radicalisation and violent extremism.

Community engagement and cooperation can be compromised by certain incidents and events, such as the use of CCTV cameras in Sparkbrook, Birmingham (see the case study on the Safer Birmingham Project in Chapter 8, page 125). Another example is the high-profile raid in Forest Gate, London, in 2006, when the Metropolitan Police, while executing a search warrant under the Terrorism Act, shot and wounded one of the two male Muslim residents. Both were arrested, but were later released without charge and the raid appeared to have been totally unjustified, a fact not lost on Assistant Commissioner Ghaffur, then the highest-ranking Muslim police officer in the country, who cautioned that an incident like this:

> *drip feeds into vulnerable communities and gradually erodes confidence and trust; the impact of this will be just at the time we need the confidence and trust of these communities, they may retreat within themselves.*

> (Pantazis and Pemberton, 2009, p659)

Despite the very best efforts of neighbourhood policing under Prevent, and officers and other partners operating in that environment, it appears that Muslim communities are the new 'enemy within' (Pantazis and Pemberton, 2009). This was confirmed by the then Minister Hazel Blears in her evidence to the Home Affairs Select Committee in 2005:

> *The fact that at the moment the threat is most likely to come from those people associated with an extreme form of Islam, all falsely hiding behind Islam, if you like, in terms of justifying their activities, inevitably means that some of our counter-terrorist powers will be disproportionately experienced by people in the Muslim community. That is the reality of the situation.*

> (Pantazis and Pemberton, 2009, p658)

It appears that Muslims are now a 'suspect' community, perceived that way by the public and police alike. This has laid them open as targets for hate crime, motivated simply by the hatred of Islam and the activities of an extremely small minority within the Muslim community.

In the three-week period following 7/7 there were 269 religious hate crimes compared with 40 during the same period in 2004 (Pantazis and Pemberton, 2009). While this could be seen as somewhat of an aberration in the immediate aftermath of 7/7, the Muslim Council of UK provided this evidence to the Home Affairs Committee:

Victimisation of Muslims under the anti-terrorism legislation has led to increased incidences of Islam phobia and racism against Muslims. This has manifested itself in the form of vandalism of mosques, Muslim graves and homes. The increased hostility towards Muslims has also seen an increase in hate campaigns against Islam and Muslims from far right groups (HAC 2005: Vol. 2, ev. 30).

(Pantazis and Pemberton, 2009, p661)

While the neighbourhood policing model under Prevent offers opportunities for enhanced relationships with Muslim communities and fosters the type of relationship that is crucial in encouraging mutual trust that will result in credible information or intelligence regarding persons at-risk of radicalisation, other policing strategies are at odds with this approach.

High-profile events such as 7/7 have resulted in the Muslim community at large being perceived as involved in terrorism. This has coalesced into a situation where Islamic communities are victims of some police strategies (e.g. stop and search) that are bordering on stereotyping all Muslims as being involved in violent extremism, while at the same time they are themselves being subjected to increased crime, motivated purely by hate.

This needs to be addressed, especially when some very effective strategies have originated from within the Muslim community itself, as in the case of the Brixton mosque. The media coverage of the mosque featured radical preachers such as Abu Hamza giving sermons outside in the street, and the mosque was linked with extremism.

The mosque elected a new administration, which involved several new measures such as setting up a trust status with elected trustees, purchasing the actual building, preventing unofficial study groups and challenging the extremist ideologies publicly in sermons (Baker, 2008). These measures were seen as being effective and discouraged known extremists from attending the Brixton mosque.

Another facet of the problem is online radicalisation, with the onset of 24/7 media and the internet bringing the influence of radicals based in areas like the FATA in Pakistan a lot closer. To counter this, in 2010 ACPO established a Counter Terrorism Internet Referral Unit (CTIRU) with a view to blocking attempts to radicalise people online. Their task is simple – to scan the internet and remove inappropriate sites from servers by using terrorist legislation (Blain, 2011).

PRACTICAL TASK

To conclude this chapter, research the internet to find out more about the problem of radicalisation in UK prisons and universities, establish what strategies are being adopted and assess their effectiveness.

C H A P T E R   S U M M A R Y

This chapter has looked at some of the key Islamic texts that inspire radicalisation and violent extremism. It has also identified some of the major events that have triggered an upsurge in this aspect of the Islamic religion. The close links between the UK and Pakistan have been discussed, along with the fact that it is not just the USA and UK that have witnessed an upsurge in extremism, but that it is a global phenomenon.

Neighbourhood policing and a multi-agency approach have been identified as key elements of the Prevent strategy, along with the need to develop good relations with the community to inspire confidence and maximise intelligence opportunities.

Within the final chapter, details are provided about a new Prevent strategy, published by the Government in June 2011 following a review by Lord Carlile of Berriew, who found a number of failings in the 2009 strategy:

> *It confused the delivery of Government policy to promote integration with Government policy to prevent terrorism. It failed to confront the extremist ideology at the heart of the threat we face; and in trying to reach those at risk of radicalisation, funding sometimes even reached the very extremist organisations that Prevent should have been confronting.*
>
> (Carlile, 2011, p1)

REFERENCES

Archetti, C (2010) *Constructing the AQ Narrative: Media and Communications in the Radicalisation Process*. New Orleans: International Studies Convention, February, 2010.

Baker, AH (2008) A View From the Inside. *Criminal Justice Matters*, 73: 24–5.

Bell, S (2007) Cold Terror: Toronto, Canada: John Wiley & Sons.

Bettison, Sir Norman (2009) Better than Cure. *Police Review*, 6 November.

Blain, M (2011) Terrorism Trawlers. *Police Review*, 20 May.

Blake, C, Sheldon, B and Williams, P (2010) *Policing and Criminal Justice*. Exeter: Learning Matters.

Burke, J (2003) *Al-Qaeda: Casting A Shadow of Terror*. London: IB Tauris.

Burleigh, M (2009) *Blood and Rage: A Cultural History of Terrorism*. London: Harper Perennial.

Carlile of Berriew, Lord (2011) *Prevent Strategy*. Available online at www.homeoffice.gov.uk/publications/counter-terrorism/prevent/prevent-strategy/lord-carlile-report?view=Binary (accessed 20 September 2011).

Gunaratna, R and Iqbal, K (2011) *Pakistan: Terrorism Ground Zero*. London: Reaktion Books.

Hamilton, D and Rimsa, K (2007) *Terror Alert: International and Home-grown Terrorists and their Threat to Canada*. Toronto: Dundurn Press.

Hewitt, S (2008) *The UK War On Terror.* London: Continuum.

Husain, E (2007) *The Islamist.* London: Penguin.

Musharraf, P (2006) *In the Line of Fire: A Memoir.* London: Simon and Schuster.

Norfolk, A (2010) Hate and Violence Taught at Muslim Schools. *The Times*, 12 February.

Pantazis, C and Pemberton, S (2009) From the Old to the New Suspect Community. *UK Journal of Criminology*, 49(5), September: 646–66.

Rehman, J (2010) Freedom of Expression, Apostasy, and Blasphemy within Islam: Sharia, Criminal Justice Systems and Modern Islamic State Practices. *Criminal Justice Matters*, 79: 4–5.

Roberts, S (2009) Ideas to Prevent. *Police Review*, 9 July.

Rumsfeld, D (2011) *Known and Unknown: A Memoir.* London: Penguin Books.

Silber, M and Bhatt, A (2007) *Radicalisation in the West: The Homegrown Threat.* New York: New York City Police Department.

Staniforth, A (2010) Tackling Terrorism – Anti-Terrorism Training: Prisons. *Police Review*, 4 June.

Thomas, P(2010) Failed and Friendless: The UK's 'Preventing Violent Extremism' Programme. *The UK Journal of Politics and International Relations*, 12: 442–58.

USEFUL WEBSITES

http://news.bbc.co.uk/1/hi/world/americas/5044560.stm (*BBC News* (2006): Canada Charges 17 Terror Suspects)

www.homeoffice.gov.uk/counter-terrorism/review-of-prevent-strategy (Home Office – Prevent strategy)

www.icsr.info (International Centre for the Study of Radicalisation and Political Violence)

www.microconflict.eu/publications/PWP7_RB_JB.pdf (*Radicalisation among Muslims in the UK* – 2009 report)

The following two sites have details of Silber and Bhatt's radicalisation model (2007):

http://publicintelligence.net/nypd-radicalization-in-the-west-the-homegrown-threat

www.nypdshield.org/public/SiteFiles/documents/NYPD_Report-Radicalization_in_the_West.pdf

10 Protecting the UK and preparing for an attack

Barrie Sheldon

CHAPTER OBJECTIVES

By the end of this chapter you should be able to:

- outline UK protective counter-terrorism measures;
- analyse the impact and effectiveness of some of the protective measures adopted;
- understand how the UK prepares for terrorist attacks;
- analyse the impact and effectiveness of the UK's preparedness for a terrorist attack.

Introduction

Previous chapters having explored the 'Pursue' and 'Prevent' elements of CONTEST; this chapter examines the remaining two strands, 'Protect' and 'Prepare'.

The threat of terrorism from various sources is a clear and present danger and it is the state's responsibility to put measures in place to protect the country and its interests overseas from attack. The current Protect strategy aims to:

- *strengthen UK border security;*

- *reduce the vulnerability of the transport network;*

- *increase the resilience of the UK's infrastructure; and*

- *improve protective security for crowded places.*

(Home Office, 2011, p82)

These aims will be explored in more detail below and examples will be provided of protective measures both currently in place and under development.

The UK has much experience of dealing with terrorist attacks, such as those during the prolonged Irish terrorist campaign, the Lockerbie airliner attack and, more recently, the attack on the London transport system on 7 July 2005. The state's primary purpose is to prevent attacks, but it also has the responsibility to ensure that it is able to respond effectively to a terrorist attack. The current Prepare strategy aims to:

- continue to build generic capabilities to respond to and recover from a wide range of terrorist and other civil emergencies;

- improve preparedness for the highest impact risks in the National Risk Assessment;

- improve the ability of the emergency services to work together during a terrorist attack; and

- enhance communications and information sharing for terrorist attacks.

(Home Office, 2011, p98)

Elements of the Prepare strand and its supporting structures are explored in the second half of the chapter, together with how the UK is preparing to face emerging threats, such as the use of chemical, biological, radiological and nuclear (CBRN) weapons.

Protect

Following the terrorist attack on Glasgow airport in June 2007 (see pages 76–7) the Government instructed Lord West (Under-secretary of State for Security and Counter-terrorism) to carry out a review, which produced a new strategic framework for 'Protect' containing eight sectors:

- critical national infrastructure;

- crowded places;

- transport systems;

- UK border;

- hazardous sites and substances;

- hostile insider action;

- individuals at risk of being targeted by terrorists;

- UK interests overseas.

Each of these sectors will be explored in turn.

Critical national infrastructure

PRACTICAL TASK

Consider the phrase 'national infrastructure' and compile a list of facilities that a terrorist could attack to cause major disruption or serious loss of life.

The list compiled should have included a range of services essential to the public. Not everything within the national infrastructure is critical, so it is necessary to identify critical elements (assets) that, if attacked, could result in a large loss of life or have a severe economic or social impact. The critical assets make up the CNI and are referred to individually as 'infrastructure assets'. Infrastructure assets may be physical such as sites, installations and equipment, or logical such as information networks and systems (CPNI, 2011).

In 2007 a Centre for the Protection of National Infrastructure (CPNI) was introduced, with the aim of reducing the vulnerability of the national infrastructure to threats from terrorism and espionage. The role of the CPNI is to provide advice to national infrastructure sectors about protective security. There are nine sectors within the national infrastructure and Table 10.1 outlines the sectors and their respective departments, who work directly with the CPNI.

In 2009 it was reported that the CPNI had provided security advice training and threat briefings to over 200 CNI organisations and 2,000 people from public and private organisations across the national infrastructure. Topics included within the advice and training included hostile vehicle mitigation, detection systems, barriers and access control, CCTV and pre-employment screening (Home Office, 2009).

Table 10.1 National infrastructure sectors

Communications	Emergency services	Energy
Department for Business Innovation and Skills (BIS)	*Police* – Home Office (HO)	Department for Energy and Climate Change (DECC)
	Fire – Department for Communities and Local Government (CLG)	
	Ambulance – Department of Health (DH)	
	Maritime and Coastguard Agency – Department for Transport (DfT)	
Finance	**Food**	**Government**
HM Treasury (HMT)	Department for the Environment, Food and Rural Affairs (Defra)	Cabinet Office (CO)
	Food Standards Agency (FSA)	
Health	**Transport**	**Water**
Department of Health (DH)	Department for Transport (DfT)	Department for the Environment, Food and Rural Affairs (Defra)

Source: Adapted from CPNI (2011)

Crowded places

The National Counter Terrorism Security Office (NaCTSO) is a police unit based within the CPNI with responsibility for both Protect and Prepare strands of CONTEST (see Table 10.2). One of its roles is to provide advice for the security of crowded places, hazardous materials and transport. NaCTSO has over 250 counter-terrorism security advisers (CTSAs) and, in 2008/09, 70 were recruited for a governmental Crowded Places programme (Home Office, 2009).

Table 10.2 NaCTSO's areas of operation

Crowded places	Bars, pubs and clubs
	Shopping centres
	Stadia and arenas
	Visitor attractions
	Cinemas and theatres
	Hotels and restaurants
	Major events
	Commercial centres
	Education
	Health
	Places of worship
Hazardous materials	Radioactive materials
	Pathogens and toxins
	Precursor chemicals (e.g. fertiliser)
Transport security	Land
	Maritime
	Aviation

Since May 2006 it has provided advice to over 500 sports stadia, 600 shopping centres and 10,000 city/town bars and nightclubs, and has delivered over 700 scenario-based training exercises (Project Argus) to city/town centre businesses for protection against terrorist attacks (Home Office, 2009).

The Government has provided a strategic framework to reduce the vulnerability of crowded places to terrorist attack. Advice and guidance is also available for key partners, such as local government, planning authorities and police and business leaders, to develop robust and effective counter-terrorism measures.

PRACTICAL TASK

Go to the NaCTSO website (www.nactso.gov.uk/AreaOfRisks/CrowdedPlaces.aspx) and download the document Working Together to Protect Crowded Places *(March 2010). Explore the document and establish the key principles of the strategy, the range of organisations involved in protecting crowded places, the process of risk assessment, and the range of security measures identified as effective.*

CASE STUDY

Protecting crowded places

Old Trafford
On 19 April 2004 an anti-terrorist operation was executed in the north-west in which officers from Greater Manchester Police, members of the security services and the Metropolitan Police anti-terrorist branch arrested 10 Muslims of North African and Kurdish origin.

The media, responding to rumours, reported that the arrests were in connection with a plot to carry out a terrorist attack at Old Trafford – the home of Manchester United football club, who were due to play Liverpool shortly after the arrests were made.

> After 10 days in custody, all 10 were released without charge. The raids were prompted by 'credible intelligence' that consisted of Manchester United posters, used ticket stubs and a fixture list that had been seized in one of the raids. It later transpired that those arrested were Manchester United fans who happened to be Muslims.
>
> (Ansari, 2004, p11)

Fertiliser bomb plot
On 30 April 2007 five men were jailed for life at the Old Bailey, London, for conspiracy to cause explosions. They had attempted to purchase large quantities of fertiliser to make a bomb big enough to cause mass devastation. Their potential targets included a major shopping centre, the utilities network, a nightclub, Parliament and a football stadium, but fortunately, acting on intelligence, the security services mounted an operation (Crevice) and arrested the men before their plan could come to fruition. Detailed information about

the plot, the investigation and the perpetrators are contained in a BBC special report that can be found at http://news.bbc.co.uk/1/hi/in_depth/uk/2007/fertiliser_bomb_plot.

REFLECTIVE TASK

Reflect on the implications of the two case studies in relation to the challenge faced by the security services, the onus of responsibility for those who own and manage the venues, and the community impact of making arrests that are later unsubstantiated.

Transport systems

The transport system provides an attractive target for terrorists and requires considerable measures to be taken to reduce the terrorist threat. The aim of the counter-terrorism strategy for transport is to reduce risk of attack, increase resilience to attack, achieve minimal disruptive impact and maintain the confidence of transport users. Table 10.3 outlines some of the measures currently in use to protect the transport system.

Table 10.3 Transport system – protective measures

Transport locations	Examples of measures adopted
Aviation (e.g. airports, aircraft)	In-flight armed police capability
	Strengthening of cabin doors
	Restriction on liquids
	Security of landside areas
	Electronic scanning
	Passenger screening
	Explosive trace detection
	Behaviour analysis
Maritime (e.g. ports, containers, ships)	Intruder alarm systems
	Access control systems
	Container-scanning technology
	Radiation scanning (Operation Cyclamen)
	Long-range acoustic devices (LRADs)
	Gamma and neutron sensitivity scanning
	Surveillance systems and radar
Railways and London Underground (e.g. rolling stock, rail track, stations)	Explosive detection devices
	Explosive sniffer dogs
	CCTV
	Scanning devices
	Vehicle access controls
	Barriers

The measures highlighted illustrate the range of equipment that is available to security services but these are not exclusive to each section, such as CCTV, which is used at all locations. The Government recognises that science and technology have a key part to play in developing effective counter-terrorism measures and works with both industry and academia to develop new ideas. The current UK science and technology strategy identifies seven areas key to reducing the terrorist threat:

- *understanding the causes of radicalisation;*
- *protecting the national infrastructure;*
- *reducing the vulnerability of crowded places;*
- *protecting against cyber terrorism;*
- *improving analytical tools;*
- *identifying, detecting and countering novel and improvised explosives;*
- *understanding and countering chemical, biological, radiological and nuclear threats.*

(HM Government, 2009, p5)

UK border

The UK Border Agency (UKBA) is an executive agency of the Home Office and was introduced in April 2009, combining a number of organisations to create a single immigration and customs detection force at the border. It is a global organisation with 25,000 staff, including more than 9,000 warranted officers working in local communities, at our borders and in 135 countries worldwide (UKBA, 2011).

The agency has a number of responsibilities, including the prevention of drugs, weapons, terrorists, criminals and would-be illegal immigrants reaching the UK. It uses intelligence, technology, a skilled workforce and a range of UK and international partners to deliver its objectives, which include the protection of our borders and national interests (UKBA, 2010).

New technologies have been introduced, such as biometric visas, travel tracking systems and electronic devices such as facial recognition gates. The Government reported in 2009 that a £1.2 billion e-border system was able to screen over 80 million passengers travelling to the UK from 105 carriers using over 185 routes, resulting in 32,000 alerts and 2,800 arrests for all crimes (Home Office, 2009). It is important that the police work effectively with the UKBA on issues relating to counter-terrorism and organised crime and, to this end, a memorandum of understanding was agreed in April 2008 between the two organisations, UKBA and ACPO. The agreement recognises that the police have primary responsibility for general and protective policing at ports and airports, and that the police Special Branch have primacy for intelligence gathering and interdiction in support of national security (ACPO, 2008).

The threat of terrorists building a dirty bomb using CBRN materials is very real and, in 2003, the Government introduced Operation Cyclamen, which uses fixed and mobile technology to detect, deter and intercept nuclear and radiological material at points of entry to the UK. Detection units can be used by UKBA officers to check ships, vehicles and passengers for traces of plutonium or enriched uranium that can be used to create a dirty bomb.

Hazardous sites and substances

The threat of terrorists using weapons of mass destruction (WMDs) is a real concern and, as technology develops and becomes more accessible globally, the potential use of CBRN weapons by a terrorist group remains a problem. In Chapter 3 (pages 44–6) the possibility of terrorists obtaining and using CBRN weapons was considered and found to be a feasible threat.

History provides examples of CBRN use, such as the Japanese terrorist group 'Aum Shinrikyo', who carried out five coordinated attacks on the Tokyo Metro railway system by releasing a poisonous gas, 'sarin', killing 13 people in March 1995. More recently Ian Davison, a British white supremacist, was convicted in March 2010 at Newcastle Crown Court for producing the deadly poison 'ricin' and preparing for acts of terrorism.

Following a review in 2008 to consider what more could be done to improve the security and storage of legally held chemicals, biological, radiological and explosive substances, an action plan was formulated to provide extra safeguards. The plan includes reducing access to hazardous substances, raising security awareness and identifying gaps within the regulatory regime (Home Office, 2009).

The UK is engaged internationally with other countries to reduce the CBRN terrorist threat. The Global Threat Reduction Programme (GTRP) aims to improve the security of fissile material around the world by reducing the number of sites containing radiological and nuclear material, destroying chemical weapon stocks, and providing sustainable employment to former weapon scientists who could otherwise be used by terrorist groups. The Department of Energy and Climate Change (DECC) is responsible for the programme and produce a yearly report of progress.

PRACTICAL TASK

Go to the DECC website at www.decc.gov.uk/publications, access the publications link and search for the latest GTRP annual report. Download the report and find out how the UK is currently tackling CBRN risks.

Other initiatives within the UK include Operation Cyclamen (see above); NaCTSO and the CPNI providing advice to industry on the security of hazardous materials; and the Office of Security and Counter Terrorism (OSCT) working with the DECC, the Office of Civil Nuclear Security and the Civil Nuclear Constabulary to ensure that the nuclear sector is robust enough to mitigate the terrorist threat.

Hostile insider action

Staff with legitimate access to organisational assets or premises can exploit their position to carry out unauthorised or malicious acts of a criminal nature, including terrorism. Personnel security is essential for any organisation and part of the CPNI role is to provide personnel security advice across the national infrastructure. Issues such as pre-employment screening, personnel security risk assessment and ongoing personnel security are addressed within the advice provided. The Department of Transport provides extensive advice on personnel security and criminal record checks that can be found on their website (see 'Useful websites').

Individuals at risk of being targeted by terrorists

Some terrorist groups choose symbolic targets, such as royalty, state ministers, diplomats and other high-profile public figures. The Home Office is responsible for the protective security of public figures and their residences and is assisted by the Police Service, which has protective duty responsibilities.

The Metropolitan Police have a dedicated Special Operations Department that includes SO15 (Counter Terrorism Command), SO1 and SO14 (Protection Command) and SO2 (Protective Security Command). SO1 provides specialist personal protection for ministers and public officials at threat from terrorism, including visiting heads of government and other public figures. SO14 provides protection for the monarch and other members of the royal family.

UK interests overseas

The Foreign and Commonwealth Office (FCO) is responsible for providing and developing protective measures for UK interests overseas. It provides timely and accurate travel advice on threats from domestic and international terrorism, and advises British companies abroad. It also supports key foreign governments to develop their ability to protect areas such as aviation and maritime security, energy infrastructure, crowded places and 'soft' targets.

PRACTICAL TASK

Go to the FCO foreign travel website at www.fco.gov.uk/en/travel-and-living-abroad/ travel-advice-by-country and check out the extent of the information provided for travellers abroad.

Cyber terrorism

Many definitions of cyber terrorism are offered by governments and academics. One example defines it as unlawful attacks against computers, networks and the information they store with the aim of intimidating or coercing government or its people to achieve certain political or social objectives (Cavelty, 2010). A well-planned cyber attack could have a devastating impact, for example by destroying equipment or shutting down key services such as water, electricity or gas with the potential of loss of life, serious social disruption and economic damage. Imagine the chaos and potential for disaster if air traffic control systems were compromised through a cyber attack.

Within CONTEST the threat of cyber terrorism is assessed as low (Home Office, 2011); however, when the Government published its national security strategy the previous year it highlighted that *cyber security has been assessed as one of the highest priority national security risks to the UK* (HM Government, 2010a, p29).

Another definition of cyber terrorism provided by a US agency (the National Infrastructure Protection Center) describes it as a criminal act through use of computers and telecommunications capabilities that results in violence, destruction and/or disruption of services to create fear, confusion and uncertainty, with the goal of influencing government or the population to conform to a particular social or political agenda (Denning, 2010).

The definition provided includes non-violent attacks; however, governments and academics have been reluctant to label non-violent acts as cyber terrorism because they have yet to cause the scale of damage or psychological effects attributed to bombings and other acts of violence, and as a result cyber terrorism is often dismissed as fear-mongering (Denning, 2010). Understanding definitions is important to differentiate between types and levels of cyber attack. Figure 10.1 shows the rungs of a ladder, with each step signifying a level of escalation as to the severity of any potential attack. The author (Cavelty, 2010), when referring to her definition of cyber terrorism (see above), makes comment that the world is yet to see an act of cyber terrorism, hence providing some credence to the risk assessment provided within CONTEST.

What is clear is that the threat of a significant cyber attack, particularly at the lower ends of the scale, makes cyber security an essential element of any national security strategy.

The internet provides terrorist groups with many opportunities, such as publicising and promoting their cause, communicating globally with sympathisers and supporters,

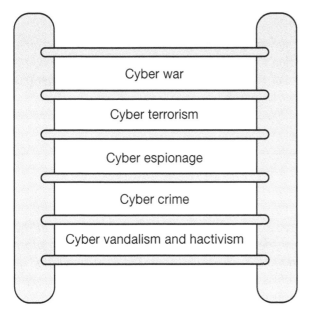

Figure 10.1
Cyber escalation ladder

Source: Adapted from Cavelty
(2010)

recruiting and engaging in criminal activity to raise funds. These are all areas of concern for governments, and strategies are required to counter the range of threats posed by the internet from both cybercrime and cyber terrorism. Globally, measures have been adopted to tackle the problem through international collaboration and cooperation, and legislative powers that enable the closure of websites linked to terrorism.

In 2009 a police Counter Terrorism Internet Referral Unit (CTIRU) was introduced for the purpose of making the web a more hostile place for terrorists to operate in and to exploit. The CTIRU works with the Police Service, the public and the internet industry and develops links with international partners to locate and shut down unlawful UK-hosted content (Thomas, 2011). In the 12-month period prior to July 2011, the CTIRU removed material from the internet on 165 occasions (Home Office, 2011).

The Government now has a cyber-security strategy that sets out the following vision:

> Citizens, business and government can enjoy the full benefits of a safe, secure and resilient cyber space: working together, at home and overseas, to understand and address the risks, to reduce the benefits to criminals and terrorists, and to seize opportunities in cyber space to enhance the UK's overall security and resilience.
>
> (Cabinet Office, 2009, p3)

In support of this a Cyber Security Office (CSO) was introduced to provide strategic leadership and coherence, together with a Cyber Security Operations Centre (CSOC) based at GCHQ with monitoring, coordination, information, intelligence and advisory responsibilities. Other initiatives include a cross-Government programme with supporting finance to develop innovative future technologies, protect UK networks, and promote and develop the growth of critical skills. The Government plans to work closely with the wider public sector, industry, civil liberties groups, the public and international partners (Cabinet Office, 2009).

REFLECTIVE TASK

Islamists have developed and used new forms of cyber warfare known as 'electronic jihad'. Complete an internet search using the search parameter 'electronic jihad' and find out more about the nature and impact of this type of cyber attack. Consider whether this type of attack could be defined as cyber terrorism.

CASE STUDY

Cyber attacks in Estonia

In April and May 2007 Estonia suffered a series of cyber attacks where websites of the President, Parliament, Government ministries and political parties were targeted, together with banks, mobile telephone networks and news organisations. The attacks consisted of overloading websites with thousands of visits, causing servers to crash. The Russians were strongly suspected of the attack following their open condemnation of the removal of a Second World War monument to the Red Army in the capital Tallinn. The NATO Secretary, General Jaap de Hoop Scheffer, made a comment following the attacks in Estonia that he believed that no member states are protected from cyber attacks (Halpin, 2007).

National Identity Register

Within CONTEST details were provided of a proposed national identity scheme. History has shown that terrorists use false or stolen papers and passports to conceal their real identity, and in some cases adopt multiple identities. The scheme, through use of biometric technology, would capture an individual's unique fingerprint and iris to be stored within an electronic chip on an identity card and recorded in a National Identity Register.

The first identity cards became available in November 2008 and were issued to foreign nationals applying to extend their stay within the UK on the grounds of being a student, fiancé(e) or spouse. The plan was for all new entrants and those extending their stay in the UK to have an identity card within three years. It was estimated that, by 2014/15, about 90 per cent of all foreign nationals residing in the UK would have an identity card (Home Office, 2009).

The scheme attracted much controversy and ultimately the Government's plan failed. As a result of the Identity Documents Act 2010 the UK National Identity Card and the Identification Card for European Economic Area (EEA) nationals were cancelled and the National Identity Register destroyed.

REFLECTIVE TASK

Consider why the UK Government failed in its attempt to introduce a national identity scheme. What were the pros and cons of the scheme and will the fact the scheme failed compromise national security?

The internet link, www.trevor-mendham.com/civil-liberties/identity-cards/hac.html, provides access to a document submitted to the Home Affairs Committee in 2004. It is a civil liberties document and outlines a comprehensive list of cons that can be considered in conjunction with the exercise.

Prepare

It is now more important than ever, following events such as 9/11, 7/7 and the Mumbai terrorist attacks, that states are fully prepared to deal effectively with a diverse range of terrorist attacks. The problem is not abating and key locations continue to be attacked, such as the metro underground railway system (March 2010) and Domodedovo airport (January 2011) in Moscow, targeted by suicide bombers and resulting in many fatalities.

The UK is no exception and during the twenty-first century considerable progress has been made to prepare the country for future terrorist attacks.

REFLECTIVE TASK

Consider the position of the Government in relation to providing a sufficient and effective response in the event of a terrorist attack. What would public expectation be of the Government and what would you consider to be a reasonable response?

CONTEST sets out four aims of the Government for the period 2011–15 to:

1. *continue to build generic capabilities to respond to and recover from a wide range of terrorist and other civil emergencies;*

2. *improve preparedness for the highest impact risks in the National Risk Assessment;*

3. *improve the ability of the emergency services to work together during a terrorist attack;*

4. *enhance communications and information sharing for terrorist attacks.*

(Home Office, 2011, p98)

At the start of the twenty-first century, government was faced with a series of national emergencies such as severe flooding, a fuel crisis, and foot and mouth disease, with the additional looming threat of further disasters caused by terrorist acts following the events of 9/11. An integrated response with robust structures, effective organisation, sufficient resources and appropriate training and development was necessary.

Civil Contingencies Secretariat

In July 2001 a Civil Contingencies Secretariat (CCS) was established within the Cabinet Office to improve the resilience of government and the UK. The Secretariat works in conjunction with a Civil Contingencies Committee responsible for managing and exercising arrangements in emergency situations. The CCS is responsible for a range of activities designed to enhance preparedness for emergencies, such as providing plans and systems enabling public services to deliver and function during a crisis; supporting ministers with development of policy; developing partnerships; sharing best practice; and improving capability at all levels of government, the wider public sector and the private sector (Cabinet Office, 2011a).

The CCS is made up of four groups (capabilities team, local response capability team, international team and emergency planning college) (Cabinet Office, 2011a) and each contributes to the aims of the Secretariat by:

- providing support for a cross-Government Capabilities Programme (see Table 10.4);

- managing local response, community resilience and recovery capability workstreams;

- liaising with international partners;

- developing through its college the skills and awareness required to improve emergency capability and resilience.

Capabilities Programme

The cross-Government Capabilities Programme provides a framework to drive forward a series of actions designed to build, develop and enhance resilience across the UK. Its aim is to provide a robust infrastructure of response that can effectively deal with civil devastation and widespread disaster. It has 22 'capability' workstreams that fall into three groups (see Table 10.4).

Table 10.4 Capabilities Programme workstreams

Groups	Workstreams
Structural x 4	Central response
	Regional response
	Local response
	Resilient telecommunications
Functional x 12	CBRN resilience
	Infectious diseases – human
	Infectious diseases – animal and plant
	Mass casualties
	Evacuation and shelter
	Warning and informing the public
	Mass fatalities
	Humanitarian assistance in emergencies
	Flooding
	Recovery
	Community resilience
	Site clearance
Essential Services x 6	Health services
	Food and water
	Transport
	Energy
	Telecommunications and postal services
	Financial services

PRACTICAL TASK

Consider the list in Table 10.4 and identify those areas that are relevant to providing a response to a terrorist attack and its aftermath. More detail can be found in relation to each workstream at www.cabinetoffice.gov.uk/content/22-capability-workstreams.

Each workstream is the responsibility of a designated lead department, which appoints a senior civil servant to manage the programme set out in a delivery plan agreed with the relevant Government minister and the CCS. Within the Cabinet Office a senior civil servant, who reports directly to a Director of Civil Contingencies, is responsible for the overall management of the programme on behalf of the Permanent Secretary, Intelligence, Security and Resilience (Cabinet Office, 2011b).

Civil Contingencies Act 2004

The Civil Defence Act 1948 and the Civil Defence Act (Northern Ireland) 1950 preceded the Civil Contingencies Act (CCA) 2004 and provided civil protection at a local level, designed specifically to afford defence against hostile attacks by a foreign power. The legislation was further limited by the fact that requirements for civil protection only applied to local authorities, police authorities and certain fire authorities.

Change was long overdue and the CCA widened the scope of civil protection to include terrorism and other emergencies that threaten serious damage to human welfare or the environment (section 1(1)), and extend responsibility to other organisations. The act imposes certain duties on 'responders', set out in Table 10.5.

Category 1 responders have the main responsibility for civil protection duties, which include risk assessment, business continuity management, emergency planning, maintaining public awareness and arrangements to warn, inform and advise the public. Local authorities are specifically required to provide business continuity advice and assistance to the commercial sector and voluntary organisations, assess the risk of an emergency occurring and maintain plans to respond to an emergency. Category 2 responders are required to cooperate with and provide information to category 1 responders in connection with their civil protection duties (National Archives, 2011).

Table 10.5 Responders – Civil Contingencies Act 2004

Category 1 responders	Category 2 responders
Local authorities	Utilities (water, electric, gas, communications)
Emergency services (police and fire)	Transport (railways, airports, ports)
Health (ambulance, hospitals, services)	Health and safety executive
Environment agency Secretary of State (coastal and maritime emergencies)	Strategic health authority

Note: Examples are provided in brackets.
Source: Adapted from Schedule 1, CCA

Risk assessment

The Government provides a National Risk Assessment (NRA) contained within a National Risk Register (NRR) of Civil Emergencies that sets out the likely and potential impact of a range of risks that may directly affect the UK. It is a five-year assessment that attempts to predict the most likely emergencies the UK and public may face, and is split into three categories:

- accidents;

- natural events (hazards);

- malicious attacks (threats).

The NRA complements Community Risk Registers (CRRs), produced and published by Local Resilience Forums (LRFs), which were introduced as a requirement of the CCA. Members of the emergency services and public, private and voluntary organisations are represented on the forums and contribute to the local risk assessment (Cabinet Office, 2008). Figure 10.2 shows an example of how the risk assessment is presented within the NRR.

Risks associated with terrorist events show a high relative likelihood, with attacks on both crowded places and transport assessed as having a fairly high relative impact.

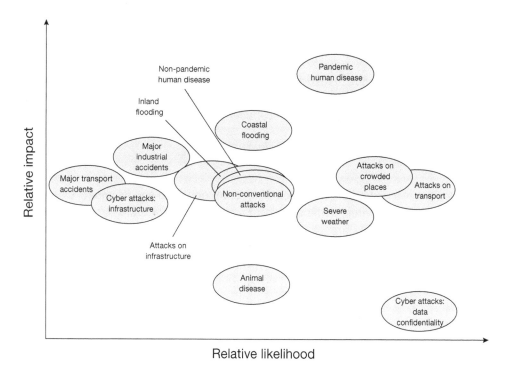

Figure 10.2 National Risk Register: illustration of high-consequence risks facing the UK in 2010

Source: Cabinet Office (2010, p5)

Local Resilience Forums

The CCA (s2) requires level 1 responders, supported by level 2 responders, to assess the risk of an emergency occurring and to maintain plans to deal with it. Plans must outline the measures necessary to prevent an emergency, reduce, control or mitigate the effects of an emergency, or take other action in connection with it. The CCA also requires publication of plans, outline arrangements to warn the public, and the provision of information and advice.

As a result, Local Resilience Forums (LRFs) were introduced to provide emergency planning at a local level to deal with a range of major incidents, including those related to terrorist attacks. At the local level a Community Risk Register (CRR) is produced that assesses risks so that the LRF can prepare, validate and exercise contingency plans, and allows it to focus on a rational basis of priority and need.

Risk assessment is based on the likelihood of an event occurring and its impact on health, social, economic and environmental aspects of a community. For example, in the London CRR the three highest risks are assessed as severe weather, pandemic flu and power or telecoms failure (Mayor of London, 2010). The CRR is concerned with non-malicious events (hazards) rather than threats (e.g. terrorist incidents), but that does not mean that terrorist incidents are not considered. On the contrary, preparation for a terrorist attack is paramount, and at both a local and national level considerable work is taking place, particularly in relation to the threats of a CBRN attack, or an electronic attack that could cripple key utilities and communications. Preparations related to tackling certain terrorist issues are not published as they may be misused; however, it is important to understand local emergency planning processes and their contribution to CONTEST. Table 10.6 provides an example of the range of emergencies that an LRF prepares for, including contingencies essential for dealing with a terrorist attack, e.g. mass casualties or evacuation.

Table 10.6 Local Resilience Forums: areas of operation

Categories	Emergency plans
Human health	Responding to a mass casualty incident Mass vaccination Flu pandemic
Humanitarian assistance	Mass evacuation plan Immediate response centres Vulnerable people
Telecommunications	Telecomms resilience
CBRN	Chemical, biological, radiological and nuclear attacks
Mass fatalities	Mass fatalities Emergency mortuary Excess deaths
Recovery and site clearance	Recovery and site clearance
Warning and informing	Major incident media strategy
Local search and rescue	Silver cell (command)
Miscellaneous	Flooding Animal diseases Coastal pollution

Source: Adapted from Devon, Cornwall, Isles of Scilly LRF (2011)

The LRFs are supported by Regional Resilience Teams and Forums whose main role is to improve coordination and communication between central government and local responders and other organisations. They are also responsible for ensuring that a region is prepared for and capable of responding effectively to any regional emergency.

7 July 2005

Questions have been asked of the Government about our preparation, response, and the support provided to survivors. Identifying and addressing lessons from the response to any major emergency is vital to improving our ability to respond to future emergencies.

(Home Office, 2006, p1)

Following the events of 7/7 the London Regional Resilience Forum carried out a multi-agency debrief following the emergency response and produced a report, *Looking Back, Looking Forward* (2006). The purpose of the debrief was to learn lessons from the response and to put in place a plan of action to update and improve future emergency responses (see Table 10.7).

Table 10.7 Issues identified as requiring action (Key lessons 7/7)

Sustainability	Chemical, biological or radiological (CBR) contamination
Strategic Co-ordination Centre (SCC)	Central Government
Telecommunications	Family Assistance Centre
Warning and informing the public	Resilience Mortuary
Communication to business community	Voluntary sector
Common information picture	Disaster Fund
Cordons	Arrangements for future event debriefs

Source: Adapted from London Regional Resilience Forum (2006, pp5–16)

REFLECTIVE TASK

Read the London Regional Resilience Forum report at www.londonprepared.gov.uk/ downloads/lookingbackmovingforward.pdf and find out more about the key lessons learned (pages 5–16). Consider how prepared London was for this type of attack and whether the key lessons learned provide evidence of a lack of preparation.

The London Regional Resilience Forum report focused on the response by London emergency services and other key agencies involved. The Government produced another report in September 2006 that considered the response from a national and central government perspective. The report recognised the importance of the Civil Contingencies Act 2004 in providing the foundation for long-term resilience across the UK, and acknowledged the value of multi-agency planning, training and exercising (Home Office, 2006). Five broad areas were identified for improvement following the lessons learned:

- providing better support to the bereaved and survivors;
- developing a more resilient telecommunications network;
- providing timely information to the public;
- keeping London moving safely;
- enhancing crisis coordination arrangements.

These reports are evidence of a commitment by the Government to learn from experience and take appropriate action to improve emergency responses. Whether this is sufficient remains to be seen, but the cycle of development will continue to enhance the effectiveness of response and deal with the aftermath.

REFLECTIVE TASK

Consider the recommendations made within the two reports mentioned above and assess the overall effectiveness of the emergency response and later management of the aftermath. Question and provide evidence as to whether London was properly prepared for 7/7, and whether the response would be improved should a similar incident occur now.

Chemical, biological, radiological and nuclear weapons

Terrorists obtaining and using CBRN weapons remain a real threat to the world and it would be very short-sighted if states did not prepare for such an event. Terrorism is inevitable and the West is currently a valid target for international terrorists, and should a terrorist group develop or obtain CBRN weapons and have the capability of deployment the vivid spectacle of the 9/11 attacks may even be surpassed.

It is crucial that governments prepare thoroughly for this type of attack and have the capability to deploy rescue services quickly and safely, deal with mass fatalities and casualties effectively, provide humanitarian assistance, restore critical services and quickly create order from the chaos.

The cross-Government Capabilities Programme provides the vehicle for developing our resilience for a CBRN attack. In 2010 the Government published a CBRN strategy with a 'Prepare' objective to *respond promptly and effectively to a CBRN attack and recover as quickly as possible from its impact* (HM Government, 2010b, p12). Considerable progress has been made and work continues to enhance resilience, such as reviews of plans, processes and procedures, provision of national guidance, delivery of multi-agency training, and developing and acquiring equipment.

A National Police CBRN Centre based at four sites within the UK (London, Coventry, Winterbourne Gunner and Edinburgh) provides multi-agency CBRN training and exercises. It also provides a command, control and communications capability that can be used in the event of a CBRN attack, and provides support for live operations. The Centre has briefed over 5,000 partners on how to respond to a CBRN attack, trained 650 emergency service commanders and police responders, trained over 10,000 police officers, and has advised and supported over 100 live incidents (HM Government, 2010b).

Police and emergency planning

To conclude this section, the Police Service has a long history of dealing with a range of major incidents and has dedicated departments that plan and train for emergencies in conjunction with level 1 and 2 responders in accordance with LRF plans.

PRACTICAL TASK

Complete an internet search using the parameter 'police emergency planning UK'. Explore the links across a range of police organisations and discover what services are provided and how links are made to the CCA, the Capabilities Programme and LRFs.

The Police Service allocates considerable resources to emergency planning and, in conjunction with other agencies, is able to provide a well-considered and professional response to most major incidents, including terrorist attacks. A recent report highlighted areas of concern following an inspection of 22 police forces responsible for high-risk sites such as airports, power stations and major transport hubs. The inspection carried out in

2008/09 assessed performance in planning to deal with civil contingencies, and in keeping the plans robust, dynamic and up to date. A number of failures were found that potentially represented a vulnerability to the Police Service or risk to the public (HMIC, 2009).

There is no room for complacency and the Police Service, together with all the other agencies and organisations responsible for emergency planning, needs to maintain a vigilance and ensure that all plans are fit for purpose.

C H A P T E R   S U M M A R Y

The Protect and Prevent strands are an integral part of CONTEST and are essential to reduce vulnerabilities in key areas, such as the critical national infrastructure, crowded places and UK borders, and to minimise the impact of any terrorist attack through the provision of robust and effective emergency measures.

Government departments work closely with the public and private sectors, and organisations such as the CPNI and NaCTSO have been created to support the delivery of protective security. A wide range of protective measures have been introduced, including publicity, advice, training, target hardening, situational crime prevention, planning and design interventions, and the use of sophisticated technology.

CBRN weapons and cyber terrorism are two specific protective security issues to be considered. CBRN weapons are a significant future threat and work continues both locally and internationally to enhance protective measures through the development of technology and other security interventions. Cyber security is identified as a key national security issue; even though the threat of cyber terrorism has not materialised, it remains a potential future threat.

The proposed introduction of a National Identity Register and its subsequent failure provides further evidence of the need to ensure a balance between national security requirements and civil liberties when considering certain counter-terrorism measures.

The introduction of the Civil Contingencies Act 2004 created a national network of emergency planning forums based locally and regionally, supported by central Government. Emergency planning is conducted through a process of risk assessment at both national and community levels, and much of the planning for terrorist attacks is integrated within generic emergency planning processes; for example, the plan to recover bodies and set up mortuaries could be as a result of a major accident or natural disaster, rather than a terrorist attack.

CBRN weapons provide their own challenge and special measures have been introduced to specifically prepare for this type of terrorist attack, such as the introduction of the National Police CBRN Centre. CBRN resilience is part of the cross-Government Capabilities Programme, with resources targeted at developing strategies to tackle the problem of the CBRN threat and provide a capability to effectively respond to an attack.

The attacks of 7/7 provided evidence of Government and emergency planners reviewing and enhancing plans, following lessons learned during and after the event. This is good practice and a learning cycle that must be repeated at every opportunity to ensure that any emergency response is appropriate and fit for purpose.

The content of the chapter is limited in its scope and further reading is recommended to obtain the detail contained within relevant legislation, strategies, plans, risk assessments and organisational websites referred to throughout the chapter.

ACPO (Association of Chief Police Officers) (2008) *Police and United Kingdom Border Agency Engagement to Strengthen the UK Border.* Available online at www.bia.homeoffice.gov.uk/sitecontent/documents/aboutus/workingwithus/Policeandukbaengagement/memoofunderstanding.pdf?view= Binary (accessed 11 May 2011).

Ansari, Fahad (2004) *Terror in the Name of Anti Terrorism: The UK in 2004.* Wembley: Islamic Human Rights Commission.

Cabinet Office (2008) *National Risk Register.* London: COI Communications.

Cabinet Office (2009) *Cyber Security Strategy of the United Kingdom: Safety, Security and Resilience in Cyber Space.* Norwich: The Stationery Office.

Cabinet Office (2010) *National Risk Register of Civil Emergencies.* Richmond: The Stationery Office.

Cabinet Office (2011a) Civil Contingencies Secretariat. Available online at www.cabinetoffice.gov.uk/content/civil-contingencies-secretariat (accessed 20 May 2011).

Cabinet Office (2011b) Capabilities Programme. Available online at www.cabinetoffice.gov.uk/content/capabilities-programme (accessed 20 May 2011).

Cavelty, Myriam Dunn (2010) *The Reality and Future of Cyberwar.* Parliamentary Brief. Available online at www.parliamentarybrief.com/2010/03/the-reality-and-future-of-cyberwar#all (accessed 17 May 2011).

CPNI (Centre for the Protection of National Infrastructure) (2011) The National Infrastructure. Available online at www.cpni.gov.uk/about/cni (accessed 10 May 2011).

Denning, Dorothy E (2010) Terror's Web: How the Internet is Transforming Terrorism, in Jewkes, Yvonne and Yar Majid (eds) *Handbook of Internet Crime.* Uffculme: Willan Publishing.

Devon, Cornwall, Isles of Scilly LRF (2011) *Combined Agency Emergency Response Protocol.* Available online at www.dcisprepared.org.uk/visual_map-2.pdf (accessed 23 May 2011).

Halpin, Tony (2007) Putin Accused of Launching Cyber War. *The Times*, 18 May. Available online at www.timesonline.co.uk/tol/news/world/europe/article1805636.ece (accessed 17 May 2011).

HM Government (2009) *United Kingdom's Science and Technology Strategy for Countering International Terrorism.* Norwich: The Stationery Office.

HM Government (2010a) *A Strong Britain in an Age of Uncertainty: The National Security Strategy.* Norwich: The Stationery Office.

HM Government (2010b) *The United Kingdom's Strategy for Countering Chemical, Biological, Radiological and Nuclear (CBRN) Terrorism.* London: Home Office.

HMIC (Her Majesty's Inspector of Constabulary) (2009) *An HMIC Report on Civil Contingency Planning by Forces in England and Wales.* London: HMIC.

Home Office (2006) *Addressing Lessons from the Emergency Response to 7th July 2005 London Bombings.* Norwich: The Stationery Office.

Home Office (2009) *Pursue Prevent Protect Prepare: The United Kingdom's Strategy for Countering International Terrorism.* London: Home Office. Available online at www.official-documents.gov.uk/document/cm78/7833/7833.pdf (accessed 24 September 2011).

Home Office (2011) *The United Kingdom's Strategy for Countering Terrorism.* Norwich: The Stationery Office.

London Regional Resilience Forum (2006) *Looking Back, Looking Forward.* London: London Resilience Team.

Mayor of London (2010) *London Community Risk Register.* London: London Fire Brigade. Available online at www.london-fire.gov.uk/Documents/LondonCommunityRiskRegister.pdf (accessed 23 May 2011).

NaCTSO (National Counter Terrorism Security Office) (2008) *Counter Terrorism Protective Security Advice for Aviation.* London: ACPO.

National Archives (2011) *Civil Contingencies Act 2004: Part 1: Local Arrangements for Civil Protection.* Available online at www.legislation.gov.uk/ukpga/2004/36/notes/division/2/1 (accessed 20 May 2011).

Thomas, Karen (2011) In Focus: Countering Internet Terrorism. *Police Oracle*, 17 May. Available online at www.policeoracle.com/news/In-Focus:-Countering-Internet-Terrorism_33634.html (accessed 18 May 2011).

UKBA (United Kingdom Border Agency) (2010) *Annual Report and Accounts 2009–10.* London: The Stationery Office.

UKBA (United Kingdom Border Agency) (2011) About Us. Available online at www.ukba.homeoffice.gov.uk/aboutus (accessed 11 May 2011).

USEFUL WEBSITES

www.cabinetoffice.gov.uk/content/local-resilience-forums (Local Resilience Forums)

www.cabinetoffice.gov.uk/news/national-risk-register-civil-emergencies-2010-edition (National Risk Register of Civil Emergencies)

www.cabinetoffice.gov.uk/ukresilience (UK Resilience)

www.cpni.gov.uk (Centre for the Protection of National Infrastructure)

www.decc.gov.uk/publications (Department of Energy and Climate Change – publications)

www.dft.gov.uk/pgr/security/personnelsecurity (Department of Transport – personnel security advice)

www.fco.gov.uk/en/travel-and-living-abroad/travel-advice-by-country (Foreign and Commonwealth Office – travelling abroad advice)

www.imo.org (International Maritime Organisation)

www.londonprepared.gov.uk/downloads/lookingbackmovingforward.pdf (London Regional Resilience Forum – *Looking Back, Looking Forward* report)

www.nactso.gov.uk/AreaOfRisks/CrowdedPlaces.aspx (National Counter Terrorism Security Office – various documents on security in crowded places)

www.ukba.homeoffice.gov.uk (United Kingdom Border Agency)

LEGISLATION

Civil Contingencies Act 2004

Civil Defence Act 1948

Civil Defence Act (Northern Ireland) 1950

Identity Documents Act 2010

11 Future perspectives

Christopher Blake, Barrie Sheldon and Peter Williams

CHAPTER OBJECTIVES

By the end of this chapter you should be able to:

- understand aspects of the future international and domestic terrorist threat and potential implications within the UK;
- appreciate how globalisation and the development of new technologies may impact on the future of terrorism;
- outline the latest developments in counter-terrorism policy within the UK.

Introduction

> *The organization of terrorism is complex and sometimes contradictory. There is no single uniform model, no one type of 'terrorist organization,' whether past or future. Instead groups are adaptive and flexible. Continued organizational development and thus more surprises can be expected in the future. Different structures of terrorism require different policies. Oversimplification of the threat cannot lead to an effective response.*
>
> (Crenshaw, 2007, p127)

The purpose of this chapter is to consider briefly how the international and domestic terrorist threat may develop during the next decade, with a specific focus on the UK and its counter-terrorism response. The questions posed in the task below form the basis of the chapter content.

REFLECTIVE TASK

Consider the above statement made by Martha Crenshaw and reflect on the range of terrorist groups that are currently active globally. What do you believe will be the future terrorist threat to the UK, and what manifestations are likely should terrorist groups continue to be adaptive and flexible? What might the surprises be and how effective is current policy to tackle any future threat effectively?

The main international threat in many parts of the world and the UK is that posed by Islamic jihadist terrorist groups. The threat to the UK can be divided into four primary sources:

- *al-Qaeda leadership and their immediate associates located on the Pakistan/Afghanistan border;*

- *terrorist groups affiliated to al-Qaeda in North Africa, the Arabian Peninsula, Iraq and Yemen;*

- *self-starting groups or lone individuals motivated by ideology, similar to al-Qaeda but not connected to them;*

- *terrorist groups whose ideology is similar to al-Qaeda's but who have their own identity and regional agenda.*

(Home Office, 2009a, p32)

Osama bin Laden's death is a significant, if perhaps mostly symbolic, achievement in the fight against international terrorism. It does not spell the end of al-Qaeda, but there is much uncertainty about its future and the terrorism that it inspires. It is unclear whether there will be a succession crisis at the centre of al-Qaeda and/or whether a resultant split in the organisation will weaken its capabilities, so this chapter will examine the future implications for international security.

Domestically, the threat of Irish dissident terrorism is resurfacing and has the potential to escalate further. The nature of the current threat is explored in the context of the peace process, policing, counter-terrorism measures and the implications for all three.

New technologies are developing at a rapid pace, contributing to a digital revolution with many positive aspects for the world's population. Unfortunately the technology is quickly utilised by both the criminal and the terrorist, and this potentially has severe implications for global security. The implications of the new technology are explored in the context of the terrorist threat.

Finally, the chapter provides a brief summary of revisions made to the 'Prevent' element of the current UK counter-terrorism strategy following a review by the Coalition Government and its potential implications for policing.

Theoretical considerations

History demonstrates the tenacity, creativeness and determination of terrorists to achieve their goals. Who would have envisaged the hijacking of jet airliners to cause mass murder (9/11), coordinated suicide bomb attacks within major global commuter hubs (Madrid, London, Moscow), the use of nerve gas (Tokyo) and holding a city hostage with a prolonged and coordinated murderous attack (Mumbai)?

When considering a future threat, a distinction can be made between *projecting* future trends and *predicting* specific events. Projections relate to theoretical constructs of trends based on the data available, whereas predictions relate to practical applications of data such as intelligence that are able to anticipate specific behaviours by extremists (Martin, 2009).

Predicting a terrorist threat is inherently challenging as, very often, data are generic rather than specific. Prior to both the 9/11 and 7/7 attacks intelligence agencies had certain information that indicated a serious threat but did not have the important details of timings, location and type of attack.

Martin suggests the use of a longitudinal framework to evaluate the future of political violence. The framework considers history, trends and cycles to project future near- and long-term trends of terrorism. Trends are considered in the light of contemporary data with near-term projections more likely to be realistic than long-term trends, which may be less realistic owing to the changing nature of contemporary terrorism (Martin, 2009).

Rapoport's theory

Terrorism analysts have attempted to define historical patterns of terrorism and one, Professor David Rapoport, provides a theoretical model that suggests that modern terrorism can be divided into four distinct waves (see Table 11.1).

The model has its limitations as many terrorist groups fall outside the chronological boundaries of the four waves; however, it does provide significant historical patterns. What it does highlight is one of the biggest challenges faced today in combating and controlling religious extremists and the brand of terrorism that has developed. It is within this context that the future problem of international religious terrorism is considered.

Al-Qaeda and affiliates

The fundamentalist warriors, flushed with victory, needed no other proof that 'god was with them', as if only the hand of God could have changed the balance of power so profoundly and led them to victory.

(Ganor, 2005, p273)

This is how Ganor (2005) describes the end of a ten-year conflict between the Afghan National Resistance Movement and Soviet forces. Some ten years prior to this, communists had assumed power in Afghanistan and in 1979 Soviet forces invaded Afghanistan to secure Moscow's influence. Gunaratna (2002) reports how this served as a rallying point and training field for Muslims who flocked to Afghanistan from around the world, joining as volunteers in a 'holy war' against the Soviets. Among them was Osama bin Laden, who understood better than most volunteers the extent to which the continuation and

Table 11.1 Historical patterns of terrorism

Period	Pattern	Purpose
Late nineteenth century to 1920	Anarchist wave	Revolutionary weapon
1920 to 1960s	Colonial wave	Weapon in an arsenal of revolutionary activity
1960s to 1980s	New left wave	To oppose neo-colonial and oppressive regimes
1979 to present day	Religious wave	To promote and enforce religious ideology

Source: Adapted from Mockaitis (2008, p38)

eventual success of the jihad depended on an increasingly complex, global organisation. Financial support was channelled through a 'golden chain', put together by financiers in Saudi Arabia and the Persian Gulf states. Bin Laden and the Afghan Arabs were able to draw largely on funds raised by the network, whose agents *roamed world markets to buy arms and supplies for the Mujahidin, or 'holy warriors'* (Gunaratna, 2002, p16).

PRACTICAL TASK

Before continuing, research and chart the rise of al-Qaeda from 1989. Pay particular attention to its homeland bases, its affiliates and major attacks.

During the Afghan–Soviet conflict al-Qaeda operated mainly out of Pakistan along the Afghan border but later moved its 'Centre of Operations' into Afghanistan (Azzam, 1998). A global network of radical Islamist groups then emerged as al-Qaeda established its 'credentials', with the destruction in 1998 of US embassies in Nairobi, Kenya and Dar es Salaam, Tanzania, and its attack on the US ship *Cole* in October 2000.

After defeating the Soviets, the mercenaries divided into three groups. The first returned to their native countries and joined with other Islamic fundamentalist organisations. The second returned to the West, mainly as political refugees, having been refused entry to their native countries for fear of their negative and dangerous influence. The third group remained in Afghanistan to be united by bin Laden, who went on to recruit, train and finance many thousands of fundamentalists to continue the 'holy war' beyond Afghanistan (Ahmed, 2005).

It is widely acknowledged that the 9/11 attacks earned bin Laden considerable acclaim among a significant minority in the Muslim world (Pew Research Center, 2003). It also galvanised al-Qaeda's allies to join the fight against the 'far enemy'. The wave of incidents that followed the World Trade Center and Pentagon attacks have been described as *the most intense and sustained global campaign of terror in modern history* (Benjamin and Simon, 2006, p19).

Following the 9/11 attacks and the US declaration of 'war on terror', 'Operation Enduring Freedom' was launched by the USA. Its aim was to disrupt, dismantle and defeat the al-Qaeda organisation and remove the Afghan Taliban. The operation forced al-Qaeda's leading operatives and key operational elements to shelter in Pakistan's Federally Administered Tribal Areas (FATA), previously discussed in Chapter 9. Others were dispersed globally, effectively decentralising control and franchising its extremist efforts to affiliated groups (McConnell, 2008). Today the FATA continues to serve as a staging area for al-Qaeda's attacks in support of the Taliban as well as a location for training new terrorist operatives, for attacks in Pakistan, the Middle East, Africa, Europe and the USA (McConnell, 2008).

The international crackdown following 9/11 was successful in removing the Taliban Government and cutting into al-Qaeda's resources. Many of al-Qaeda's former leaders were captured or killed and the organisation has been transformed from a hierarchical organisation with a large operating budget into an ideological movement. Whereas al-Qaeda once trained and deployed its own operatives to carry out attacks, it is just as likely to inspire individuals or small groups, often without support from the larger organisation but rather as part of state-sponsored operations (Ahmed, 2005).

Who are al-Qaeda's leaders and affiliates?

Al-Qaeda is administered by a council, formerly headed by bin Laden. Ayman al-Zawahiri, the head of Egyptian Islamic Jihad, is currently thought to be al-Qaeda's ideological adviser, while Abu Yahya al-Libi is described as the 'public face' of al-Qaeda, a top strategist and theological scholar who has helped to engage much of al-Qaeda's Arab audience. Some experts believe that this makes him one of the most effective promoters of global jihad (Brachman, 2009). As a senior member of al-Qaeda in the Arabian Peninsula, Shaykh Anwar al-Awlaki has openly and directly called for violence against the USA and the UK. Mustafa Abu al-Yazid is an original member of al-Qaeda's leadership council and a previous adviser to bin Laden. He served time in prison in the early 1980s with deputy leader al-Zawahiri for their role as conspirators in the 1981 assassination of Egyptian President Anwar Sadat. Abu Ayyub al-Masri joined the Egyptian Islamic Jihad in 1982 and is believed to have succeeded Abu Musab al-Zarqawi after his death in 2006.

Headed by Abdelmalek Droukdel, al-Qaeda in the Islamic Maghreb (AQIM) is based in Algeria and remains one of al-Qaeda's robust affiliates. A protracted civil war in Libya may well give al-Qaeda affiliates there opportunities to establish another base, while fully free and fair elections may eventually result in governments more sympathetic to al-Qaeda's narrative if not its tactics.

The Yemeni resurgence of al-Qaeda operatives since 2006 is also seen as a UK and regional security challenge. In Yemen, al-Qaeda in the Arabian Peninsula (AQAP) is headed by Nasser al-Wahishi, a former secretary to bin Laden. As a regional affiliate, AQAP aims to destabilise the Al Saud regime in Saudi Arabia and eradicate a Western presence in the Gulf. It has acquired capabilities of global reach and has been involved in various international terrorist plots over the past few years. Umar Farouk Abdulmutallab, the Nigerian suspect behind the attempted 2009 Christmas Day bombing aboard a US airliner, confessed to receiving weapons training from al-Qaeda terrorists in Yemen. The group has also claimed responsibility for the September 2008 attack on the US Embassy in Sana'a, which killed 18 people.

Al-Qaeda: what next?

Since 9/11 America's domestic and international counter-terrorism policies have been both aggressive and extensive. Addressing the nation in May 2011, President Obama confirmed that US Special Forces had launched a targeted operation in Abbottabad in north-west Pakistan, killing bin Laden, whom he described as a *leader and symbol of terrorism* (White House, 2011). Bin Laden's death comes at a time when al-Qaeda has been sidelined by the democratic surge that has unsettled the Arab world, although Hamas's mourning of bin Laden may be an ominous sign, and clearly one that poses another threat to what is already a fragile Middle East peace process. Ayman Al-Zawahiri, founder of the Egyptian Islamic Jihad, and other al-Qaeda leaders have attempted to frame these changes as an Islamist awakening. It is suggested that with bin Laden's death we are now enabled to test the truth of the observation that radical Islamist terror is a manifestation of the repressive governments that dominate the region. The somewhat pessimistic bottom line is that al-Qaeda as an organisation has grown far beyond bin Laden, which potentially limits the impetus that can be gained for the fight against international terrorism (Wright, 2011).

REFLECTIVE TASK

Consider the ramifications of the death of Osama bin Laden and its implications for the West, specifically the UK. How do you see the international terrorist threat unfolding and how prepared is the UK to deal effectively with it?

Irish dissidents

Given the long history of Ireland and its struggle by republicans against what they see as the British occupation, divisions within the republican ranks should not be seen as a surprise.

Gerry Adams, President of Sinn Fein, stated during the peace process that *one of our goals was to keep the republicans united* (2003, p317). The Irish writer and former IRA activist, the late Brendan Behan, once said that the first thing on any republican agenda is the split. Clearly, in the past this has been the almost inevitable outcome of divisions within the republican ranks and in the recent past has spilled over into violence, especially among the Irish National Liberation Army (INLA). During the 1970–90 period this became bitter and deadly factionalism (Adams, 2003).

So splinter groups within the Irish dissident movement should be no surprise to us, despite the fact that, since the 1998 Good Friday Agreement, relative normality has prevailed across Northern Ireland.

There are two main republican factions that are maintaining a terrorist threat and are clearly capable of terrorist operations, such as bombings and the targeted shooting of police and military personnel, all of which have been witnessed in recent years. They are the Continuity IRA (CIRA) and the Real IRA (RIRA).

Continuity IRA

The background to the CIRA concerns the republican abstention policy regarding the three parliaments: Stormont, Westminster and the Dail Eireann. In 1986 Gerry Adams, as the leader of Sinn Fein, proposed that the Irish element of this, the Dail Eireann, should be rescinded. This caused a split and Republican Sinn Fein was established from the dissenters. They went on to form a military wing, but it was some years before the CIRA as a terrorist force revealed its hand (Moloney, 2002).

Real IRA

This group was born from the necessity of Sinn Fein to sign up to what was called the 'Mitchell Principles' in order to enter the formal peace process in 1997. However, to do so would have meant that an IRA volunteer would be breaching the IRA constitution and would therefore be liable for expulsion (Moloney, 2002). Gerry Adams had agreed on behalf of Sinn Fein to agree to the Mitchell Principles – that was not the issue; but some of Sinn Fein were IRA members and that was. A series of conventions was arranged that culminated in a split in the IRA and the dissenters formed a group called Oglaigh na hEireann, which the media dubbed the Real IRA (Moloney, 2002).

Given the circumstances of the origins of both organisations, it is unlikely that a cessation of violence along the lines of that of the Provisional IRA was realistic, and that is what has been seen.

The significance of the two groups continues to grow and MI5 has raised the threat level regarding these groups from 'moderate' to 'substantial' (Frampton, 2010). Their overall objective is to create opposition to 'normalisation' (Frampton, 2010). This is the final stage in the process from the situation before the onset of the peace process and the Good Friday agreement, and total cessation of dissident activity and total peace.

Total cessation appears unlikely at the moment and greater dissident activity appears to be a real possibility; in 2009 there was 22 attacks by these groups; in 2010 this had increased to 37 (Frampton, 2010) and police and military personnel are once again key targets.

In the wider concept of policing and the objective of the Police Service of Northern Ireland (PSNI) to move towards community policing within Northern Ireland, this has been impaired by this increased dissident action (Frampton, 2010).

REFLECTIVE TASK

Consider the ramifications of increased activity by Irish dissident terrorist groups and how it might impact on the ability of the PSNI to develop effective community policing.

New technologies

The twenty-first century continues to witness the growth of new and exciting technologies that are becoming more sophisticated, but also more accessible globally to the general population, criminals and terrorists alike.

PRACTICAL TASK

Consider how the terrorist has grasped new technologies and then write down a list of those technologies that enable the terrorist.

Raman (2000), in an analysis of new technologies, suggests how they have unwittingly contributed to strengthening the capability of the terrorist in the following areas:

- communications;
- weapons concealment;

- psychological warfare;

- mass disruption;

- weapons of mass destruction.

Communications

Transnational terrorists need to communicate and will want to conceal any communications related to planning an attack or to thwart security services following an attack. Use of sophisticated encryption software and innovative concealment of messages embedded within digital pictures (steganography) are just two examples of how this can be achieved. A whole range of communication devices is currently available, including cellular and satellite phones, internet (chat rooms, chat clubs, bulletin boards, newsgroups, etc.), internet telephony (skype), email and social networking (Facebook, Twitter, linkedIn, Flickr, etc.).

Weapons concealment

As new technologies develop, the terrorist is continually looking for ways to conceal weapons that cannot be detected. Odourless Semtex explosives were popular with terrorist groups because they were not easily detectable by detection devices and dogs trained to detect explosives. Operation Cyclamen (see pages 158–9) provides an example of technology introduced to detect radioactive devices at ports and already terrorists will be looking for new technologies to overcome this obstacle.

Psychological warfare

Modern technology can be used to assist or publicise the terrorist cause, to discredit a government or put the general population in fear. This is easily achieved through use of a wide range of mediums such as the internet, websites, radio and television. TV stations such as Al Manar, in Lebanon, and Al Jazeera, in Qatar, have been effectively used by terrorist groups to convey their messages and the internet has provided a wealth of opportunity to target global audiences. Websites are easy to create and some terrorist groups employ hackers to access and destroy or distort government sites to promote their own propaganda. The organised terrorist group will embrace and maximise the use of available technologies to promote their cause and apply psychological pressure.

Mass disruption

The critical national infrastructure relies on sophisticated technologies to support daily operations and, should terrorists succeed in finding the means and technology to attack key installations, computers, networks and the information they store, mass disruption would result. Cyber terrorism is a distinct possibility and, although there is little evidence at the moment of viable attacks, incidents of cyber terrorism in the future may become more of a reality.

Weapons of mass destruction

WMDs were considered in Chapter 3 (page 44) and the development and use of CBRN weapons was identified as a potential future threat. AQ has made clear their intentions to harness and use CBRN weapons in the future, and other terrorist groups are likely to grasp the opportunity if they are able to obtain the required materials, develop a viable weapon and have the capability of deploying it.

Counter-terrorism responses to technology

Technological development provides many opportunities for the terrorist, so it is important that states are able to respond accordingly to counteract the threats posed:

> *CONTEST recognises that aspects of modern technology have been exploited by terrorist organisations. The strategy also argues that science and technology have a key part to play in our counter-terrorist work.*

(Home Office, 2009b, p4)

The UK Government is aware of the threat new technology poses and has produced a Science and Technology Strategy to support and tackle the threats posed by international terrorism. The Strategy (Home Office, 2009b) has three objectives, briefly summarised as follows:

- to understand future threats and opportunities;

- to develop and deliver effective counter-terrorism solutions;

- to enhance international collaboration.

The strategy identifies a number of challenges that reflect Raman's (2000) analysis above and includes understanding the causes of radicalisation, protecting the national infrastructure, reducing the vulnerability of crowded places, protecting against cyber-terrorism, improving analytical tools, identifying, detecting and countering novel and improvised explosives, and understanding and countering the CBRN threat (Home Office, 2009b).

PRACTICAL TASK

Read through the Government's Science and Technology Strategy (see 'Useful websites' for link or search online) and identify the seven broad science and technology domains where future developments may have a significant impact on terrorist activities and counter-terrorism work.

Counter-terrorism

The Government's new Prevent strategy was launched on 7 June 2011 by the Home Secretary, following a lengthy consultation period. It acknowledges that, since 2007, 1,120 people have been referred to Project Channel (see Chapter 8, page 147) under the previous Prevent strategy as being at risk of violent extremism. This is four times the previously released figure (Travis, 2011) and most were referred by schools, colleges, police and youth-offending teams.

The new strategy contains three overall objectives:

- respond to the **ideological challenge** of terrorism and the threat we face from those who promote it;

- **prevent people from being drawn into terrorism** and ensure that they are given appropriate advice and support; and

- work with **sectors and institutions** where there are risks of radicalisation that we need to address.

(Home Office, 2011, p7)

The Home Office intends to prioritise 25 areas where Prevent will be coordinated via the local authority. Resources will be targeted where it is perceived the greatest need lies and the priority areas will be subject to frequent Home Office reviews.

There will be an enhanced role for the CTIRU (see Chapter 10, page 162) in respect of inappropriate material on the internet and far more proactive action will incorporate international internet providers, colleges, schools and libraries in attempts to minimise exposure to radical online material.

Health workers will have a key role to play within the strategy. The Government sees this sector as crucial in detecting early signs of radicalisation and intends to launch a training programme aimed at health professionals, mainly operating at community level. As a principle, this is not new to health workers, who are trained and have a front-line role in respect of child protection within communities, and who are well versed in multi-agency approaches to specific community problems. However, given the workload of the National Health Service, this additional work may present some difficult challenges for them.

REFLECTIVE TASK

Read the Home Office Prevent Strategy (see 'Useful websites') and consider whether it is a comprehensive approach to tackling the problems of radicalisation and violent extremism. Do you consider, for example, the 25 priority areas to be a realistic policy in relation to managing risk, or does each individual local authority area deserve a similar amount of resources allocated to it?

Policing

Since the General Election in 2010 and the ramifications of the Comprehensive Spending Review (CSR), the Police Service, in line with other public services, is witnessing massive cuts to its budget. Compulsory redundancy is being implemented in most police forces and recruitment has ground to a complete halt. Although the Government has stated that the counter-terrorism budget has not been reduced, in reality operational police officers deal with whatever they need to at the time, irrespective of who is paying the bill. But it is clear there will be a lot fewer of them.

In attempts to ease the funding situation, most forces are collaborating for some specialist and support functions, such as training. This measure and others announced by the Coalition Government, such as disbanding the Serious Organised Crime Agency and replacing it with a National Crime Agency, may just be the early steps towards the creation of a national Police Service. This would not enjoy unanimous support and, historically, would go against the features of British life that have singled out British policing as being somewhat unique in the world – that it is largely unarmed, is locally based and is performed with the consent of the public.

In the area of counter-terrorism, however, there would be support for such a move to enhance our capability, which is becoming more and more reliant on technology. Currently the constabulary-style structure has produced diverse information technologies and communications systems. Depending on the operational needs of individual forces, the expertise and capabilities of specialists such as firearms officers, surveillance officers and crime scene investigators vary, and it is proposed by some that a slim-line single configuration would resolve these issues (Hayman and Gilmore, 2009). Irrespective of any enforced budget cuts, in the area of counter-terrorism there are clear signs that a certain template has already been laid down, with the introduction of Counter Terrorism Command (SO15), regional counter-terrorism units and counter-terrorism intelligence units set up as a national policing resource (see Chapter 8, page 119).

Inadvertently, the financial cutbacks are forcing the Police Service to seriously consider what services it provides and at what cost. Staffing costs equate to 85 per cent of the policing budget and this realistically is the only area where significant cuts can be made to meet Government targets. The provision of substantial funding and resources for counter-terrorism is likely to remain a priority; however, as the cuts continue to bite and decisions become more challenging, there is potentially a threat to the maintenance of adequate funding and resource levels.

C H A P T E R   S U M M A R Y

The concept of projecting future trends and predicting specific events was initially considered, together with a longitudinal framework to assist in evaluating the future of political violence. Rapoport's theory provided a useful four-stage model to define historical patterns of terrorism that identified a 'religious wave' for the current era, reflecting the challenges faced today in tackling religious extremists and the brand of terrorism they purvey.

Consideration was given to how the international and domestic terrorist threat could develop and impact on the UK in the future. Al-Qaeda and its affiliates were identified as the main international threat, and the dissident terrorist groups, the Real IRA and Continuity IRA were identified as the main domestic threat.

The death of Osama bin Laden has posed further questions about the viability of al-Qaeda and its future; however, its growth into a fragmented and global network is likely to continue to cause international problems in the foreseeable future. Hence, international terrorism with a particular focus on AQ remains a priority for counter-terrorism policy.

Despite the peace process, Irish dissidents continue to provide a domestic terrorist threat to the UK and it is a problem that it is not going to diminish in the near future. This threat is also recognised by the Government and will impact on future counter-terrorism policy.

New scientific and technological opportunities were briefly discussed and identified as a continuing threat. The terrorist will continue to embrace new sciences and technologies and it is important that counter-terrorism policies are flexible and dynamic enough to meet new challenges. The Science and Technology Strategy provides evidence of the Government's commitment to meeting the challenges of the modern technological age.

In respect of counter-terrorism policy, the revised Prevent strategy was considered, which focuses on responding to the ideological challenge, preventing people being drawn into terrorism, and working with sectors and institutions to tackle the problem of radicalisation. This policy is in its infancy and only time will tell whether it will have an appropriate impact to stem the growth of radicalisation within the UK.

Finally, the future of policing was briefly discussed in the context of the age of austerity that is having a significant impact on police resources. Whether the cuts will have an impact on the policing counter-terrorism structure remains to be seen, but some solutions to the challenges faced are available, such as collaboration and the pooling of resources.

Future studies

This book is aimed at higher education (HE) students completing terrorism-related subjects at levels 4, 5 and 6. The tasks throughout the book should provide stimulus, sources and evidence for the completion of HE assignments. It is an introductory text and further academic reading and research are essential to provide a more detailed understanding of the subject matter. Students undertaking level 5 and 6 HE qualifications will be required to provide evidence of wider research and analysis to attain a first-class grade.

FURTHER READING

Hoffman, Bruce (2006) *Inside Terrorism*. New York: Columbia University Press.

Mahan, Sue and Griset, Pamala L (2008) *Terrorism in Perspective*, 2nd edition. London: Sage.

Martin, Gus (2009) *Understanding Terrorism: Challenges, Perspectives and Issues*, 3rd edition. London: Sage.

REFERENCES

Adams, G (2003) *Hope and History: Making Peace in Ireland.* London: Brandon.

Ahmed, NM (2005) *The War on Truth: 9-11, Disinformation and the Anatomy of Terrorism.* Northampton, MA: Olive Branch Press.

Azzam, A (1998) Al-Qaeda al Sulbah: The Solid Foundation. *Al Jihad*, April: 46.

Benjamin, D and Simon, S (2005) *The Next Attack.* New York: Henry Holt.

Brachman, J (2009) The Next Osama. *Foreign Policy*, 10 September.

Crenshaw, M (2007) The Organization of Terrorism, in Ellis, JO III (ed.) *Terrorism: What's Coming – The Mutating Threat.* Oklahoma City, OK: Memorial Institute for the Prevention of Terrorism.

Frampton, M (2010) *The Return of the Militants: Violent Dissident Republicanism.* London: International Centre for the Study of Radicalisation and Political Violence.

Ganor, B (2005) *The Counter-terrorism Puzzle: A Guide for Decision Makers.* New Brunswick, NJ: Transaction Publishers.

Gunaratna, R (2002) *Inside al-Qaeda: Global Network of Terror.* New York: Columbia University Press.

Hayman, A and Gilmore, M (2009) *The Terrorism Hunters.* London: Bantam.

Home Office (2009a) *Pursue Prevent Protect Prepare: The United Kingdom's Strategy for Countering International Terrorism.* London: Home Office.

Home Office (2009b) *The United Kingdom's Science and Technology Strategy for Countering International Terrorism.* London: Home Office.

Home Office (2011) *Prevent Strategy.* Norwich: The Stationery Office

Martin, G (2009) *Understanding Terrorism: Challenges, Perspectives and Issues*, 3rd edition. London: Sage.

McConnell, JM (2008) *Annual Threat Assessment of the Intelligence Community for the Senate Armed Services Committee.* Available online at www.dni.gov/testimonies/20080227_testimony.pdf (accessed 3 June 2011).

Mockaitis, TR (2008) *The 'New' Terrorism: Myths and Reality.* Palo Alto, CA: Stanford University Press.

Moloney, E (2002) *A Secret History of the IRA.* London: Allen Lane.

Pew Research Center (2003) America's Image Further Erodes, Europeans Want Weaker Ties. Available online at http://people-press.org/reports/display.php3?ReportID=175 (accessed 4 June 2011).

Raman, B (2000) Terrorism: The Technological Imperative. South Asia Analysis Group. Available online at www.southasiaanalysis.org/%5Cpapers2%5Cpaper104.html (accessed 5 June 2011).

Travis, A (2011) Official Review Finds Scant Evidence of State Funds Going to Extremists. *The Guardian*, 8 June.

White House (2011) Barack Obama's Address on Osama bin Laden. *The New Yorker*, 1 May. Available online at www.newyorker.com/online/blogs/newsdesk/2011/05/osama-bin-laden-dead-obama-address.html (accessed 6 June 2011).

Wright, L (2011) Bin Laden: Hey, Hey Goodbye. *The New Yorker*, 2 May. Available online at www.newyorker.com/online/blogs/newsdesk/2011/05/bin-laden-hey-hey-goodbye.html (accessed 5 June 2011).

USEFUL WEBSITES

www.homeoffice.gov.uk/counter-terrorism/review-of-prevent-strategy (Prevent Strategy)

www.homeoffice.gov.uk/counter-terrorism/science-and-technology/science-and-technology-strategy (Science and Technology Strategy)

Appendix A

Answers to task questions in Chapter 4

Pages 53–4

1. To quieten Ulster and secure the province against the risk of further native uprising and foreign invasion.

2. Undertakers: English or Scots who had taken the Oath of Supremacy in that they were Protestant.

3. Former rebellious inhabitants.

4. Religion, justice and civility.

5. To colonise the province with loyal British subjects.

Page 54

1. Land.

2. To convert a Protestant to become a Catholic.

3. Irish woollens, due to English jealousy.

4. Protestant.

5. Payment of rent and tithe.

Pages 55–6

1. Attacks on Protestants in County Armagh at the Battle of Diamond.

2. 1798.

3. To defend culture and traditions.

4. 'Ireland is not a nation but two peoples, separated by a deeper gulf than that dividing Ireland from Great Britain.'

5. Threat to Protestant supremacy in Ireland.

Pages 58–9

1. Irish Republican Army.

2. National Service Act 1916.

3. Being an American citizen.

4. Rebellion must occur at some stage of the First World War.

5. Irish War of Independence.

Page 60

1. The Black and Tans.

2. Due to the distinctive uniform they were first issued with.

3. 1,900.

4. Assaults on IRA suspects, occasionally causing death.

5. Further repressive measures.

Page 64

1. Irish Republican Army (IRA).

2. IRA.

Answers to task questions in Chapter 9

Page 142

1. Sir Henry Mortimer Durand.

2. Foreign Secretary to the Colonial Indian Government.

3. British.

4. 1893.

5. Afghanistan and the British Indian Government.

Appendix B

Glossary of Islamic terms

Ayatollah	A leading Shi'a scholar
Caliph	Leader of the Muslim faith
Hadith	Acts and sayings of the Prophet
Ijtihad	Process of interpreting Islamic text
Jihad	Struggle, strain, effort
Madrassas	Religious schools throughout Islam
Mujahidin	Holy Warriors
Salaf	Forefathers of Islam
Salafist	Salafi Muslim who supports jihad
Sharia	Islamic law
Shi'a	Follower of Ali, a direct descendant of Mohammed
Sunna	Examples given by the Prophet
Sunni	Orthodox version of Islam; a follower of Abu Bakir as Mohammed's successor
Sura	Chapter in Qur'an
Tafseer	Study on the commentary of the Qur'an
Taliban	Seekers of knowledge
Tauhid	Unity within Islam
Ulema	Learned clergy within Islam
Umma	Muslim community
Zulm	Tyranny

Index